D1478629

Right Hand Man

Right Hand Man

How Phil Lind Guided
the Genius of Ted Rogers,
Canada's Foremost Entrepreneur

Phil Lind
with Robert Brehl

BARLOW BOOKS
fine books for enterprising authors

AURORA PUBLIC LIBRARY

Copyright © Philip Lind, 2018

All rights reserved. No part of this publication may be reproduced,
stored in a retrieval system or transmitted, in any form or by any
means, without prior written consent of the publisher.

Library and Archives Canada Cataloguing in Publication data available
upon request.

978-1-988-02533-9 (hardcover)
978-1-988025-37-7 (paperback)
978-1-988025-36-0 (ebook)

Printed in Canada

To order in Canada:
Georgetown Publications
34 Armstrong Avenue, Georgetown, ON L7G 4R9

Publisher: Sarah Scott
Book producer: Tracy Bordian/At Large Editorial Services
Cover design: Paul Hodgson
Photography: All photographs (including cover) courtesy Phil Lind
            unless credited otherwise
Interior design and layout: Rob Scanlan/First Image
Copy editing: Karen Alliston
Proofreading: Eleanor Gasparik
Indexing: Wendy Thomas

For more information, visit **www.barlowbooks.com**

Barlow Book Publishing Inc.
96 Elm Avenue, Toronto, ON
Canada M4W 1P2

AURORA PUBLIC LIBRARY

For my children, Sarah and Jed, and for my young
granddaughter. James, may you find inspiration that there are
no limits in what you can achieve in the same way I found
inspiration from my grandfather.

———————

For those who at various times in my 50-year career acted
as my indispensable right hand: Vernon Achber, Ken Engelhart,
Missy Goerner, Bob Buchan, Alison Clayton, Jan Innes,
Michael Allen, and Adrian Montgomery.

———————

And, finally, for my mentor and friend, the late Ted Rogers.
It was a pleasure and a wild ride to serve as his lieutenant.

Contents

Foreword by John H. Tory ix

Prologue 1

1 Johnny Lind 11

2 The Bridgman Family, a Society Wedding, and St. Marys Cement 29

3 Garbage Trucks, Hymnbooks, Christmas Trees,
   and Other Hijinks 41

4 The Art and Science of Politics 57

5 "You're Hired, but Friends Don't Last Long Working Together" 71

6 David and Goliath 85

7 Cable, the Constitution, and a Cheshire Cat Grin 97

8 Southward Ho 107

9 Minnesota 119

10 Texas 127

11 Oregon 135

12 California 143

13 Exit Stage Left 151

14 Be Careful What You Wish For 163

15 Whew! 179

16 Farm and Family 193

17 CPAC Man 205

18 The Stroke and the Road Back 219

19 Changeup: The Jays Purchase and My Evolving
    Relationship with Ted 235

20 Regional Sports and a National Dream 251

21 The Buffalo Bills in Toronto Series 265

22 The Brand and Other Battles 273

23 Art and the Beauty of British Columbia 287

24 Post-Stroke Campaigns and CRTC Chairs 297

25 Close Calls, Gender Equality, and Loyalty 313

26 Reflections 327

Index 345

About the Author 357

Foreword

by John H. Tory, 65th Mayor of Toronto

Phil Lind will always be linked to Ted Rogers, Canada's greatest post–World War II entrepreneur. Phil and Ted worked together for 39 years building the country's largest telecommunications and media company, Rogers Communications Inc. They were yin and yang: Ted's relentless drive to grow, grow, grow regardless of cost and Phil's relentless drive to execute campaigns and cajole partners and competitors to help further that growth.

They didn't always agree, and sometimes fought like an old married couple, but they complemented each other like no one-two punch in Canadian business. I know because I was there and witnessed it, at both the board and operations levels at RCI.

Though Ted Rogers and his company are integral to Phil's story, neither the man nor the brand encompasses the entire Phil Lind story. To suggest otherwise would be like remembering Barack Obama simply as a best-selling author or Alfred Nobel as merely the inventor of dynamite.

Phil's fingerprints are all over Canada.

With more appearances before the Canadian Radio-television and Telecommunications Commission than any other person (100-plus panel appearances and before every single CRTC chair in its history), Phil has left a mark on our broadcasting and telecommunications policies like no other.

His impact on Canadian sports is enormous, and includes ensuring that another Canadian Major League Baseball team wouldn't fly south, bringing National Football League games to Toronto, broadcasting a smorgasbord of live games every

Sunday with NFL Sunday Ticket, introducing regional sports net-works to Canada, and building Sportsnet into the biggest sports television entity in the country.

And then there's arts and culture, from sitting on the boards of the most prominent galleries in Canada to collecting some of Canada's best contemporary art and tirelessly promoting Canadian artists like Jeff Wall, Rodney Graham, Stan Douglas, and a host of others. Way back in 1980, Phil spearheaded Rogers Telefund, which for 36 years has provided financing assistance to producers to help fund the production of thousands of hours of quality Canadian television programming.

No need to stop there. There are backroom advisory roles with prominent politicians dating from the days of John Diefenbaker and on to Darcy McKeough, Bill Davis and the Big Blue Machine, Peter Hyndman, Bill Bennett, Davie Fulton, Brian Mulroney, and others. I count myself fortunate to have received many provocative ideas and opinions from Phil over the years, both in politics and business. His sound advice and diplomacy always ring true, whether for political or business campaigns. And you won't find a more loyal political partner. Phil proves the wise saying that you know who your real friends are on your worst days, not on your best.

Speaking of diplomacy, few Canadians know as much about the United States as Phil, who studied in the U.S., led the charge to build a successful cable company in the U.S., and has travelled that country as much or more than any Canadian alive. I'm just glad he never decided to move there!

On numerous occasions many high-profile thinkers—on both sides of the border—have called Phil "the best ambassador to the United States that Canada never had." Indeed, the University of British Columbia's Phil Lind Initiative furthers understanding of the two countries by inviting prominent American scholars, writers, and intellectuals to UBC to discuss important issues of our times. Like the millions of dollars Phil has given to various cultural and educational causes, he opened his wallet widely to UBC as well.

There is also Phil's influence on such social issues as diversity, gender equality, and environmental awareness, long before most of us were doing anything about them. No one in Canada did more to further multilingual television programming in our diverse Canada than Phil. He has always promoted women to senior executive levels and relied on their counsel. He has often pushed for more women on the boards of directors he serves on, and on more than one occasion Phil would accept a board appointment only if the organization promised to appoint women to serve along with him.

As an avid conservationist, outdoorsman, and environmentalist, Phil is the founder of Sierra Club Ontario, a volunteer organization that funds leading-edge projects to restore and preserve the environment. He's also a director of the Atlantic Salmon Federation, a body dedicated to the conservation, protection, and restoration of wild Atlantic salmon and the ecosystems needed for their survival.

And he is a man dedicated to his family. He's proud of his roots, the distinguished Canadian history of his ancestors, and proud of his children, grandchild, and extended family of nephews, nieces, and siblings. Even tough, competitive Phil softens when it comes to family.

Yes, Phil has many accomplishments, but one thing stands taller than all the rest: his steely determination to not only survive a horrific stroke that left him permanently paralyzed on his right side but also prove beyond reasonable doubt that a productive life is much more than possible after a stroke. How inspiring is that to those surviving strokes and their families? He had to relearn how to walk, talk, and read, and learn to write with his left hand. No easy tasks. For more than two years he underwent strenuous daily physiotherapy, and he returned to Rogers and 14-hour workdays only a year after the stroke.

He stirred in all of us who worked with him loyalty and respect, and he humbled competitors who worked against him. And he was no token executive when he returned to the corporate offices. Some of his greatest campaigns took place in the two decades following the stroke, always with the same clear, methodical thinking and strategies, and always mixed with fun and hard work.

I have counted Philip Bridgman Lind a dear friend and irreplaceable mentor for closing in on 50 years, and it's my honour to say these few words to open his memoir.

Just before I first met Phil in the 1970s, Randolph S. Churchill, the son of Sir Winston Churchill, uttered these immortal words: "Beneath the mighty oak no saplings grow."

I can tell you that Phil worked beside a mighty oak for four decades, and he proves Randolph Churchill wrong. Phil has stood tall on his own, gone out on more than one limb, and had a spectacular view of so many things that have taken root in Canada over the last half of the twentieth century and well into the twenty-first. And beneath the mighty oak that is Phil Lind many people have grown in many ways and have gone on to shape Canada and the world with his guidance and support.

Ted Rogers and Phil Lind forged a relationship that created opportunity and success for many Canadians. I know the pages of this book will be just as valuable to many more.

Prologue

C anada Day, July 1, is that annual day of national celebration when businesses close, barbecues fire up, faces
are painted red and white, the Maple Leaf is waved, and
fireworks explode high above in the night sky. This particular
Canada Day, in 1998, was a Wednesday, and seemed like the perfect time to take the rest of the week off and fly to Vancouver for
a short fishing holiday on the West Coast, one of my favourite
places in the world.

Fly fishing is in my blood; it's in the Lind family blood.
My grandfather, John Grieve Lind, started it all in 1932 when
he bought a farm on the Rocky Saugeen River in Durham, Ontario,
and later built a fishing camp there. I remember my dad teaching
me techniques in the early 1950s; later I would pass along the art
to my children, Sarah and Jed. Sarah never cared much for it, but
Jed fell in love with fly fishing and has become a far better fisherman than his old man. My father, also named Jed, was better
at it than me (and it used to drive him crazy when I'd out-fish him
through luck or happenstance), so maybe the prowess skipped
a generation, but the love of it certainly did not.

All recreational fishing is fun, but fly fishing is an art, from the
addictive nature of tying the feathers, fur, and thread to pulling
on hip waders and feeling the initial freeze of the icy water before
tugging the line for that first cast of the day. Standing in a cold
stream or on the shoreline and rhythmically casting a fly line

back and forth creates a satisfaction that's difficult to describe. It's as if all your worries, stress, and problems fall away. It's a great feeling.

I simply love fly fishing. For a guy who spends most of his life in glass-and-iron office towers, aboard airplanes, and eating at restaurants, nature's draw and power is humbling, always exhilarating. The fly line takes me to that physical and mental state every time as it delicately moves through the air, floats, seemingly weightless, and rolls along as if defying the law of gravity. Then there's the wait, the anticipation of when the salmon or trout will strike. Atlantic salmon and steelhead trout—or trout of any kind, whether rainbow, speckled, brook, or brown—are my favourite adversaries. Yes, fly fishing is an art, a beautifully romantic art.

It's unlikely that such thoughts were in my head that Canada Day, but it's a safe bet that I was excited about getting on that plane, given that I always look forward to fly fishing. But before I headed to Pearson International Airport, a friend dropped by for lunch. Just as we were about to sit down to eat, a phone call came, and I retreated to the den of my apartment at the corner of Avenue and Lonsdale roads in Toronto's Forest Hill neighbourhood.

Not unusual for Rogers, where business for our senior team is a 24/7 endeavour, I seem to recollect that it was a business call, one of those routine snags in a deal that can get worked out through dialogue. Over the years I've closed deals on handshakes, on verbal agreements over the phone, even on cocktail napkins—one of those was for $25 million in Texas and written on a breakfast napkin.

Anyway, this deal involved Canada's first regional sports network, Sportsnet. South of the border, Fox and others had proven throughout the 1990s that such networks were fast becoming gold mines when it came to things like college and high school football, Major League Baseball, and basketball at all levels. As a lifelong sports fan, I hoped the same could be done in Canada to compete against the national sports monopoly TSN (The Sports Network), even if Canada is one-tenth the size of the U.S. and high school and university sports aren't nearly as important here in driving viewership. Hockey, of course, would be the linchpin of Sportsnet's success.

Suddenly a sensation came over me, as if I were spinning. I ended the call and tried to get my wits about me. It wasn't dizziness; it was more like I was somehow inside a sort of strange, personal tornado and spinning, spinning, spinning. I collapsed and hit the floor with a loud thud. My friend came running into the den and immediately dialed 911.

Had I been alone you wouldn't be reading this; there would have been no way I could have survived such a severe stroke without help.

At this point in my life I'd been single for almost five years after the end of my marriage with Anne. Though we'd never stopped loving each other, we just couldn't live together after the pain we'd caused each other. I was living alone, but I've always craved company—being with people, eating together, telling tales, working together. Though I'm not a regular churchgoer, it was by the grace of God that I wasn't alone at that moment. I was only 54 years old, and everything would have ended without immediate help.

Much of what follows are my memories as I slipped into and out of consciousness, but some things I was told later, either because they occurred while I was unconscious or the stroke permanently erased certain recollections. (For example, my longtime friend and colleague Missy Goerner later told me that, in the days before, she'd noticed my eye drooping and my irritability rising, both telltale signs of impending danger and something we'd all learn about after the event.)

In my apartment, I lay on the floor helpless. The stroke didn't feel as though it came as a thunderclap but rather as a series of events, crippling events. Paramedics arrived and asked me many questions. Did I know where I was? Did I know what had happened? Could I move my legs, my arms, my head?

I could barely talk; I merely mumbled. I'd been a healthy person my entire life, but for some reason at that moment I remembered being in Mount Sinai Hospital in downtown Toronto with a broken foot 10 years before. I somehow made the ambulance attendants understand that this was where I wanted to go. Why there? I don't know. It's a fine hospital, but it was probably a mistake. In hindsight, I likely should have gone northeast to Sunnybrook Health Sciences Centre, which has a regional stroke unit.

As the ambulance raced to Mount Sinai I could see nothing but an attendant beside me and some medical machines blinking and flashing. I could hear the siren screaming outside and feel the jostling of the vehicle, presumably slowing down at red lights to make sure the path was clear to proceed and then quickly accelerating.

I drifted between the realm of realization and this strange, dreamlike, out-of-body feeling. The best way to describe it is like lying in the bathtub, the plug being pulled out and the water draining from the tub, just as if life were draining from my body.

In recovery—days, weeks, and months later—I would have similar but very different out-of-body feelings: of being extricated from the world, of watching life from afar and in an unfamiliar place. I'll get into more detail about that later, but during these frantic moments, all I wanted to do was get the plug back in the bathtub drain.

I wanted to survive. I wanted to live and see Sarah and Jed again. I wanted to kibitz, debate, scream, argue, and laugh with close friends and colleagues like Missy, Ken, John, Jan, Alison, Colette, Bob, Pam, Tony, Robin, and, of course, my boss and partner, Ted. (In the coming pages, you'll read more about these important people in my life.) Was I thinking these things at that very moment or are these later thoughts I've imagined happening at the time? I don't know, but I do know that I wanted to live, and that I had unfinished business.

The next 24 hours or so don't belong to me. I remember being wheeled around to places for a whole bunch of tests; for one examination, I was even wheeled across the street to Toronto General Hospital. Everything else I now know only through what I was told later.

Clearly I'm no doctor, so I'll put this the best way I can: a stroke is an injury to a part of the brain after something goes wrong with the blood flow to the brain. Blood vessels, or arteries, carry blood and nutrients through the body. One way the brain may be injured is when an artery to the brain becomes blocked and the blood supply is cut off. Without a supply of blood, the brain doesn't get the oxygen and nutrients it needs. Permanent damage results when the blood supply is cut off for more than a few hours.

Believe it or not, up until the early 1990s, strokes weren't even considered a priority call for medical responders. Even though every 10 minutes a Canadian suffers a stroke (more than 50,000 people a year), until that time, very little could be done to help patients other than stabilize them in hospital and wait and see. If you stroked, the attitude was, "That's too bad; if you survive, we'll offer physiotherapy and see if you can get back some of your speech or the use of your arms and legs." "Barbaric" is too tough a description, and yet with all the scientific advancements in the late twentieth century, such treatment does sound like an anachronism from the Dark Ages.

But in 1995—just three years before my stroke—a study demonstrating the benefit of tissue plasminogen activator (tPA) in acute stroke changed everything. The study showed that tPA, a protein involved in the breakdown of blood clots, was effective in treating ischemic strokes, the most common type of stroke in which blood is prevented from flowing to the brain. There have been other advances over the past 20 years, too.

These super-drug "clot busters" were a major breakthrough in helping restore the blood flow to the brain and lessening the disabilities brought on by strokes, especially when administered less than four and a half hours after the onset of the stroke. The problem is that they're risky, even deadly, if used on a patient whose stroke was caused by bleeding in the brain, a ruptured artery, which was my type of stroke.

On Thursday, July 2, a neurologist came to see me. Now, I admit that I was in and out of delirium, but what this doctor told me rocked my world, especially given everything I'd been through during the previous 24 hours. I am not imagining what he said. His words are ingrained in me, and I've never forgotten them. He explained that secondary strokes are probable, that they're kind of like aftershocks following an earthquake. And that sometimes these secondary strokes can be worse than the initial one.

"I'm going away to the cottage now for the long weekend," the doctor went on. "If you survive all that, I'll be around on Monday to see you."

I'm a guy who likes the truth. I hate it when someone bull-shits me or sugarcoats things. But given the weakened state of both my mind and body, this bedside manner was borderline cruel. I couldn't speak very well at all. When I had to, I'd muster what I could to talk to people, but I didn't know what to say to this doctor. After he left I just lay there, forming different thoughts in my head. This was the only thing I could control: thoughts in my head. And I was going places I shouldn't have gone. I was convinced, at that moment, that I'd be gone, or if I did make it to Monday, that I'd have only a couple of years at best. It felt as though that doctor's words had flushed every-thing out of me.

The next day my personal physician, Bernie Gosevitz, who was also Ted's doctor, came to see me; he also talked to the med-ical staff and went over my hospital charts. It's worth repeating that Canada Day had been on the Wednesday, meaning that only a skeletal staff remained, since many had arranged for the next two days off to make it a very long weekend.

Also on Thursday, Ted Rogers ordered a conference call so that Bernie could brief my Rogers executive team on where things stood. On the call with Bernie were Ted, Ken Engelhart, Robin Mirsky, Michael Allen, Jan Innes, Missy Goerner, and John Tory. Others simply couldn't be tracked down.

By all accounts, it was a sombre call. Ted was bawling at times, as befitting such an emotional man in a situation like that. I don't blame Bernie because he was relaying the facts pre-sented to him at the time. In a nutshell, he reported that it was touch-and-go whether I would survive, but he thought I would. However, he said, "Phil will never work again."

"It was dire, so dire," says Jan Innes, my communications adviser, who was on holiday with her family in Nantucket.

"I heard it all and had difficulty digesting it," says John Tory, then the president of Rogers Media, and vacationing in Italy at the time. "There was little to be optimistic about, but this was my friend Phil, possibly the most determined person I know next to Ted, and if anyone could overcome this, it was him. I had to keep thinking that way."

There'll be a place later to detail the rigours of rehabilitation and the incredible support and love of friends and family, but the point of starting this memoir with the stroke is to underline how significant Canada Day 1998 was to me. I had to learn or relearn how to talk, to read, to walk dragging a right leg that often feels like a log, to write with my left hand, to dress myself, to drive a car, to do so many everyday things that everyone, including myself, takes for granted until something happens.

That day defined my life. It changed me forever. It changed my relationship with Ted Rogers. But it did not end my life. I can honestly say that I've done some of my best work since the stroke, and I'm proud of what I've accomplished.

Some have held me up as some sort of poster boy for stroke victims, an example that a life can be lived with purpose and fulfillment after a stroke. And that's okay, but I've never sought that status and don't think of myself that way. I don't like the terms "victim" or "disability." Sure, I've had to work a lot harder at some things, but I still got the job done through sheer determination. I never wanted people looking at me and thinking, "Poor Phil. He's doing the best he can, all things considered." I wanted to do the job and achieve positive results, just as I'd done all through my career during the 25 years before the stroke.

My mother always drilled into us the importance of never giving up, of always finding ways to fight adversity. And if this book leaves the reader with only one message, it would be this: Listen to my mother—no matter what, never give up hope and never give up trying to come back.

The effects of a stroke can be ameliorated. There are wonderful, ongoing advances happening in medicine. Therapy and rehabilitation can make a big difference. Always remember to never underestimate the importance of your own inner strength.

My mother instilled this dogged determination in me from an early age. Other things helped it flourish, too. Maybe it was in my genes from my grandfather. Possibly it came from my high school years at Ridley College in St. Catharines, Ontario, where in those days verbal abuse of students was common and teachers told me I'd never amount to anything. Or maybe it came from working side by side for 40 years with such a complex and relentlessly driven man as Ted Rogers. Who knows? But it's been a wild ride, and it's not over yet.

1

Johnny Lind

I met the man, likely several times, but I have no memories of him. Still, his influence on my life is immeasurable and very real, with the greatest impact being on my family's fortunes. His name was John Grieve Lind, also known as Johnny Lind, and he was my grandfather.

He died from a stroke in 1947, just weeks before my fourth birthday. I can't recall ever sitting on his lap or walking to the park in St. Marys, Ontario, a park he paid to have refurbished during the Great Depression so that he could create jobs and help those townspeople who were struggling to find work. He was that kind of man. In fact, he opened a line of credit with the local St. Marys grocer, telling him to use it for anyone who couldn't pay for their food.

He was an adventurer with a heart of gold who made a small fortune by risking much and working even harder during the Klondike Gold Rush of the late 1890s. At the turn of the twentieth century, he took his gold and money with him and returned to Ontario, where he bought homes for all his unmarried sisters. He invested in a business that would eventually become St. Marys Cement, and that would grow into what would be the largest independent cement company in Canada for many years. He took pride in knowing the name of virtually every employee who worked for him at the plant, treated all with respect, and did not lay off a single person during the deepest, darkest days of the Depression.

Throughout my life I've revelled in his accomplishments; as a young boy, I remember listening with rapt attention to stories passed down from my father, Jed, my mother, Susie (who admired him greatly and was more than just a daughter-in-law to him), and other relatives. I still get a little misty-eyed recalling Mother describing his funeral. Virtually the entire town of St. Marys was there, along with many other people from nearby towns and cities, even places like Toronto, where he was known in some circles. But the image that stuck with me was her description of the hundreds of workers, many in overalls covered with cement dust, weeping while paying their last respects before returning to the factory to finish their shifts.

In my eyes, and for many others, John Grieve Lind was a giant of a man. He was such a towering figure in southwestern Ontario that the *St. Marys Journal* ran his obituary on the front page, above the fold. It began: "St. Marys lost its most prominent and colourful citizen over the week-end when death came to John Grieve Lind, a farmer's son, bridge builder for the pioneer railroad in Montana, Sour Dough of the Klondike, cement company president, fishing enthusiast, amateur gardener and benevolent townsman."

Because of him, I've compiled one of the largest private collections of books about and artifacts from the Klondike Gold Rush. My collection includes thousands of photographs, more than a thousand books on the subject published from 1896 to 1905, and hundreds of original cheques, posters, and other memorabilia. After my death, the entire collection will be given to a museum in British Columbia. I would have liked to donate it to Dawson City, but facilities capable of preserving such rare artifacts aren't available there.

My grandfather inspired me, and he still does. The grit and sheer determination of the man! In the North he lived in unbearable conditions, especially during the early years before Dawson City's population exploded and goods and services became available. As he wrote some years after leaving the North, "Of all the gruelling hardships, probably, there is nothing that will sap your energy as freighting [provisions] with the temperature constantly from 45 to 65 degrees below zero ... time did appear endless, the cold intense."

The winters were long and hard. They lived in cabins they'd built themselves with no glass for windows, just narrow slits they tried to plug with glass bottles. The cold blew in relentlessly; the only heat came from burning wood. In today's luxury-filled world, it's difficult to imagine such conditions. For visionary dreamers like my grandfather, it was a life filled with unbelievable hardships: months of darkness, disease, isolation, and monotony. It could be awful but it could also be wonderful, such is the lure of gold.

It was first discovered in August 1896 on Bonanza Creek near Dawson City, but the world didn't hear of it until 1897. Word spread like wildfire, with a stampede of more than 100,000 people from all over the globe descending upon the Klondike, many of whom weren't prepared for its harsh conditions.

And if there's one story that epitomizes Johnny Lind, it would be the one about the Christmas Eve baby. I'm so proud of my grandfather for his role in saving that newborn baby's life on December 24, 1897.

The story is recorded in a little-known book published in 1938 called *I Was There: A Book of Reminiscences* by Edith Tyrrell, a rather extraordinary woman whose husband holds an interesting place in Canadian history, too. Joseph Burr Tyrrell was a geologist, cartographer, and mining consultant who in 1884 was the first to discover dinosaur bones and coal in Alberta's Badlands. The Royal Tyrrell Museum of Palaeontology in Drumheller, Alberta, is named in his honour. In retirement, he owned and operated a huge apple orchard in Scarborough on the land now home to the Toronto Zoo. Edith Tyrrell, founder and first president of the Women's Association of the Mining Industry of Canada, shared her husband's interest in geology. Twice she went to the Yukon during the gold rush, and it was on her first visit that she heard of this Christmas story involving my grandfather.

According to Edith Tyrrell, on Christmas Eve 1897 three men—Johnny Lind, Skiff Mitchell, and Bill Wilkinson—travelled 25 kilometres from their cabin on Eldorado Creek to Dawson City for supplies. Upon their return their dogs were weary, having hauled the heavily laden sleds, so they took a short breather. My grandfather noticed a faint light coming from what he thought was a deserted cabin. They went to investigate, and as they got closer they could hear a moaning sound.

Inside, they discovered a dying young woman who had recently given birth to a baby girl. They started a fire in the stove and fetched a bottle of brandy from their supplies. They tried to give the mother a teaspoon of it, "but she was past swallowing, and as they looked she gave a last quivering sigh and was gone," Tyrrell writes.

They took the baby from the dead woman's arms and Wilkinson wrapped the child in soft woollen underwear. The three men then lined a packing box with newly purchased blankets to create a makeshift bassinet.

Just then, the husband arrived with a doctor from Dawson. Having looked for help all day in extreme minus-45 cold, and now seeing his dead wife, the man collapsed and died. It was pleurisy, or lung infection, the doctor said. The couple was from the American Midwest; months earlier they had headed out on their Klondike adventure unprepared for the North. After the doctor told my grandfather and his two friends how to feed the baby and keep her warm, he departed for another call.

The miners headed back to their own cabin with bassinet and baby. "Never had so strange a load gone along the Eldorado trail, or any trail for that matter, as went that Christmas Eve," writes Tyrrell. "The dog team, the three men and the baby, while the northern stars shone brightly on their pathway." Back at their cabin, the men took shifts through the night, holding the sleeping baby and feeding her teaspoons of tinned milk, warm water, and brandy.

On Christmas morning, word spread along Eldorado Creek of this miracle baby. Sixteen women miners arrived, offering help. A Nova Scotia woman named Mrs. Brock, who'd gone to the Klondike with her husband after their own infant died, took charge while the three men began collecting gold dust from miners. Their initial collection amounted to $400, and it was sorely needed: a pint of milk in Dawson cost $2, or roughly $50 today.

The baby was christened Edna Eldorado. Tyrrell doesn't say what ultimately happened to her, but she brought joy to many that Christmas long ago. And the story of "how Bill, Dave and Johnny had been led by the Christmas star to the place where the young child was" became folklore in the Klondike.

The story holds obvious parallels to the original Christmas story and underlines the goodness in humanity, especially amid adversity. It's amazing what these three wise men did for that baby, and it makes me—and all my family—proud to be descendants of a man like Johnny Lind.

———

In the Klondike, my grandfather worked long hours and found pleasure in reading books like Edward Gibbon's *The History of the Decline and Fall of the Roman Empire* and anything by Thomas Carlyle, Victor Hugo, or Thomas Hill Green.

He had an eclectic taste in authors—from novelists and biographers to philosophers and scientists—and a thirst for knowledge. His formal education had ended after Grade 8, so in 1898 he hired a tutor up in the Klondike to help him while other miners headed to the saloons, card tables, and brothels for their own forms of relaxation.

Genes are often remarkable, and the parallels between our lives—two lives that barely intersected—are noteworthy. A stroke killed my grandfather, and very nearly did the same to me. Wanderlust was part of his DNA—he left home at 15 to make his fortune, eventually landing in the Yukon at the right time— just as it's part of mine, chasing the cable franchising "gold rush" of the 1980s across the United States.

I like to think I share other qualities and attributes my grandfather exhibited over his 80 years: dogged determination and hard work, fierce loyalty and deep friendships, sportsmanship, appreciation of the outdoors and protection of the environment, and, of course, the importance of family.

Johnny Lind obviously wasn't my only familial influence, and I'll get to some others. But his story is fascinating and well worth exploring in a little more detail.

John Grieve Lind, the eleventh child of Adam and Ann Grieve Lind, was born on February 8, 1867, mere months before Canada became a country. His twin brother, George, was minutes older; the two boys had nine older sisters. The family lived on a hundred-acre farm near Pond Mills, today a neighbourhood in London, Ontario.

Not interested in farming, teenager Johnny Lind headed down to the United States and landed a job working with the Great Northern Railway Company, controlled by the famous railway magnate James J. Hill, who during the late nineteenth century was expanding across the American Northwest from the Great Lakes to the Pacific Ocean.

Johnny Lind worked hard, and quickly rose to foreman of a crew of 200 men. He became proficient in designing and overseeing the construction of trestle bridges over rivers, canyons, and gullies. In essence, this tenacious, self-taught teen was an engineer without the papers. It was the first of many self-taught skills he would acquire over the years.

At age 27, by now an independent contractor building bridges in and around Missoula, Montana, and after more than a decade of railroad work, he was anxious for a new adventure. One morning, he pondered two opportunities: join an oil-prospecting expedition to Venezuela or head to Alaska where gold had reportedly been discovered. He flipped a coin and up came Alaska.

From that moment forward, the Lind family fortunes would never be the same.

In Seattle, Johnny purchased enough supplies for a venture to the Great White North. Then he boarded a coastal steamer, and after stopping briefly in Victoria, arrived in Alaska on May 1, 1894, three years before the Klondike Gold Rush. (The big Bonanza strike occurred in August 1896, but the stampede of men didn't start until word reached the outside world in July 1897.)

In Dyea, Alaska, he hired Chilkat Indians to assist in moving his supplies inland, via the treacherous Chilkoot Pass, to the headwaters of the mighty Yukon River at Bennett Lake. Johnny had one year's worth of provisions, according to a journal he wrote 40 years later, around 1934.

> Everything had to be packed, each pack made up of 100 pounds. We had to organize a small army of Indians at one dollar a pound to pack our plunder to the summit of the pass which is called "stone house" … this is supposed to be the stormiest pass in the world. There is never over two or three hours at a time that it does not snow or blow and when it storms, no one can stand it, but immediately throw down their beds and crawl into their fur robes and wait for the storm to pass, sometimes for as long as a week or two at a time.
>
> The only water you could get was from snow, which must be melted by lighting candles under your frying pan. Many a man perished here, as this was the shortest way over the range known to white man…. It took three days to get our Indians with their loads up to the top and from there, we sledded our stuff down hill to the head of Lake Lindeman. Then on to Bennett Lake, where there was lots of fine timber.

It's difficult to describe the vastness and the remoteness of this area, especially then, more than 120 years ago. Dyea is on the Alaska Panhandle, south of both a sliver of northern British Columbia and the massive Yukon Territory. Back then, there was

talk of gold in creeks and rivers almost everywhere, but the boun-
tiful gold fields were 720 kilometres or so north and accessible
only via river.

These early years in Alaska and Yukon were important for
Johnny, who learned gold prospecting up and down their various
creeks, where sometimes the dust and nuggets were plentiful and
sometimes not so much. All the while he was making new friends
and acclimatizing himself to the rigours of living in the North.
And two of those friends, Johnny Crist and Skiffington Mitchell,
would become his partners.

Upon arrival at Bennett Lake, Johnny felled trees and
cut the wood into lumber to build a boat, no mean feat without today's power tools like chainsaws and "Alaska mills,"
a portable device used for making lumber in remote locales.
He doesn't say exactly who was with him on this initial journey,
but he wasn't alone. Our family believes that Crist and Mitchell
were with him on that first trip up the Yukon River.

They sailed the boat up to the treacherous Whitehorse Rapids,
where some of their supplies went overboard, including all the
sugar. It was time to abandon ship, so they pulled the boat ashore
and burned it to harvest the nails. Then they portaged all the supplies to calmer waters and built another boat.

Johnny soon spotted a small fur-trading post and introduced
himself to the owner, a man named Arthur Harper. "He had
no sugar, but had honey, which we bought," he wrote. They continued on, and after going days without anything sweet, they
decided to make camp and have a treat that evening. But just
as they were reaching shore the water started to roar and all the
honey "fell into the raging river, and sank before our eyes." This
story was one my father told whenever he was asked to describe

the conditions my grandfather endured. Imagine the disappointment: a year's supply of honey swallowed up by the mighty
Yukon River and you not knowing when you might taste something sweet again.

About a week later they reached a small hamlet full
of Sourdoughs called Forty Mile, the oldest town in Yukon and
80 kilometres northwest of Dawson, which in 1894 didn't yet
exist. (The Sourdough nickname was given to prospectors who
stayed in Alaska or Yukon for at least one full year and survived
the winter. "Sourdough" refers to their tradition of protecting their
sourdough bread starter, or leaven, during the coldest months
of the year by keeping it close to their body, usually by hanging
it around their neck.)

Called Ch'ëdä Dëk in the Han language, Forty Mile, located
at the confluence of the Yukon and Fortymile rivers, is historic for
two reasons. First, it was used by the ancestors of the Tr'ondëk
Hwëch'in for at least 2000 years. For the Han, Forty Mile was
important not for gold but for caribou, being one of the major
river-crossing points for the Fortymile herd. (For some reason,
the Fortymile River is spelled as one word and the outpost as two
words.) Second, in 1886, coarse (or "placer") gold was discovered
at Forty Mile. Within a year, 160 prospectors arrived looking for
gold nuggets in the gravel of rivers and creeks in the region, and
the territory's first town was formed.

After Forty Mile, Johnny, Crist, and Mitchell continued
along Fortymile River about 140 kilometres and set up camp
near Franklin Gulch, Alaska. There they cut 20,000 board feet
of lumber to build sluice boxes, used to sift the gold from the
gravel in placer mining. They had some success, but it was gruelling work in often horrid conditions.

At minus 40 degrees, Celsius and Fahrenheit meet. There were weeks and weeks during which the temperature wouldn't rise above minus 40, giving an indication of just how cold and harsh life was. The Bard of the Yukon, Robert Service, described life's bleakness best in his book of poems titled *Songs of a Sourdough*—a book that would earn him a fortune greater than most prospectors would ever realize.

> This is the Law of the Yukon, that only the Strong shall thrive;
> That surely the Weak shall perish, and only the Fit survive.
> Dissolute, damned, and despairful, crippled and palsied and slain,
> This is the Will of the Yukon, —Lo! how she makes it plain!

One of Johnny's great regrets was leaving all that lumber behind after hearing about the Bonanza strike and realizing that time was of the essence. In December 1896, he and Skiff Mitchell had gone into town at Forty Mile to buy provisions for the winter only to find that the place was near deserted. They were told that there'd been a big strike in Dawson 80 kilometres upriver, and that that's where everyone had gone. Johnny and Skiff debated whether to follow; after all, there was much talk of big strikes that often proved false, and they didn't want to waste their time. But in the end they set off for Dawson with their sleds and dogs.

But first I need to back up a bit, to the beginnings of the Bonanza strike. Months earlier, in the summer of 1896, two Tagish First Nation people—a man named Skookum Jim Mason and his sister Kate Carmack—along with Kate's husband, George Carmack, were fishing on the Klondike River with a few others when they bumped into Robert Henderson, a prospector who didn't think much of the Indigenous people. Henderson and George Carmack began a discussion in which Henderson revealed that he'd been having some luck lately. (Per the unwritten code of the miner, Henderson had to share his knowledge of potential finds with whomever he met.) Carmack asked whether there was a chance he could stake a claim. In a voice loud enough to be overheard by Skookum Jim and others, Henderson replied that Carmack was welcome, but not his First Nations relatives.

In early August Carmack took his relatives to Rabbit Creek, a tributary of the Klondike, based on what Henderson had told him; they even ran into Henderson again, who once more insulted the First Nations men, this time by refusing to sell them tobacco. His obstinacy, Carmack later recalled, would cost him a fortune.

The group headed farther up Rabbit Creek and panned for gold. It was indeed encouraging, just as Henderson had said. Then a few days later, in a place where the bedrock was exposed, someone found a nugget the size of a dime. They all scrambled excitedly, turning over rocks, and found gold—gold that lay thick between the flaky slabs "like cheese sandwiches," according to Carmack. The date was August 16, 1896.

Carmack, Skookum Jim, and Dawson Charlie, another relative, staked their claims and renamed the creek Bonanza. The next day the men headed downstream to Forty Mile to register those claims. What they didn't do was return to Henderson and tell him about their find—not after the way he'd treated the First Nations people. Without that tip, Henderson remained several miles away for another three weeks. By the time he caught wind of the great discovery, the best locations on Bonanza Creek had already been staked by prospectors who were in Forty Mile when the men registered their claims.

Four months later, Johnny and Skiff finally arrived in Dawson, where they found a good many of their old mining friends—who confirmed the news of the big Bonanza Creek strike.

That strike had been followed by a second on Eldorado Creek days later. Unfortunately for Skiff and my grandfather, by the time they arrived in Dawson all the prime locations had already been staked at both sites. They must have felt devastated. But, using the money made from the smaller amounts of gold they'd found in Alaska, they immediately set out to buy a few of the claims that had been staked.

Many of the prospectors with early Dawson claims didn't have much money, and many of these easily pissed their cash away or had arrived in Dawson quite coincidentally by changing their plans for other destinations after hearing about the Bonanza strike. In other words, they were willing to sell some or all of their claims for a quick profit, especially when no one knew at that point just how much gold was in the Klondike.

According to my grandfather's notes, a creek claim consisted of 500 feet up and down the length of the valley and from one side to the other. The place where the gold was discovered was called "discovery," and all claims were named from that point outward. For example, George Carmack's claim was deemed "discovery" on Bonanza Creek. The first claim downstream from discovery was known as No. 1 Below Bonanza, the first claim upstream from discovery was called No. 1 Above Bonanza, and so on. "After some deliberation on our part, we bought interests in about a dozen claims," my grandfather wrote. "One particular claim we got a half interest for $12,000 cash at 26 Above Bonanza."

It didn't take long to realize that this was a good piece of land. "Early in the spring we bought out the other half for $200,000, but were not to pay anything until the middle of August." That price is the equivalent of $5.5 million today. Needless to say, they worked like crazy—20-hour days—through the summer of 1897 to pay for the claim.

When the big Bonanza and Eldorado strikes at Dawson had occurred my grandfather was relatively close by, and yet in some ways he was late to the party. But he persevered, took big chances, and worked incredibly hard. And once word had spread, imagine how late those stampeders were who travelled thousands of miles from as far away as Europe, South America, Australia, and all across the United States.

So many of these stampeders had no idea until they got there that the stakes were claimed and the conditions unbearable. But through his difficult work on the railroad and his pre–gold rush arrival, my grandfather was, if not prepared, at least fully aware of the dangers and hardships. To put things in perspective, when he first arrived there were only several hundred non-Indigenous (and fewer than 5000 Indigenous) people in Alaska and Yukon. Within a few short years, upwards of 100,000 stampeders would cross ocean waters and treacherous mountain passes, navigate raging rapids, and withstand unbearable cold—all in a craze for gold.

From the summer of 1897, my grandfather and his partners—by this point Crist had arrived in the Klondike—were running a 24-hour operation, employing 200 men with a daily payroll of $4000 (or $90,000 in today's money). Johnny Lind, Skiff Mitchell, and Johnny Crist were true entrepreneurs.

Their best days would reap $50,000 of gold dust and nuggets, although most days weren't that lucrative, and their expenses were hefty. Beyond payroll, they were paying for claims, buying expensive tools (shovels were $20 each and nails $5 a pound), building housing for workers, and paying 10 cents per pound to freight supplies to and from their various claims. Food was incredibly expensive, too. Eggs, for example, sold for $12 a dozen, or about $275 today.

"Every dollar we made, we kept investing in other properties until we were quite a large operation," Johnny wrote. "By Fall [of 1897], I was worn to a shadow, working about 20 hours a day, also doing my own cooking and household duties."

In July 1897, *Excelsior*, the first boat filled with Klondike gold, arrived in San Francisco with more than $500,000 of the precious metal (almost $13 million in today's dollars). Three days later, another $1 million worth of gold arrived in Seattle aboard the steamer *Portland*.

By 1898, Dawson had swelled to 30,000 people and was being called "the Paris of the North." For a price, almost anything could be bought, from French champagne and Paris fashions to oysters and imported delicacies. Such wealth naturally attracted scoundrels and grifters, who were more than willing to lighten miners of their gold and dollars. One man named Pope lost $75,000 in a hand of cards! That's about $2 million today, and the guy bet that in poker. Ludicrous, but there was this feeling that, thanks to the gold, money was in endless supply.

And then there's the story of Charlie Anderson, nicknamed the Humpback Swede, who worked for my grandfather for a brief time in Alaska. Two Americans got Charlie really drunk in a saloon one night and sold him what they thought was a worthless claim they owned for all the money he had left in his pocket, which happened to be $600 (about $13,000 today).

When he was sober again, Anderson was furious. Still, he went to the claim, put down a shaft—and found some of the richest pay dirt on the Eldorado. In all, he pulled out $1 million worth of gold, which would be about $25 million today. His nickname then became "the Lucky Swede." He bought a large cabin in Dawson, bathed in champagne (at $65 a bottle), and spent lavishly on himself and others. Eventually he married a dance hall girl, who took most of the money he had and left him penniless. By this point he'd lost the "Lucky Swede" nickname.

"Poor Charlie went to work in a saw mill," my grandfather wrote. "There was probably 75 per cent of all the wealth taken out of the Klondike that was dissipated in a similar way. Too much sudden wealth went to a great many men's heads and ruined them forever. Very few were ever able to come back. I could name dozens and dozens of fine men in adversity, with fine principles, utterly ruined by a little brief wealth and usually they put on all the airs of a Prince of the Blood, while it lasted."

It's estimated that only about 2000 men found gold. Of these, only about 200 found significant amounts, and only 40 or so left the Klondike with their wealth. Fortunately, John Grieve Lind was one of those 40.

By 1898, with operations and procedures firmly in place, my grandfather and his partners no longer needed to work 20 hours a day. He relished his off-hours and rarely went into town, preferring the company of books: "I never in all my life, had a chance to read just what I wanted to." Such was the life of a self-made man who had to read books to teach himself the skills needed to build bridges or mine gold or make cement.

In July of that year Johnny returned home to Pond Mills for a time; then, in the spring of 1899, he went back to the Klondike with two of his sisters, Ada and Wilhelmina. Within a year Wilhelmina would marry Skiff Mitchell, and Ada would eventually marry Johnny Crist.

With the new century came the arrival of the huge gold-mining companies and their heavy machinery. In 1901 that spelled the departure of my grandfather, who could see the writing on the wall: smaller operators couldn't compete against the likes of the Guggenheim's Yukon Gold Company, which, with government help, bought up claims and churned through the creeks and rivers with large floating dredges.

Though he never returned to the North, so many of Johnny's descendants have done so over and over, both to experience the beauty of the area and to imagine the hardships our trailblazing ancestor endured so that we would have so much.

In 2001, after we'd donated $275,000 to the Dawson City Museum, in part to pay for the John G. Lind Storage Facility and the Lind Gallery, local historian Michael Gates wrote this in *The Klondike Sun*:

> The Lind family is neither new nor unfamiliar to the community of Dawson. They have been actively involved in the centennial celebrations of the past few years, starting in 1996, and continuing to the present. Characteristic of their visits is the energy and enthusiasm they display, and the numbers of the clan who descend upon the community at once. They don't just visit Dawson, they invade, invariably heightening the energy level around town during their stay.
>
> Significant about their involvement with the community has been not only their enthusiasm, but the continuity. It is also rare to find a family so aware of the origins of its good fortune, and a willingness to return that to the community in a meaningful and lasting way. In that regard, the family has set a shining example of philanthropy and generosity, which will be a challenge for others to follow.

My dad, Jed, made five trips to the Yukon. He walked, canoed, drove, and flew to the Klondike, all to capture just a hint of what his father must have gone through. On one of our trips, *The Klondike Sun* again wrote about us:

> Phil Lind talks of the Klondike as if he wants to be laughing all the time he's here, as if he's full of energy and good will for the place. "It's been kind of a tradition in our family," Lind says. "What was told to us was that you could do anything if you set your mind to it, because that's how grandfather did it. I think it's about the spirit of what is encompassed here rather than the actual [fact] that he went and mined for gold. There's a lot of philosophy behind this thing ... the spirit of the Yukon, which is that there are opportunities available, but it's not easy. Life isn't easy so you have to work to succeed." That work may be hard, but it has rewards that may be passed on through generations.

Yes, it was passed on through generations. The spirit of the Klondike—hard work, perseverance, big dreams, and humbly giving back when good fortune smiles—never left my grandfather, but the twentieth century brought new business dreams and life adventures he was ready to fulfill, and so would his children and grandchildren.

2

The Bridgman Family, a Society Wedding, and St. Marys Cement

As fortune continued to smile on the Lind family, even through the Great Depression, the opposite occurred to the Bridgman family when my mother's father died young and unexpectedly in 1936. My mother, Susan (Susie) Bridgman, had just finished high school at the time.

My maternal grandfather, Philip Ashley Bridgman, was a gregarious man from Belchertown, Massachusetts, a quaint place between Springfield and Amherst, 135 kilometres due east of Boston. (Somewhat awkwardly named, the town's designation is in honour of Jonathan Belcher, a wealthy local landowner and the royal governor of Massachusetts from 1730 to 1740.) Now a sleepy commuter town for places like Hartford, 80 kilometres south, and Boston, Belchertown is rich with history.

Because the rocky soil wasn't great for crops, the town's first industries were lumbering, cattle, sheep, and hog farming. But in the 1800s it became known for building carriages and stage-coaches, peaking midway through that century with as many as 10 carriage shops. By 1845, in one year Belchertown produced 677 wagons that were shipped all over the eastern United States and as far south as Virginia. Local legend has it that one carriage went all the way across the Atlantic to London for Queen Victoria. In his book *The History of Western Massachusetts*, nineteenth-century American writer and poet Josiah Gilbert Holland said that Belchertown made the best carriages of any town its size. "The finest make of carriages proudly bore the label 'Made in Belchertown,'" he wrote. The railroads, however, hurt the coach and carriage manufacturing business in the late 1800s, and then automobiles killed it.

Belchertown also has a strong military history, producing some of the first Minutemen to take up arms against the British in the Revolutionary War. Unlike militia, men-in-arms who protected their towns, Minutemen—"ready in a minute" soldiers—were a small, hand-picked, elite force of patriots who had to be highly mobile and able to assemble quickly. The men from Belchertown fought at many of the most important and pivotal battles of the Revolutionary War—Bunker Hill, Dorchester Heights, and West Point, to name a few—and they were there with George Washington at Yorktown when Cornwallis surrendered.

The Bridgmans came to this area in the mid-seventeenth century, when Springfield was the first settlement in the Connecticut Valley. Soon afterward, more and more Bridgmans made their way north 30 kilometres to Belchertown, atop a hill overlooking the Connecticut Valley to the west and Quaboag

Valley to the east. Today, Belchertown's church spires can be seen for miles in all directions.

I travelled around the area back in the 1970s, and at my mother's suggestion, I drove into Belchertown. It's quite a pretty place; I was especially taken by its four attractive churches aligned along the Town Common, or square, in its centre. And in the backyard of the Congregational Church I found all sorts of huge plaques and monuments to the various Bridgmans of Belchertown. This was obviously a family that had had an impact on the town and region for many years.

My Bridgman ancestors were postmasters, merchants, farmers, militiamen, and politicians. There was even a preacher who became America's first "China expert" and the first person to translate the Bible into Cantonese. "One of Belchertown's most illustrious sons was Elijah Coleman Bridgman born in Belchertown in 1801," the town history proclaims. "He graduated from Amherst College in 1826 and from Andover Theological Seminary in 1829. He was ordained in Belchertown in 1829 and was sent by the American Board of Commissioners for Foreign Missions to China and arrived in Canton, China in February 1830. He was the first American missionary to be sent to that country. He spent 14 years translating the Bible into Chinese." As editor of *The Chinese Repository* from 1832 to 1851, my distant cousin contributed greatly to America's knowledge and understanding of Chinese civilization through his extensive writings on the country's history and culture. His work laid the foundations for American Sinology and shaped the development of Sino-American relations through the late nineteenth and early twentieth centuries.

Like Elijah, my grandfather Philip Ashley Bridgman graduated from Amherst College, in his case in 1906 with a bachelor of arts. A decade later, on July 29, 1917, in Belchertown, he married my grandmother, Blanche Watson from Boston. My mother, Susie, was born on May 27, 1918. (Fifteen years later Ted Rogers would be born on the same day, May 27, one of several peculiar coincidences between Ted and me.)

In the early 1930s my mother's family moved to Toronto after my grandfather was named national sales manager for General Foods in Canada. With his big job and good salary the family lived well, and yet they remained on the fringes of Toronto's establishment. Back in those days, before World War II, Toronto's high society looked more across the ocean to Britain than south to the States as they do today. Americans like my mother and her family were thus considered interlopers by the city's self-anointed aristocracy.

Nonetheless, everyone loved my grandfather, with his big personality and genuine interest in others. I'm told that even dogs loved him—something he and I definitely do not have in common. But like me as well as my son, my father, and my paternal grandfather, Philip Ashley Bridgman loved to fish, except that his preference was going after the lunkers—muskie—not fly fishing like the Linds.

One day, while fishing on the French River, the unofficial dividing line between northern and southern Ontario, he appeared jaundiced, his eyes were said to be yellowed, and he collapsed and soon died. That was August 19, 1936.

It was some sort of liver disease, and yet he wasn't a drinker. In acute liver failure, people may go from being healthy to being dead within a few days, and sometimes their blood pressure gets so high that a heart attack or stroke could be the ultimate killer. We don't know for sure about Grandfather. There was no autopsy performed, nor was there a reputable hospital up there at the time, so no one really knows what happened. He probably noticed some symptoms, such as fatigue, weakness, nausea, and loss of appetite, and ignored them so as not to miss a beloved fishing trip. He was only 51 years old.

I was born seven years later, almost to the day he died, on August 20, 1943, so naturally I was named Philip Bridgman Lind in his honour.

Needless to say, the family fortunes changed dramatically that day on the French River in 1936. Susie, my mother, had just completed high school at Bishop Strachan School, Canada's oldest private school for girls in Toronto's Forest Hill neighbourhood. She was all set to attend Smith College in Northampton, Massachusetts, a private women's liberal arts school 25 kilometres from Belchertown and loosely affiliated with Amherst College, when her dad's tragic death scuttled all that. (At the time her only sibling, younger sister Ann, was at Havergal College, a private girls' school in North Toronto.)

Instead of college at an exclusive private school, Mother went to the University of Toronto, where she graduated with a bachelor of arts. At U of T she met my father, Walter (Jed) Lind, while he was in law school; he had returned to Toronto in 1937 with a BA from McGill University in Montreal. Susie was beautiful, social, and—despite the family's fortunes having changed—very much sought after.

My dad's legal education at Osgoode Hall Law School would be interrupted by World War II, but not his courtship with Mom and their eventual nuptials. They married on January 15, 1941, during the deepest and darkest days of the war. The United States was almost a year away from entering on the side of the Allies, and the Soviet Union was still on the sidelines under the German-Soviet Nonaggression Pact. Britain and its empire, including Canada, were alone against the tyranny of the Axis powers.

By this time my dad had become a pilot in the Royal Canadian Air Force. He'd gotten his wings at Ottawa's RCAF Station Rockcliffe despite having broken the rules about getting married. At the time, you weren't allowed to marry unless you were an officer or had special written permission from way up the chain of command. My father, naturally, didn't think that made sense since he'd soon be an officer anyway, so off he went to Toronto on leave to get married. The thing is, the wife of Rockcliffe's commanding officer, Bill McBrien, was one of my mother's good friends and a member of the wedding party. So it wasn't a secret to Dad's C.O., who kindly looked the other way. But then the next problem arose: it was a big, splashy wedding in Toronto that made the society pages of *The Globe and Mail*, the *Star,* and the *Telegram.*

After a very brief honeymoon, Dad returned to Rockcliffe to finish his pilot training. Well, his buddies got their hands on a few copies of the newspapers with the wedding spread, and knowing that he hadn't had official permission to marry, started posting them on strategic bulletin boards around the base. Just a silly prank, but with potentially serious repercussions. My dad ran around frantically pulling down the newspaper clippings in case a higher-up in the military was visiting the base and started asking questions.

He survived that little episode and a few weeks later did get his wings, learning a critical lesson mid-flight at the same time. McBrien, the C.O., had taken Dad up to test him and sat in the back seat. Before takeoff, for whatever reason, Dad hadn't strapped himself in properly. (I bet it was nerves that caused him to make that mistake, because nerves plagued him his entire life.) When it came time for the rollover manoeuvre, Dad slipped far enough out of his seat while upside down that his feet could no longer reach the pedals to turn the plane back into the right-side-up position. After a few harrowing seconds, from the back seat McBrien righted the plane. Fortunately he overlooked that buckle-up mistake, and Dad got his wings. It was a hard lesson learned, though, and Dad would never forget it; he would pass it along to other trainees over the years.

After all this, however, Dad would never get to a combat theatre. He had awful stomach and ulcer problems. Once, while training over Prince Edward Island, he got terribly ill in flight, and afterward they told him that with such a condition he couldn't go overseas into combat. This bothered him a great deal.

Dreadfully disappointed, he ended up serving the entire war as a flight lieutenant training bomber pilots at the huge air base in Brantford, Ontario, southwest of Toronto. Meanwhile, his older brother, John Skiffington Lind, would go on to become a war hero during the campaign through Italy, winning both the Distinguished Service Order (DSO) and the Efficiency Decoration (ED). According to the famed Perth Regiment's records,

Lieutenant-Colonel Lind throughout the operation led the Perth Regiment with great dash and dogged determination, and although he was continually under intense enemy shellfire for several days on end was never deterred from the task in hand. At the crossing of the Liri River near Caprano on the 27th May 1944, with his battalion being subjected to steady enemy artillery fire, he went forward to the leading platoons, who were assembling in an area which was under observed enemy shell and machine gun fire from the far bank, and, ignoring his own safety, personally directed and supervised the crossing in assault boats of his entire Battalion.

If you've seen the movie *A Bridge Too Far*, imagine the scene where Robert Redford leads his men of the 82nd Airborne Division on a dangerous daylight river crossing in flimsy wood-and-canvas boats. That's not too different from what my uncle did: "His courage, determination and personal disregard for his own safety set a high example to his men and resulted in the formation of a bridgehead across the river thus allowing the engineers to bridge and the remainder of the Division to cross and continue the advance."

My uncle "Jenny" was a good man, and tough as nails. I liked him a lot. (To digress briefly, it was that toughness that earned him the nickname back at boarding school, where they liked to call you something the opposite of what you were; "Jenny" derived from Jenny Lind, the famous Swedish soprano. My father, Walter, also had his nickname "Jed" hung on him at boarding school. The school's bus driver at the time was an incredibly obese man named Jed, and since my dad was rake-thin, he got called after him. And although both nicknames—Jenny and Jed—stuck for life, their mother detested them. She refused to call her sons anything other than their given names, John and Walter—but she was the only person who did.)

Uncle Jenny was promoted to brigadier-general before the war's end. I don't believe Dad resented his brother's wartime heroics, but he would have loved to have seen action himself. No doubt "second son" insecurities were naturally felt, too.

After the war, those feelings would have been cemented when Dad returned to Osgoode Hall Law School while John S. Lind (Uncle Jenny) was named president and general manager of St. Marys Cement Ltd., succeeding their father, John Grieve Lind.

This would be a good time to step back and look at what John Grieve Lind did upon his return from the Yukon.

My grandfather Lind looked around for opportunities, as was his way, and envisaged a future in cement. He foresaw an explosion of economic growth coming to North America—and that as the continent quickly became more and more urban, less and less rural, cement would be the backbone of the necessary infrastructure. No skyscraper, subway system, dam, or highway could have been built without it.

First, John Grieve Lind invested some of his Klondike money in the Grey and Bruce Cement Company, and soon became the principal owner of its Owen Sound cement plant. The venture wasn't altogether successful, though, mostly because the plant wasn't equipped to produce a new type of cement developed in England in the mid-1800s called Portland, named for the limestone Isle of Portland in the English Channel. But there were other pressures, too, including the dubious business practices of Max Aitken of New Brunswick (later Lord Beaverbrook), who misled both his Canada Cement shareholders and the owners of smaller cement companies he was buying up in a bid to consolidate the industry. Grandfather refused to sell, but he really felt the sting of anti-competitive pricing and other dirty tricks.

Believing in this new cement called Portland, Grandfather and his brother-in-law, A.G. Larsson, a chemist at the Durham Cement Company, started researching and learning everything they could about it. This goes back to the self-taught aspect of my grandfather's personality and his dogged determination to succeed.

He and Larsson decided in 1910 that St. Marys, Ontario, with its abundance of limestone, clay, and water nearby, would be an ideal location for a new factory. It was also situated on two national railway lines, had access to hydroelectric power from Niagara Falls, and was close to the giant U.S. market. Next, John Grieve Lind rounded up investors such as Alfred Rogers (a relative of Ted Rogers whom he knew through the cement industry) and John Gooderham in Toronto.

They called the company St. Marys Portland Cement Company Limited. The original plan was to disassemble the Owen Sound plant and move it to St. Marys, but when this proved impractical, construction began on a new plant, costing $250,000 ($5.5 million today). That plant went into production in November 1912, employing 90 people; with two 165-foot rotary kilns, its initial capacity was 180 tonnes a day. The product, named "Pyramid Brand" Portland Cement, sold for $9 a tonne. It was an immediate success.

My grandfather, who by this time had married Gertrude Heming of Owen Sound (after asking her father for her hand during a game of bridge), moved his young family to St. Marys just before the plant's official opening. He was a minority owner and the plant manager, and the only owner to live in the town. He and my uncle Jenny would go on to grow St. Marys Cement into the largest independently owned cement company in Canada. (Later in these pages, I'll delve into the messy and short-sighted sale of the company, which, as a board member, I unsuccessfully tried to stop.)

Over his 35 years living in St. Marys, Grandfather became one of the biggest supporters of the community and its institutions. Indeed, the St. Marys Museum says this: "No one had greater impact on the Town of St. Marys in the 20th Century than John Grieve Lind."

Beyond running the cement plant, the largest employer in the region, and helping put bread on the table for hundreds of families, John Grieve Lind was father of the St. Marys public parks and recreation system, becoming its first parks commissioner. When the town bought the baseball-diamond lands called the "Flats" (now Milt Dunnell Field, named for the famed *Toronto Star* sports columnist who grew up in St. Marys), he bought property immediately north of the Flats so that he could expand the facility for other sports, including lacrosse and hockey.

And, during the Depression, Grandfather purchased the seven-acre Cadzow Park on Church Street South, including the century home on the property, and built the Cadzow swimming pool. (On opening day he sat by the pool and tossed pennies to the bottom so that children could dive for them.) He also donated the property's stone house, which eventually became St. Marys Museum. "He envisioned municipal parkland all along the Thames River and Trout Creek," says Amy Cubberley, the museum's curator. "Although this did not happen in his lifetime, he would have approved of today's system connecting walkways and parks along the waterfront."

One of the best examples of John G. Lind's community building was purchasing derelict lots near his home on Church Street during the early 1930s—in the depths of the Great Depression—and turning them into a lovely park, now called Lind Park. He hired a landscape architect and used labourers from the cement plant to do the heavy work, like building the stone walls on the south and west sides with pillared entrances into the park. This brought twofold benefits during the Depression: he provided more hours of work for hungry men while creating a lasting beautification for the town.

In 1942, the year before I was born, John Lind donated the park to the people of St. Marys. Our family has continued his legacy over the years by supporting parks and recreation in the town with donations to the development of the Quarry, the tennis courts, the swimming pool, the Sportsplex, and the Canadian Baseball Hall of Fame. The Lind family has given millions of dollars in total, and may I say, humbly, that we've contributed more to St. Marys than the famous Eaton family, which also got its start in St. Marys after Timothy Eaton opened his first store there in 1856.

I am proud of the Linds for giving back to the communities—the Klondike and St. Marys—where so much good fortune was bestowed upon our family. I think my grandfather would be proud, too. Through his deeds and his dreams, John Grieve Lind instilled these feelings of thanks and appreciation in each of his descendants.

3

Garbage Trucks, Hymnbooks, Christmas Trees, and Other Hijinks

After World War II, our family moved to uptown Toronto while my father was still at Osgoode Hall Law School. Once he'd graduated and begun his career, my younger brothers and sister soon came along: Ron, then Jenifer (Jenny), and finally Geoff.

My childhood was a happy one—at least until I was sent off to boarding school. I played hockey for the Beavers in the Lawrence Park Athletic Association, got bored at school, and managed to find trouble at most every turn. I was not unlike most boys growing up in the postwar years, except that trouble seemed to find me more easily than others. As a youngster, I was what some of the older folks would call "a going concern," or perhaps a "hellion" to those more blunt.

At Bedford Park Public School they threatened to hold me back a year, which caused consternation in our home, especially with my father. So I was tested, and when my IQ score came back high, instead of holding me back they had me skip a grade.

My mother and I had a special bond. All my siblings would agree that I was her favourite, no matter how hard she tried to conceal it. She loved my stories and antics. Although in hindsight, she probably wasn't too fond of my more mischievous pranks—like pushing cream pies into the faces of unsuspecting strangers on the street, especially when my little brother emulated my bad example. (Poor Ron. Instead of using a fast getaway car like my friend Gordie Chaplin's Ford convertible, he used our family's Nash Rambler station wagon. So when he went out one time and "pied" an innocent person, the car was so slow in getting away that the guy had time to wipe off the pie and take down the licence plate number. By the time Ron got home, the police were already at the house. And believe me, my mother and especially my father were not amused in the least.)

But most of the tomfoolery was just the silliness of boys from well-to-do families exercising their privileges of the day. One time a police officer nabbed us for some stunt, but released us when he found out Thor Eaton was in our group. Things are sure different today; there's no way police would look the other way simply because the kids are from Forest Hill, Rosedale, or any other tony neighbourhood with well-connected parents.

My most vivid early memories were the long talks with Mom and making her laugh. Sometimes she'd laugh so much that Dad would accuse her of condoning my bad behaviour. She'd sheepishly agree with him, look down at the floor in shame, and then glance over at me with a twinkle in her eye, almost as if there was a secret between the two of us. I loved her so much, as I also loved my dad, but there was something special about her. Looking back, she expertly walked the tightrope between mother and best friend to her eldest child during those impressionable years. (My son, Jed, has very similar memories about his mother and their long talks together. "Dad and I are very close but very different people," Jed says. "Mom wanted every bit of news, all the details. She had a great ear and great wisdom. I lost that when I lost her.")

During my middle-school years at Upper Canada College, my classmate and lifelong friend John Godfrey would battle me for the bottom position in every subject. John's parents, Jack and Mary, and my parents were good friends. Both our dads were lawyers and had been pilots during the war. But while the Godfreys were dedicated Liberals like my grandfather Lind, my parents were Tories, as I would become. (John's dad ended up as a senator and John himself was a member of Parliament for 15 years, even serving as a parliamentary secretary for Liberal prime minister Jean Chrétien.)

Perhaps the best way to describe my feelings about and memories of UCC would be "benign." There was definitely some weird shit going on then—as future convictions of teachers on counts of sexual assault would prove. But for me, nothing really bad happened. The worst creepy feeling I ever had was a shoulder rub during class from one of the teachers.

It was during these years that I met my first real girlfriend, Susan Dunlop, who was attending the private girls' school Bishop Strachan, near the all-boys UCC. We were very young and very naughty, or so we thought at the time. Girls fascinated me far more than schoolbooks did.

With two scholastic strikes against me—grade school and middle-school years—Dad shipped me out of UCC after Grade 9 to Ridley College, the military-style boarding school that both he and Uncle Jenny had attended. Ridley is in St. Catharines, Ontario, about an hour's drive down the QEW highway, but it felt like a world away. It was a place that meted out corporal punishment, and life was dominated by arcane rules and regulations.

My feelings about Ridley are far more emotive than those about UCC. To paraphrase Charles Dickens, it was the best of times and the worst of times—with the emphasis on worst. Although I do need to add a proviso here: most of the things I detested about Ridley no longer exist there now. And many of my friends and relatives who attended, including my dad and my brother Geoff, loved the place. (Given my experiences and views, my mother put her foot down and wouldn't allow Dad to send Ron to Ridley, but later Geoff wanted to go.)

The other thing Ridley had going against it was that, from ages 14 to 18, only two things occupied my mind, and schoolwork wasn't one of them. Those two things were girls and politics. As for the first, there were no girls at Ridley back then. (My daughter, Sarah, went to Ridley for Grade 11 when her mother decided she needed more discipline in her life. Sarah did not enjoy it either.) But as for the second, the name Ridley "College" would work in my favour when, in the late 1950s, I was able to gain access as a young delegate to the national Progressive Conservative convention in Ottawa. Convention organizers thought I was a postsecondary student, not a high school student. I was only 15 years old at that first of many political conventions, and I loved the excitement, the wheeling and dealing. (A couple of years later, in October 1961, I attended the

Ontario Progressive Conservative leadership convention where John Robarts was elected after six ballots. Barely 18, I was a "runner," or gopher, for convention chairman and backroom legend Eddie Goodman. These were the early days of my life-long fascination with politics and politicians.)

But what I loathed so much at school was Ridley's strict regimen and Victorian-era rules. The older students could make the younger ones carry their books, shine their shoes, or clean up the seniors' room. When we had free time on Wednesday and Saturday afternoons they'd often make us "duck walk" around the indoor pool while carrying heavy unloaded rifles. And the masters, or teachers, not only allowed this to occur but endorsed it.

Physical and mental abuse was rampant. Canings were commonplace, with six whacks being the maximum. I remember one master making me memorize a 400-line poem over a weekend when I should have been studying for my final exams. That punishment was borderline sadistic.

There was one master named Jack Swift whom we called "Jack Rat." (Apparently, during World War II he'd been a British tank commander in North Africa, part of an armoured division dubbed the "Desert Rats," hence the nickname.) We pulled one of our greatest pranks on him when we had kids throughout the school fill out magazine orders for all sorts of different items, mark them "Bill Me Later," and address them to Jack Swift, Ridley College. For months thereafter, literally hundreds of things arrived in the mail for Swift. He was beside himself.

I was cheeky, and so the stricter the discipline, the more I'd organize crazy things in some sort of rebellious counterattack. Such antics at Ridley are probably the only reason I survived the place. There are so many stories, and most of these lend themselves better to the oral tradition than the written word, but I've got to write a few down for posterity.

One time, the night before family day when parents and siblings would visit Ridley, my pal Russ Jones and I strung a long metal chain and huge padlock around the Marriott Gates at the front of the property, blocking access to vehicles entering the grounds. With none of the visitors able to get in, dozens and dozens of cars lined up outside on Ridley Road, honking away. Frantic Ridley staff scurried about, trying to locate a cutter big enough to clip the chain and open the gates, but they couldn't find anything that would work. They ended up having to use a torch to get the chain off the gate. The whole thing took a good couple of hours, and all the while Russ Jones and I were dying of laughter.

Another time, after we'd all peed into bottles for tuberculosis testing, my friend Gordie Chaplin and I added liquid sugar to quite a few sample bottles. When the results came back the school thought it had an "outbreak" of diabetes and immediately sent several boys to be quarantined. I can still hear the public-address announcements calling one kid after another down to the infirmary.

For me, the best thing about my time at Ridley was the trouble I could cause with friends like Gordie Chaplin, Ross Poyntz, and a handful of others. To this day, Gordie is like a brother to me. There's probably no one in the world who can make me laugh as much as Gordie can.

He and I had befriended Ridley's garbageman, Mr. Shelby. He also worked as a pig farmer, and we'd help him load 45-gallon drums of slop (which he'd use for feed) from the Ridley kitchen onto his truck. One time, just for fun, we asked to borrow his truck, and to our surprise he agreed. Gordie and I loved to take it to drive-in restaurants. These weren't drive-through restaurants like today; back then, you'd pull your vehicle into a parking slip, and the wait staff would come out with your tray of food and hook it to a rolled-down window. "That truck stunk," reminisces Gordie. "We'd pull in and all the cars nearby would look at us, get a whiff of the smells, and pull their cars out as far away from us as possible."

Another guy named Mowat Robinson, who died in 2011, pulled off one of the best pranks in Ridley's history. One of the teachers, an insecure little man named Jack Matheson ("Mad Jack"), used to shake us down for any pennies in our pockets. He had a huge jar in his office, bigger than a goldfish bowl, and he called his collection "Pennies for the Poor." Mad Jack would keep dumping his collected pennies into the jar, and when it was filled he'd roll them up and take them to the bank. There were thousands and thousands of pennies in that jar. One day in chemistry class, Mowat got the idea to take some hydrochloric acid and dump it into Mad Jack's jar. After a few hours the pennies turned into a bluish-green blob of copper chloride—and Mad Jack went ballistic. He launched himself on the warpath, looking for the culprit. I wasn't about to rat Mowat out, but I was in Mad Jack's crosshairs for a while.

I've lost track of Steve Mitchell, but he and I pulled off one prank that got us very close to being expelled—and it wasn't even that big of a deal, nor did it do any damage (unlike the time we set off a bomb on the football field). But this prank had to do with the Ridley College chapel, so it was deemed "sacrilegious" and caused an incredible fuss.

Back in those days, students were required to attend chapel a couple of times a day and sing our hearts out. Well, Steve and I decided one night to sneak into the chapel, collect all the hymnbooks, and hide them in Reverend John Hesketh's office. The next morning, when the entire school had gathered in the pews, Reverend Hesketh had the organ start up to lead us in singing. Problem was, none of the boys knew the words—and no one could find a single hymnbook. Great laughter all around. Of course, it wasn't long before all hell broke loose; they even ran a special investigation.

It was a perfect storm of bad timing. The tough but popular headmaster, Dr. John Russell Hamilton, had recently died, a fatal stroke having taken him in the Ridley chapel. And with "Hammy" gone, now Mad Jack Matheson was the acting headmaster. Matheson was an okay guy, but when he lost his temper, he really lost it. I had absolutely adored Dr. Hamilton, so in my eyes Matheson had a tough act to follow.

By then I was in my last year, and Matheson had had it with me and my antics. He'd already punished me for various crimes by skipping over me as editor of the school magazine *Acta Ridleiana*, despite my having been associate editor for two years. I'd also been in line for lieutenant of the drill team and possibly a prefect, but with Hammy gone I was denied all these honours. It would turn out to be a year of rage for me.

Matheson wanted me out. And so, after the hymnbook episode, he went to Ridley's board and declared that the prank had been disrespectful not only to the church but also to former Ridley students who'd died in the two World Wars and whose names were etched upon the walls of the chapel.

It was all such bullshit. One of the names up on that wall was Philip Frowde Seagram, a distant relative of mine and a captain in the famed 48th Highlanders. He'd been killed on March 8, 1941, when a German bomb hit the Café de Paris in London while he was enjoying an evening out with friends. I'd heard many stories about Captain Seagram, and I knew that he and his colleagues up on the chapel walls would never have been offended by our prank; they'd probably get a good chuckle out of it.

Nonetheless, Mad Jack was out for blood. But my father came to my rescue, both as a former Ridley student and as someone with friends on the board. After such a close call I should have put my head down, stayed out of trouble, and graduated without further incident. Instead, I vowed to torment Matheson even more.

We stepped up our efforts to help kids go AWOL by increasing the "excursion fund" we'd use to finance trips to visit girlfriends and buddies in places like Toronto and Ottawa, and even in far-flung places across the border in the States. Parents would call in a panic, and the school wouldn't know where the kid was. Let's just say Matheson was under a fair bit of stress when this happened.

Admittedly, I was a real shit disturber. But I just hated the corporal punishment, the favouritism shown to jocks, and the "old boys" system of reparations for rebels like me. In fact, my Ridley nickname was "Fidel" because I was viewed as such a rebel. (Thankfully, the nickname didn't stick.)

In fairness, there were teachers I did like and get along with. Headmaster "Hammy" was my favourite, even if I did feel his cane from time to time. Others were Gwen Morris (history and English), Gordon "Mickey" McLeod (English), and D.S. "Fingers" Fensom (he had long fingers and taught chemistry, fencing, and debating). We tormented them all, but Fensom took it best, and in the spirit in which it was given.

Ridley has produced many famous alumni, from politicians, businessmen, and actors to ambassadors and Bank of Canada governors (including David Dodge, who was in my class). I remember too often being told by various masters that I'd never amount to very much. That lit a fire in my belly, for which I am tremendously grateful. I was driven and determined to prove them wrong.

In 2014, "as part of the 125th Anniversary of Ridley College, the Alumni Committee researched and prepared profiles of 125 Ridleians of Distinction—Ridley alumni who exemplify Ridley's motto *Terar Dum Prosim*," which, loosely translated, means "May I be consumed in service." (Although many Ridleians translate it as "Tear down this prison.") And lo and behold, there I am, the kid who wouldn't amount to much now a Ridleian of Distinction: "Phil Lind attended Ridley from 1957–1961 ... Lind joined Rogers in its infancy and working alongside Ted Rogers managed to parlay the company into the major communications powerhouse it is today in Canada." It also mentions some of my other work in sports, arts and culture, and charities. A very nice honour, but it does make me wonder what Mad Jack Matheson and some of the others would think about "Fidel" Lind being part of such an elite group in Ridley's history.

After Ridley, I went to McGill University in Montreal and was accepted into the Zeta Psi fraternity. My dad had been in the same fraternity when he was at McGill. And by the time I got there in the early 1960s, Zeta Psi was *the* fraternity for parties and general rowdiness. To picture our fraternity house, just think back to National Lampoon's *Animal House* movie.

Every weekend was a party, either at the house or at the cool bars and hangouts around Montreal. Two places that really stand out were the Esquire Show Bar on Stanley Street and the Berkeley Hotel on Sherbrooke. Neither one exists today (and the Berkeley is now the headquarters of Alcan Aluminum). But back in the early 60s, the Esquire Show Bar was a rhythm-and-blues nightclub that attracted international artists before they were famous and even after they gained fame: people like James Brown, Ray Charles, Aretha Franklin, Tina Turner, Otis Redding, Bo Diddley, and B.B. King. We'd go to the Berkeley Hotel's bar for different reasons—once we found out that Air Canada, headquartered in Montreal, would put up their flight attendants-in-training there. It was also the place where we enjoyed a strange Friday afternoon ritual: after a hard week's work, guys would get a few drinks into them and one or two would actually eat glass. It was quite something to watch.

"I'll tell you one thing," says Jim McCoubrey, a Zete brother at McGill and a lifelong friend, "for someone who doesn't drink, no one could get you into more trouble than Phil Lind."

One Christmas, we cut down a large fir tree in the front yard of a Westmount estate and took it to the famous Bens Delicatessen on our way back to the fraternity house. We spent a night in jail, but a guy named Victor Mills was the ringleader of that escapade, not me. There was another time when we "liberated" two Kon-Tiki statues from Montreal's downtown Sheraton Hotel. Luckily, a Zete brother named T.R. Anthony Malcolm, who was a young lawyer at the time, would always help get us out of trouble. (Malcolm went on to have a long legal career, and he worked tirelessly to preserve the Scottish culture and tradition in Quebec. He died in 2013 at age 83.)

Needless to say, my grades were subpar and I flunked one subject in my first year at McGill. I loved the action, the people, and the city. I also fell in love for the first time with a woman by the name of Martha Nixon, who was smart and incredibly attractive. With Martha, I was definitely punching above my weight. But after dating for a couple of years, we broke up when I told her I was transferring to the University of British Columbia in Vancouver. She said that this "thing" we had wouldn't work cross-country. I said it *could* work, but she said goodbye.

She went on to become dean of students at McGill, which is a pretty big deal, as the dean of students is in charge of a team responsible for the quality of student life on campus. Student rights and responsibilities, academic integrity, academic advising, the student disciplinary process, and student recognition are all overseen by this office, which she ran.

It's funny what life can bring. Over the years, Martha was married and divorced twice and ended up living in Aurora, Ontario. In the mid-1990s, after my marriage had ended, I found myself there one afternoon—I'd gone to watch my son Jed and his UCC rugby team play against the town's St. Andrew's College team—and thought I'd look Martha up. We had a nice visit, but it was an eye-opener. She had multiple sclerosis and was really thin. What really got me that day was a scrapbook she pulled out with press clippings about me over the years—she'd followed my career all along. Not long after our reunion Martha moved back to Montreal, where her elderly mother looked after her until she passed. It was a really sad ending.

But back to McGill and the early 1960s. I simply had to leave for UBC; McGill was too rigid for my personality. Its antiquated rules were too much like those at Ridley College, except that Ridley's corporal punishment was replaced by McGill's psychological beat downs.

They loved to threaten to fail you. For example, I remember a professor telling us on my first day to look to our right and then to our left, and to understand that one of us wouldn't be there next year. Another time, I was flunked out of a geography course that I hadn't even registered in. Holy shit, I thought to myself, this place is so unwelcoming.

So after a couple of years at McGill, I became that person on the left or the right; I needed out, and UBC was the tonic. I loved the place. Maybe I was maturing (although the Zeta Psi fraternity house was just as fun and wild in Vancouver as it had been in Montreal), but I took to UBC like a fish to water.

I also immersed myself in B.C. politics, and met many brilliant people who'd be friends for life and political allies for years: people like Peter Hyndman, Malcolm Wickson, Jake Kerr, Bob Healey, and David Barnhill, along with prominent Tories like Davie Fulton, John A. Fraser, and Bill Macadam. (We helped Fulton try to revive the B.C. Progressive Conservative Party when he returned from Ottawa to take on the provincial leadership in 1963.) These names will appear again in these pages. They would all play roles in my life, not only in politics but also in business and personal dimensions. During these years I really got to know western Canadian politicians and what motivated them, just as in my McGill years I'd met and come to understand Quebec politicians like Brian Mulroney and Michael Meighen.

After two years at UBC, I'd attained a BA in political science and economics and made many valuable political connections. From there, I went down to the University of Rochester to complete a master's in political sociology under tremendous professors like Peter Regenstreif and William Riker, who were

doing groundbreaking political science research in voter motiva-
tions, game theory, special interest groups, and a whole lot more.

With my American background (being half American
through my mother), I was at this point exploring the American
psyche and culture, especially politics. This has been a lifelong
passion—including my spending millions in setting up two
chairs at UBC for others to study the U.S.—and in later years
would prove invaluable at Rogers Communications. I'll talk more
about the Phil Lind Initiative later, but for context, I've pulled
this description from its website:

> The Phil Lind Initiative is an annual dialogue series and course host-
> ed by the School of Public Policy and Global Affairs at the University
> of British Columbia (UBC), and is made possible by a generous gift
> from Philip Lind (BA'66, LLD'02). The initiative invites prominent
> U.S. scholars, writers and intellectuals to UBC to share ideas with
> students, faculty and the wider community on some of the most
> urgent issues of our time.
>
> Our Spring 2018 series, "The Unravelling of the Liberal
> Order," includes visits from many of the world's leading intellec-
> tuals on the subject, including Ed Luce, Francis Fukuyama, Steven
> Pinker, Misha Glenny, Susan Rice, and Anne-Marie Slaughter.
> Each speaker gives a public talk and guest teaches one session of
> the course: "GPP 591 Lind Initiative Seminar: The Unravelling of
> the Liberal Order."
>
> Previous series focused on some of the world's most pressing
> global issues. The initiative's inaugural series in 2015, "The Politics
> of Inequality," was led by Nobel Laureate Joseph Stiglitz, who taught
> and lectured at UBC in a course that explored global inequality. Our
> 2016 series, "The U.S. Election Campaign," examined the influx of
> populism into American politics, the role of 'dark money' in shaping
> the election, and the internal realignment of the Republican party.
> For our 2017 series, "The Trump Impact: Change, Challenges, Re-
> sponses," professor, author and former U.S. Labor Secretary Robert

Reich led an ongoing discussion of how such a divisive and controversial politician would shape American and world politics.

For much of my early life—up until my twenties—I was a first-
class shit disturber. Sure, I was captivated by politics and worked
my ass off on political campaigns and in getting my master's degree
in only one year, but there were definitive signs that the seeds
planted in me by my grandfather Lind and my father were not
taking root. So by the time I reached my twenties, I was determined, absolutely determined, to get much more out of life.
I'd seen too many people from wealthy families drift aimlessly,
and this was not a path for me. (As my old friend Jim McCoubrey
says, "Phil comes from the upper class, but he's always had this
innate ability to socialize with everyone and make friends easily.
He's always been connected socially and politically, and he was
always more interested in civics than studying.")

Many thought my path would be politics, and I admit that when
I was young I'd seriously considered running for public office. But
inside me were those same entrepreneurial feelings my grandfather
must have had when he ventured out to the Klondike. I just had
to find my own gold rush, just as he had found his.

It's funny how fate can smile at the most appropriate times.
One summer in the 1960s, when I was at Gordie Chaplin's family
cottage for the weekend, I met a man named Ed Cole. The son
of a dairy farmer, Cole was president of Chevrolet and would
become president of the entire General Motors. He'd also become
the driving force in eliminating leaded gasoline from North
American vehicles. The Chaplin family business was building
automotive parts, so they knew Cole well. That weekend Ed Cole

looked me in the eye and said, "Son, always act in business like you've got a million dollars in your pocket."

It was great advice—and perfect for someone like me, who always spit the bit when the reins were too tightly pulled. I knew I couldn't survive in just any old corporate environment. I needed the freedom to speak my mind.

And I'm ever thankful that Ted Rogers not only tolerated that from me, but encouraged it.

4

The Art and Science of Politics

I love life—and all the things that make up its fullness. I love music and art, especially contemporary photographic art. I'm also crazy about sports and all sorts of other things. I have a childlike (some might call it juvenile) sense of life. I was 30 years old when Bob Dylan recorded "Forever Young," and it has always resonated with me.

I really love politics and am fascinated by the political world, particularly why people do what they do and what influences them. Call it sociology, political science, or maybe marketing. But I genuinely do understand what motivates a guy like my friend John Tory to give up a high-paying executive career for an often thankless job in public service as the mayor of Toronto.

Politics has always been one of the central themes in my life, and has taken on so many various forms. Now, I understand that most don't share my interest and enthusiasm for its backrooms, so I'll keep this chapter as brief as possible and limit the details to things that helped shape my life, particularly in business.

Early on, when I was about 13 or 14, I started getting the political itch. This was likely because my father was a Conservative and politics was discussed often in my family. By that time the Liberals had been in continuous power in Ottawa my entire life, and even a decade longer. But the late 1950s were proving to be an interesting time in Canada's history.

With Louis St. Laurent's government showing its age, it was looking like the wheels were beginning to fall off the Liberal wagon. Meanwhile, a populist crusader named John Diefenbaker was agitating for breaking the bonds of this apparently perpetual state of affairs. In 1957 he managed to crack the reign and, in 1958, he scored an overwhelming majority victory. As a young Tory, I was totally caught up in this struggle. It was almost like a freedom issue. A liberation from the Liberals.

I was so carried away by this Conservative movement that I asked Ridley College's headmaster, Dr. John "Hammy" Hamilton, if I could attend an upcoming party convention in Ottawa, and he agreed. As I mentioned earlier, I used Ridley's full name not only to attend but to be recognized as a young delegate from a "college."

For me this was really quite something, and I loved every minute of it. With the Conservatives now in power, it was fascinating to see their politicians up close and to shake their hands. And then there were the policy-issue debates, and the subsequent votes on these. I ate it up.

It was also around this time that my informal education in all things American took shape, with near-annual summer road trips to various parts of the U.S. with friends Cammy McArthur and anyone else who wanted to come along. We'd travel in these trucks that looked like troop carriers, and would have such a blast. (One trip resulted in an emergency appendectomy in Alaska, though—my first of several close calls. You'll read about others later in the story.)

When I got to McGill in 1961, I became instantly involved in the Progressive Conservative party in Montreal. We did things like mock Parliament debates in which PCs, Liberals, and the NDP would fight it out on campus. I also got elected as a delegate, and ultimately a vice-president, of the Progressive Conservative Student Federation. Our campus-based PC organization then merged with the riding-based youth group (Young Progressive Conservative Association) to create the Progressive Conservative Youth Federation. PCYF was then sanctioned as the PC party's official youth wing, meaning we could vote at the national conventions that pick leaders and establish policy.

We were engaged in fantastic emotional struggles in those days because by that time Diefenbaker's regime had pretty much run its course. Dithering on decisions had replaced decisiveness. And the Bomarc missile debate was the perfect example of this.

In the fall of 1958, Diefenbaker agreed to deploy American anti-aircraft missiles in Canada as part of the 1957 North American Air Defence (NORAD) agreement with the United States. But Diefenbaker's government didn't make it clear that the version to be acquired, the Bomarc-B, would be fitted with nuclear warheads and deployed in North Bay, Ontario, and La Macaza, Quebec. When this became known in 1960, it led to anti-nuclear protests throughout the country and set off a national debate on whether Canada should adopt nuclear weapons. In a surprising move, the Liberals endorsed nuclear weapons. (Liberal leader Lester Pearson—the 1957 Nobel Peace Prize winner—was not known for having these tendencies. In Canadian politics, we've long seen that a Liberal is someone who's flexible with his or her principles.) On the other hand, Diefenbaker and his foreign affairs minister, Howard Green, were now against arming the missiles with nuclear capabilities.

The nuclear-weapons battle also became a central arguing point within the PC party. As a youth VP, I strongly backed nuclear weapons; I'd been taken by the Kennedy movement in the United States in general and by JFK's decisiveness during the Cuban Missile Crisis in particular. And at an annual Tory convention, the nuclear debate became toxic: while the Diefenbaker loyalists argued against these weapons, those of us who were becoming disenchanted with Diefenbaker argued the reverse.

It was here that I met Ted Rogers for the first time. Ted—a lifelong Diefenbaker loyalist—was leading the anti-nuclear side. In his late twenties, he was tall and gangly and had a baby face that made him look more like a member of our youth wing than of the main party, which he was by that point. I don't remember much about our very first meeting and handshake, but it was not unpleasant even though we were opponents. I do, though, remember Ted speaking for long periods; he felt he needed to filibuster. But that only bought us more time to get more delegates in the room, and we were able to overwhelm him. (Incidentally, that was the first of many political battles I would have with Ted Rogers, but few resulted in the same success I enjoyed that day when I was only a teenager.)

In the end, although our convention resolution to accept nuclear weapons into Canada passed, the government didn't act on it. Diefenbaker's dithering cost him the confidence of the House, and on February 6, 1963, his government was toppled.

Pearson's Liberals went on to win the election and have the weapons deployed (until they were phased out in 1969).

Once I got to UBC, it was an entirely different scene. There, I concentrated not on the youth wing but on the main Progressive Conservative party.

The PC party in B.C. was not a powerful entity at the time, provincially or federally—despite having such talents as Howard Green, the external affairs minister who led the anti-nuclear movement in cabinet; Davie Fulton, another Diefenbaker cabinet minister whom I came to really like and respect; and an up-and-coming MP named John Fraser. Still, B.C. was an interesting place for a young political junkie like me. As Patrick Boyer wrote in *The Big Blue Machine*, his in-depth look at the PC party, "Lind was drawn to the intelligence, modernity, and political attractiveness of Fulton and Fraser." I also became closely attached to Malcolm Wickson, a small land developer in Vancouver. I worked very hard to have him elected president of B.C.'s PC party, and later we'd work together at the party's national headquarters.

I'm still drawn to B.C. for its beauty, its culture, its fishing, and its people. One of my big regrets—and my biggest fight with Ted—was his swapping our B.C. cable assets with the Shaws. More on that later.

My next foray into politics began when I was studying for my master's in political sociology at the University of Rochester. To get to Rochester I'd even turned down Davie Fulton's offer to be his executive assistant in Ottawa. It was a difficult choice, but I really wanted to learn from Peter Regenstreif, who was a Canadian and an outstanding teacher. He'd taken his doctorate at Cornell, and after becoming a professor at Rochester, he developed a sophisticated polling method for forecasting amazingly accurate Canadian election results. And as fate would have it, during my year in Rochester, Davie Fulton opted to run again for the federal PC leadership in 1967. I decided to leverage my on-the-ground political work by making my thesis all about Fulton's leadership bid.

After completing my course work, in 1967 I became a member of the Fulton team at the national convention in Toronto. The members of that team were excellent; among them were Brian Mulroney, Lowell Murray, and Joe Clark. Nonetheless, the winning candidate was Robert Stanfield—although Fulton proved pivotal in Stanfield's election after moving his delegates in that direction. But I often wonder whether, given Stanfield's record, we made the right choice. Certainly Stanfield's team, led by Dalton Camp and Big Blue Machine architect Norman Atkins, was formidable and deserved the victory.

I then formally went to work for the PC party in Ottawa under Malcolm Wickson, whom Stanfield had chosen as national direc- tor. Shortly after my appointment I received a lovely note in the mail from Ted Rogers, who congratulated me and said the party would surely benefit. It was a nice gesture, and typical of Ted; I was on the side of the party that had worked to dump his hero Diefenbaker, but for him none of that mattered.

We were in full election mode now, the Liberal party having chosen Pierre Trudeau for the election expected in 1968. And that campaign was incredible. We worked our tails off, but with limited success. Trudeau was so attractive to the electorate— recall Trudeaumania—that we were roundly defeated. Their win marked the first Liberal majority since 1953.

Some good did come from the 1968 election, though: we elected a strong opposition. Guys like Albertans Steve Paproski and Don Mazankowski, Lincoln Alexander from Hamilton, and a whole series of other MPs enabled us in four years to come within a whisker of defeating Trudeau.

But back then, right after the 1968 election, the PC party organization was decimated. We'd run up considerable debt, and had no early signs of optimism. To compound matters, the party we'd inherited from John Diefenbaker was in disarray. The national headquarters had been, for all intents and purposes, ignored for 10 or 20 years. We had to build a whole new political organization. Fortunately, we had Norm Atkins, Eddie Goodman, and Malcolm Wickson. But Stanfield wasn't a strong leader and Diefenbaker was still there, resisting any and all efforts to work with us.

So, with my American roots, I began looking south of the border for ideas. Through sheer brazenness I became an associate of the Republican Party, whose chairman at the time was the famous Ray Bliss; he took me under his wing and introduced me to many important people, among them Robert Teeter, the pollster from Michigan. And with Wickson, we hired Teeter to come and work with us in Canada.

It was a relationship that would last years beyond my time. Through Teeter's research, Wickson, Atkins, and I changed the party colours from blue and white to red, white, and blue. This represented an enormous change, one that Diefenbaker certainly didn't like. We were putting the "Progressive" part of our name at the fore. And our efforts were certainly yielding results; a newer, flashier political party was emerging.

It wasn't easy: I worked from eight a.m. to midnight every night. (This was good training for later years at Rogers!) There were so many problems, and so many things that had to be fixed. (More good training for Rogers!) To make matters worse, at age 25 I was running the office while my boss Wickson was away for months in a sailboat race to Australia. I felt under siege. With Eddie Goodman's help, we managed to increase the staff somewhat and got a bunch of younger people in there, including Janis Johnson, who later became a senator herself. My main problem centred on, believe it or not, Janis's future husband, Frank Moores, who was both a newly elected MP and the party president. I never really cared for him; I thought Frank was full of bravado but lacking in substance.

The first thing he did after being elected party president was call on me to send out a letter introducing himself to the entire party across Canada. This would have cost a lot of money, and in those days we had none, so I resisted the idea until Moores could tell me how such an expense was going to be paid.

He told me to send it out now and that we'd worry about the money later. I refused. Later, this became a central issue at a board meeting of the Progressive Conservative party, and, to my chagrin, neither Goodman nor Wickson adequately backed me up. So, I resolved there and then to leave the party as soon as I could. I hadn't been planning on staying there beyond a year anyway. As it turned out, I left just before a PC policy conference in Niagara Falls in October 1969.

It's worth noting that on my office wall at PC headquarters hung a poster of Robert Kennedy. I was totally taken by him. Even though I leaned Republican, I'd been transfixed by RFK, and remain so to this day. He was the most attractive politician I've ever known, and that includes quite a few. I would have loved working for him.

I'll never forget the speech he gave the night Martin Luther King Jr. was assassinated in 1968, two months before he himself was gunned down. Kennedy stood atop the trailer of a flatbed truck in Indianapolis and announced that King was dead. Most people in the crowd knew only that MLK had been shot. Kennedy began by saying that King had dedicated his life to justice and non-violence.

> We can move in that direction as a country, in greater polarization— black people amongst blacks, and white amongst whites—filled with hatred toward one another. Or we can make an effort, as Martin Luther King did, to understand, and to comprehend, and replace that violence, that stain of bloodshed that has spread across our land, with an effort to understand, compassion, and love.
>
> For those of you who are black and are tempted to be filled with hatred and mistrust of the injustice of such an act, against all white people, I would only say that I can also feel in my own heart the same kind of feeling. I had a member of my family killed … by a white man.

Since his brother's death, Bobby had grown into a leader who transcended politics and inspired people to do things they didn't know they could do. He closed his speech that night by urging people to go home and say a prayer for King's family and for the country. Incidentally, Indianapolis was the only major American city that had no riots following Martin Luther King's murder.

In my mind, there is only one Canadian politician I hold in anywhere near as much reverence, and that is Darcy McKeough, my political mentor, friend, and brilliant Ontario cabinet minister throughout the 1960s and 70s. He was initially a hard right-of-centre politician who progressively moved to the centre with integrity and compassion for those less advantaged.

In early 1971, Darcy invited me to play politics in the real world again—and I was still only 27 years old. I didn't really know Darcy well at this point, other than that he was the uncle of Joy McKeough, who was married to a good friend of mine, Ross Poyntz. In any case, Darcy phoned and invited me to a meeting at his ministerial office at three p.m. on Sunday, January 3, 1971. We were to discuss whether he'd run for leader of the ruling Progressive Conservative party in Ontario.

Despite the many prominent Tory businessmen in the room, I was surprised to see how few people there were with any real experience in a leadership contest. Besides me—and my experience was limited—there was Joe Martin, who'd worked the 1967 federal leadership campaign for Duff Roblin (who finished second to Bob Stanfield), and an old friend of Darcy's from the Windsor area named Dick Walker.

I was even more surprised by what came next. As Darcy recounts in his memoir *The Duke of Kent*, "I named Richard Walker as my campaign manager with Phil Lind and Joe Martin in charge of the convention organization."

The role of convention chairmen can be as narrow or as broad as the campaign allows, and we interpreted it very broadly. So, along with other offices elsewhere, Joe Martin and I set up a campaign office at the Westbury Hotel near Maple Leaf Gardens, the site of the convention to be held on February 12, 1971, in six weeks' time.

The run-up to the convention was eventful, and incredibly stressful. Every day we'd hear that Darcy had been visiting various places in the province on targeted missions to round up delegates. Unfortunately, we didn't have a solid base anywhere in the province. Darcy was from southwestern Ontario, but the bulk of those delegates had already been scooped by Bill Davis, who'd entered the race a few weeks before Darcy. Tory MPP Charlie McNaughton, also from southwestern Ontario, pointed delegates in Davis's direction.

As convention day approached, we found Darcy McKeough neck-and-neck with Bob Welch for third place, but you never know how things will play out on the floor. Bill Davis and Allan Lawrence were the frontrunners, and Bert Lawrence was also in the field.

At the convention itself we had a tremendous amount of fun, including our "spontaneous" demonstration on the floor. Darcy gave a very good speech about how the role of government is to create incentives for individual and collective success, but that the government is not to be expected to solve every problem by itself. We thought we had some significant momentum, although neither Joe Martin nor I thought we'd win the convention. Still, our team was very spirited and enthusiastic.

In *The Duke of Kent*, Darcy describes some of the hijinks: "Whenever any of my people saw Bert Lawrence, they said 'Hello, Al,' and they said 'Hello, Bert,' to Al, just to drive them both crazy. I'm told one of my workers, who was in the trucking business, moved an Allan Lawrence trailer in the middle of the night from a parking lot opposite Maple Leaf Gardens to a shopping centre in North Toronto." (Just to flesh out Darcy's stories, Joe Martin and I had instructed everyone on the team to call each Lawrence by the other's name; and the trailer that was moved was filled with campaign materials like placards, buttons, and hats.)

Darcy put up a strong fight and made it to the third ballot. But the writing was on the wall, so he dropped out before the fourth ballot and endorsed Davis, the eventual winner. Just as Davie Fulton had done in 1967, my candidate backed the winner.

Darcy had some tremendously good people working for him, among them John Thompson, Joe Martin, Tom Kierans, and Paul Curley. After the campaign, Paul Curley and John Thompson became integral to the Big Blue Machine. As for me, I stayed very close to Darcy as an outside adviser. He seemed to welcome this, as did a number of people who worked for him, including Paul Little and later Tom McMillan. Darcy served as an MPP and cabinet minister from September 25, 1963, to August 16, 1978.

As I mentioned earlier, Darcy McKeough became a tremendously progressive politician. And he certainly covered a lot of ground in key roles as treasurer, minister of municipal affairs, minister of economics and intergovernmental affairs, and energy minister. His reputation was that of a bellicose, old-line conservative, but his actions were entirely different. Beneath the surface of this brash right-winger lay the heart of a sensitive, thoughtful, caring man who gave Ontario some of its best and most progressive policies, many of which are still prominently in place almost 50 years later and form the basis of what has become modern urban Ontario.

Looking back, it took courage and sheer guts to do many of the things Darcy did, especially introducing regional government across the province. Without Darcy McKeough, I'm not sure any of this would have happened, but kudos to Bill Davis in allowing Darcy to do what he did.

Darcy never rose to top-dog status, but he served premiers John Robarts and Bill Davis tirelessly and loyally—especially the latter, during which time Darcy matured as a politician, leader, and thinker. Both premiers were brilliant at setting courses and overall policies and then allowing Darcy to do the job. Ted did the same thing with me. When the boss places near unconditional trust in his proven subordinates, it raises their confidence and hence their performance.

Over the years, my work in politics has been a key reason for my success on many levels. I learned the art of organizing and executing campaigns and of distilling communication down to the simplest, most effective terms. Understanding the art and science of politics was essential in our U.S. endeavours, in which a Canadian company took on Americans in their own backyard and won.

Most importantly, politics introduced me to so many key people in my life, not the least of whom was Ted Rogers.

5

"You're Hired, but Friends Don't Last Long Working Together"

It was cold and drizzly in Washington on January 20, 1969, for Richard Nixon's first inauguration. I was only 25 at the time, and was there as a guest of Ray Bliss, the legendary chairman of the Republican National Committee.

After the drubbing Pierre Trudeau gave the Tories in June 1968, I'd gone to the U.S. to study political tactics that might help the Progressive Conservatives next time around. And Ohio's Bliss was the master of nuts-and-bolts politics who'd reorganized the crippled Republican party following a similar drubbing Lyndon Johnson gave Senator Barry Goldwater in the 1964 presidential election.

Standing in the cold on Capitol Hill amid both presidential pomp and Vietnam War protesters, it appeared as though my career was heading deep into politics. (After the inauguration,

71

anti-war protesters threw rocks at Nixon's limousine as it trav- elled up Pennsylvania Avenue to the White House. Ironically, the next time I'd witness something like that would be 25 years later when people in Vancouver, angered over "negative option" pric- ing, hurled rocks at Rogers's red cable trucks.)

But politics would not be my path. Nine months later to the day—October 20, 1969—I'd be walking into dumpy offices on Toronto's Adelaide Street East to begin my career alongside Ted Rogers.

One day in the spring of that year, I'd had to deliver import- ant party papers to Eddie Goodman, a Tory strategist and lawyer, who was in Ottawa at a CTV network board meeting. Eddie and his legal partner, Charles Dubin, were representing CFTO-TV, Toronto's first privately owned television station and the keystone of the CTV network.

Eddie invited me to stay for the board meeting. Around the table were shooters like Ray Peters from BCTV in Vancouver, Finlay MacDonald from ATV in Halifax, a young Randy Moffat from Winnipeg, and John Bassett from Toronto. As I sat there listening to these powerbrokers talk about television, politics, and the future, I immediately knew that the media industry was the career for me. These guys were paid to read newspapers and be informed! That one meeting literally changed my life.

I actively began looking for a job in the media, and was able to line up job interviews with some of the biggest in the indus- try at the time, including Selkirk Holdings Ltd., a dynamic radio and TV broadcaster. Selkirk's president, J. Stuart MacKay, was predicting explosive growth in Canada's TV industry.

Of course, I also contacted Ted Rogers. His sister Ann Graham was a friend; we were the same age and had known each other since she'd gone to Bishop Strachan just down the road from Upper Canada College. (About five years before this job hunt, at Ann's twenty-first birthday party hosted by Ted, then 32, at his new house on Frybrook Road in Forest Hill, he and I briefly talked about perhaps someday working together. Little did I know how often I'd be in that house over the years. The debates—or more precisely Ted's berating—over key business issues would often get so heated that Rogers executives nicknamed the house the "Frying Pan.")

When we met in 1969 to discuss the job, Ted told me I'd be better off with a little company doing many things than with a big "aristocratic" company. Make no mistake, his company was small back then.

Ted had started in radio in 1960 with the $85,000 purchase of CHFI-FM. By 1969 he also owned CFTR-AM, and had a smattering of several thousand cable TV subscribers in Toronto and the nearby suburb of Brampton. As well, Rogers Cable owned a minority stake in CFTO, Toronto's first privately owned television station, which was controlled by the Bassett and Eaton families. Those families owned half of Rogers Cable and two-thirds of its debt. They were extremely important to Ted, but things would change.

I accepted Ted's offer to come and do exciting new things in cable TV programming. This would also lead to getting immersed in regulatory affairs. I was the company's 160th employee (for comparison's sake, today there are 26,000).

As we shook hands, Ted remarked that it was good to work with people you know, "but friends may or may not last long working together, so let's take it year to year and see how it goes." And that's how we handled it, throughout all the ups and downs, until his death on December 2, 2008, almost 40 years later.

Three months before I started at Rogers, the newly formed Canadian Radio-television and Telecommunications Commission—in its myopic belief that cable and broadcasters should play in separate sandboxes—had ordered the Baton group, owners of CFTO, out of the fledgling Rogers Cable and Ted out of CFTO. Ted delayed the severing for two years, but it was inevitable.

The repercussions were plentiful. The CRTC almost wiped Ted out before he could get going: without deep-pocket partners, Rogers would teeter day to day on the edge of bankruptcy for the next three years. And perhaps more importantly, the CRTC's precedent-setting order to keep cable and broadcasters separate would negatively impact Canadians' programming choices for years to come. During that time Canada's cable industry, including Rogers, was delivering so many innovative TV programming choices, and yet each time we'd offer something new and exciting, the broadcasters would complain to the CRTC and we'd get shut down. Most of the specialty-channel programming we were doing in the early 1970s—but were ordered to stop doing—would come along years later.

The CRTC would maintain this "church-and-state" mantra for more than 30 years. In doing so it upheld the broadcasters' belief that if cable were allowed into programming, cable operators would choke them out of the limited bandwidth available. Advanced digital technology killed that argument long ago. And yet even back in the analog days the broadcasters' argument was, at best, specious. The CRTC could have easily limited cable companies' amount of profitable programming without restricting them to programming that couldn't make money.

And so the cable industry was considered merely a deliverer of programming into homes, not a developer (apart from local programming, or from those things not lucrative enough for the broadcasters, like multilingual programming). The animosity broadcasters seem to hold against cable has long been a hobby horse of mine, especially when one looks at the three critical innovations cable has introduced to support broadcasters over the years.

One, cable expanded broadcasters' reach into Canadian homes with a picture quality superior to that of antennas. Cable also created a broader commercial spectrum by making weak UHF signals attain the technical quality of the scarce VHF signals in Canada. And by opening up more channels like 79, 47, and 28, cable allowed the emergence of more Canadian broadcasters like Global TV and City TV.

Two, over the years the cable industry has invested more than $1 billion in Canada's independent television and film community in order to create mandated Canadian content for broadcasters. And between 1980 and 2018, $600 million has come from the Rogers Group of Funds to help back 2000 productions.

Three, perhaps cable's greatest benefit to broadcasters is something called simultaneous substitution—the inserting of Canadian advertising into hit U.S. programs that have been purchased by Canadian broadcasters to attract audience and drive revenue. Simultaneous substitution was a guarantee by cable operators that if Canadian broadcasters owned the rights to the show, the Canadian channel would be substituted on top of the U.S. broadcast. This ensured that the aggregation of the audience size—and higher ratings—accrued to the Canadian channel, and thus the Canadian broadcaster could charge more for commercials.

So, along with providing a crisp, clear signal, cable increased the value of every Canadian licence and created a more orderly rights market for U.S. programming—the backbone of every private broadcaster's business model in Canada. Cable immediately made Canadian channels worth millions upon millions of dollars more and strengthened the Canadian broadcasting system. And with the rapid growth in broadcasters' revenue, Canadian content contributions accelerated and flowed to film and television producers, creating thousands and thousands of jobs. This revenue growth in turn meant far more money for broadcasters' news and public service programming. It made room for more competition and more investment in everything related to television. In short, with the flow of money that came from simultaneous substitution, the Canadian television industry was reborn.

I'll let Leslie Sole, former CEO of Rogers TV, speak for me here: "One of the least known accomplishments of Phil Lind is his role in the creation of simultaneous substitution. Bob Short and Ted Jarmain may have come up with the idea and Ted Rogers may have been the driving force and front man to the public, but Phil's behind-the-scenes campaign orchestration had enormous impact. I know because I was there, often in awe of his creativity and insights. And this single development had more impact on Canadian television than any other regulatory or industry agreement."

In July 1972 Ted Rogers was elected the second chairman of the CCTA (Canadian Cable Television Association), succeeding

Ted Jarmain, son of cable pioneer Ed Jarmain. Bob Short was the CCTA president at the time. (You'll read more about the Jarmains in the next chapter.) Ted Rogers used this platform to really push the initial policy of commercial deletion—the forerunner of simultaneous substitution. We'd delete commercials from U.S. channels carried on Rogers Cable. This would discourage Canadian advertisers from buying time on Buffalo stations because there was no guarantee Toronto viewers on Rogers would see the ads.

Ted stood his ground and took the heat. *The Globe and Mail* mocked him as the "defender of the Canadian way of selling soap." Canadian advertisers initially cried foul over losing money buying time on U.S. channels. American broadcasters called him a thief for illegally tampering with their signals. Even some other Canadian cable operators thought we were wrong at Rogers for stripping out U.S. commercials.

As I said, Ted publicly took the heat, but he also had the backing of the CRTC, which did the unusual thing of paying Rogers's legal bills in the fight.

Over time, and with technological improvements, commercial deletion—blacking out commercials on cable—morphed into simultaneous substitution. But American broadcasters didn't let up. They sued Rogers and the case got all the way to the Canadian Supreme Court, which in 1977 ruled in favour of Rogers and the CRTC and against Capital Cities Communications Inc., which owned WBEN-TV Channel 4 in Buffalo.

Basically, the case came down to a sovereignty issue: Canadian regulators and cable operators have the right to prop up the country's broadcasting system by stemming the flow of Canadian advertising money to U.S. stations.

Indeed, the federal government went further by changing tax laws to prohibit Canadian corporations from writing off advertising in U.S. media as a business expense. Now, Americans don't take it kindly if they feel they're being pushed around, and so this was a huge squabble back then (it would even rear its ugliness again 10 years later during the free trade negotiations). The U.S. Congress even set up a House Foreign Affairs subcommittee to examine the issue. And in May 1974, when it came time to defend our position in Washington, Ted asked me to go to Capitol Hill to face the inquisition. With my background in and knowledge of American politics and culture, he insisted that I was the natural person to represent Rogers. Ted could be charming when he wanted to be. And when your name is on the cable trucks, it's your call. So off I went.

It was a rough ride. Dante Fascell, a Democrat from Florida, headed the committee. Pie-faced and tough-talking, he could have had a role in one of the *Godfather* movies. One of his wealthy constituents owned one of the Buffalo TV stations, and he wanted answers.

He grilled me like no other. He used many of the same pejorative words American newspapers were using to describe Canadian cable operators: "robbery," "larceny," "piracy." For a 30-year-old under oath and out of his element, I was uncomfortable, to say the least.

In fact, if it weren't for an excellent young Washington lawyer named Ted Pierson, of Pierson, Ball & Dowd, a pioneer in federal communications law, I'm not sure I could have survived. In hindsight, though, it was terrific training, not only for some of the heated CRTC hearings that would soon emerge but also for the political battles to be fought during the cable franchise wars of the late 1970s and early 1980s.

Beyond the simultaneous substitution issue, the early to mid 1970s were exciting, zany times for programming, and for cable in general.

We offered 12 channels when I joined Rogers, but with the launch of the Jerrold converter box in March 1973, all of a sudden we had capacity for 30. The public loved them. It cost $4.50 a month for basic cable, but for another $2.50 per month for the Jerrold converter, customers could more than double their programming.

With today's streaming and hundreds of digital channels, it's difficult to explain how revolutionary the Jerrold converter was in its day. It was so big that Marshall McLuhan himself came to the official launch at our Adelaide Street offices. McLuhan— the University of Toronto professor and media futurist whose global village theory predicted the Internet age 35 years before it happened—was so delighted to attend that he had his agent waive his $25,000 speaking fee. At that time, I was taking his graduate course on the media at the University of Toronto. A photograph of McLuhan, Ted, and me at that event still proudly hangs in my home.

Increasing capacity from 12 to 30 channels meant finding programming to fill those channels. And we were still doing community programming on Channel 10, too. But we were never at a shortage for ideas worth trying. The first few channels to add were easy: they were the over-the-air broadcast channels the public wanted but we didn't have capacity for on basic cable, like Buffalo's PBS affiliate WNED or Peterborough's CHEX. We also created genre channels, much like today's specialty channels. We bought programming for a Western cowboy channel and a Golden Oldies movie channel. But the broadcasters went crazy—we were showing movies commercial-free!—and had the CRTC order us to stop. Basically, even though we had the capacity, the CRTC told the cable companies that they couldn't broadcast full-motion video programs in English or French. We were, however, allowed alphanumeric programming (I'll discuss those services a little further down) and multilingual shows, since the broadcasters didn't kick up a fuss about either.

As a result, we bought as much foreign-language programming as we could: Greek, Italian, Portuguese, Indian, Asian, and Croatian. The problem was that so much of it, especially the much-needed Greek, Italian, and Portuguese, was owned by state-run broadcasters with no incentive to sell to us. So we had salespeople who spoke the residents' tongue going door to door, telling them that with the new converter they could watch TV in their own language. People were signing up in droves—and the heat was on for more and more foreign-language programming.

It got so bad that I sent cable programmers to Greece, Italy, Portugal, and Brazil to record programming from their hotel televisions. (One poor guy, Al Pace, even got caught with a huge trunk loaded with illegally obtained programs.) And yet somehow we managed our way through it until broadcasters would sell us the stuff. These were madcap days for TV programming on cable.

One of the more humorous incidents involved Ted and I getting the idea to broadcast the air show that capped off Toronto's Canadian National Exhibition on Labour Day weekend.

Picture this: Ted and I hauling our equipment up to the top of the black TD Bank tower, which back then was the city's tallest building. Ted was, of course, the camera operator and I was assigned the task of spotter. As soon as I saw an approaching aircraft I was to alert Ted. Well, I did just that—and the jets zoomed past with Ted and his camera getting nothing. This happened several times during the flybys. We'd laugh about it for years afterward, but at the time we got into a pretty good row, with Ted calling me an idiot for not alerting him in time and me calling him a no-talent, wannabe cameraman.

Some of our ideas were way ahead of their time. For example, have you ever had dinner at a restaurant and noticed a "burning log" on a screen on the wall? The TV fireplace idea came from Arthur "Kip" Moorecroft one Christmas when he thought Rogers could provide a yuletide feel for those customers without a hearth. Kip was a tremendously creative guy who died way too young of cancer in 1993 at the age of 47.

We were also the first to give the LGBTQ community a voice on television by creating a program called *Gayblevision*. Community leaders and average people would discuss such issues as relations with the police. The program filled a void and was quite popular in the community. But the president of Rogers Cable, Bob Short, who'd recently come over from the CCTA, ordered it off the air. Bob was almost 20 years older than me and from a different generation; he didn't like us "promoting" the gay lifestyle. I stood firm, arguing that it was a valuable program for our community television and important to the CRTC. So Bob went to Ted and made the mistake of issuing the boss an ultimatum: either Ted orders Phil to end *Gayblevision* or he'd resign. Bob Short's career at Rogers was, indeed, short. (Even shorter than another cable president who got so liquored up at a company dinner that he loudly started dropping copious F-bombs and trying to eat the plastic fruit on the table.)

The programming ideas were endless. We created alpha-numeric channels for news, sports scores, stock prices, airport departures and arrivals, job classifieds, and even a shopping basket of local grocery stores' sale products.

The airline-flights service worked against one customer, who told his wife his flight had been cancelled. Turned out he just wanted to spend more time with his girlfriend. His wife, however, saw on TV that his flight was about to land in Toronto. After she got to the bottom of it, the man called Rogers and *blamed us* for getting him into trouble with his wife!

The shopping-basket channel was leading-edge stuff. It did hit a snag, though. There was a guy named Charles Ambler in Oakville who ran a lucrative little company that compared prices at supermarket chains. He had a battalion of housewives collecting prices on 300 different items in grocery stores across the country; his office would amass all the information and sell it to the big chains to see how they were doing against the competition's prices. The likes of Loblaws, IGA, Dominion, and A&P would pay him big bucks for this top secret information, so he wasn't about to allow us to publicly disclose it on TV. But I had the idea of pitching him on selling us maybe 25 to 30 prices per week. It was a win-win: it wouldn't impact his sales to the stores; he'd add a new revenue stream; and we'd be offering subscribers another innovative service.

I drove the half hour to Oakville to see him. After handing him my business card, he looked at it quizzically and said, "Philip

Bridgman Lind … that's odd, I knew a Philip Bridgman long ago."

"Yes," I said, "Philip Bridgman was my grandfather. He died before I was born and my mother named me in his honour. He came to Canada from Massachusetts to run General Foods' Canadian operations."

"I know," he replied. "I worked at General Foods and Philip Bridgman fired me."

Shit, I thought.

Then he smiled. "Kid, getting fired was the best thing that ever happened to me. Sure, you can use 25 or 30 items per week."

Another of our ideas was to set up a "speakers' corner" at Yonge and Adelaide streets in downtown Toronto where people could come and have their views broadcast on Rogers's Channel 10. Moses Znaimer, the progressive broadcaster who founded City TV, would later use that idea with great success—and claim credit for another Kip Moorecroft innovation. (By the way, Rogers ended up buying the City TV urban network after the CRTC got over its holy mantra of keeping cable out of broadcasting.)

Ted was steadfast in his support of trying things, but also in his belief that if we had the best technical systems and the best programming, customers would pay more for that added value.

We always wanted to do things first, to never miss an opportunity. We were broadcasting municipal council meetings long before local TV news reported on them. We also carried a live mayoral debate into the city's living rooms for the first time ever, although that turned out to be a disaster, with plenty of technical problems. But the point is, we tried and we learned from our mistakes.

Those were some of the rawest, most fun, flying-by-the-seat-of-our-pants days. And throughout it all Ted was trying to keep his head above water financially. I knew things were dicey at times, but it wasn't until years later that I found out how close we'd come to bankruptcy. To his credit, Ted kept the direness close to his vest, and the vests of his financial guys like Hugh Lewis and Bob Francis.

As the crazy 1970s wound down, some of the toughest battles and some of the best days of my business life were on the horizon.

Right: My father, Jed, and me, retracing John Lind's steps across the Chilkoot Pass.

Bottom: My gold-mining grandfather, John Grieve Lind, standing atop his "26 Above Bonanza" claim, Yukon, 1899.

Top: Ridley College pals in a *Bermuda News* photo, 1956. (L–R) Gordie Chaplin, Beau Matthews, me, and David Dodge (future seven-term Bank of Canada governor). Gordie, a lifelong friend, was my partner in frat-boy hijinks.

Left: At the University of Rochester, studying political sociology for my master's. (Note my pin-up wall.)

Right: With Prime Minister John George Diefenbaker, in my early twenties. Politics is one of the central themes of my life, and Darcy McKeough was my political mentor.

Bottom: A group of friends at Bally McKeough during a summer in the 1970s. Me, seated; my ex-wife, Anne, on my right; Darcy behind me; and Joyce McKeough in the back row, second from right. Except for Joyce and Darcy and one other pair, each of the couples in this photo would split up.

Rogers executives appearing before the CRTC for our successful 1980 takeover of Premier Cable. (R–L) Me, Ted Rogers, chairman John W. Graham, and George Fierheller. Second row, right: Colin Watson.

Fifteen years later with Colin, arguing a regulatory point with Ted during a recess in the CRTC hearing for our successful Maclean Hunter takeover.

At Ted and Loretta Rogers's winter home in Nassau in the 1980s.
(L–R) Colin; Loretta; me; Ted, my ex-wife, Anne; and Colin's wife, Barb.

(L–R) Me; Rogers's CFO Bob Francis, who deftly kept our creditors at bay;
and longtime Rogers board member David Wilson.

Below: Canadian artist Robin Collyer found a picture of Ted, Marshall McLuhan, and me and created this sculpture, entitled *Round Ceiling Diffuser 2000.* It's now part of my art collection.

Me, chairman John W. Graham, and Ted in the 1990s with Prime Minister Brian Mulroney. Decades later, Mulroney honoured me by taping an introduction about me for the U.S. Cable Hall of Fame ceremony.

With Colin Watson on the set of Rogers TV's *Ask Us*. For more than 30 years we'd take customer calls on this live monthly call-in show.

Ted and I shared many a dais and many successes during our 40 years together.

We also shared the honour of being named to the Order of Canada and being two of only three Canadians (the other is JR Shaw) inducted into the U.S. Cable Hall of Fame.

Like politics, fishing (particularly fly fishing) is one of the central themes of my life. *Top left:* Fishing with my friend Larry Black in Portland, Oregon, while franchising in the U.S. in the 1980s. *Top right:* With Ted Turner in the 1990s. *Bottom:* With my friend and the best guide I've ever met, Steve Pauli, in 2016, on one of the annual trips that my son, Jed, and I make to Big Timber, Montana.

6

David and Goliath

I n the late 1970s, Rogers's near-simultaneous takeovers of both
Canadian Cablesystems Limited (CCL) and Premier Cablevision
were two of the boldest moves by one of Canada's boldest
entrepreneurs. I marvelled at Ted's grandmaster approach, and
would map out strategies to bring his deals to fruition—which
involved gaining regulatory approval through campaigns aimed
at both Bay Street and Main Street. The ramifications were significant, not only for our company but also for the Canadian cable
industry as a whole—and later, to a lesser extent, for U.S. cable.

In fact, both takeovers redefined the cable industry.
Until then, the CRTC, under former chairman Pierre Juneau,
believed that cable should be all about local ownership and
community channels. But Rogers had other ideas. "We had
to persuade the CRTC to change policy on local ownership and approve greater concentration of ownership, and
it wouldn't be easy," says Bob Buchan, a brilliant communications lawyer in Ottawa who began his long association with
Rogers with the CCL campaign.

The interesting thing is that in both campaigns, and in all
future campaigns, I would craft our approach based on the simple
advice that Juneau himself had given me a few years earlier:

"Always endeavour to understand your opponent's point of view at all times." In other words, you won't agree with it, but understand why it's their point of view, and don't focus only on what you believe to be right, but why they believe they're right. The advice was simple and yet deeply strategic, even if the answers weren't immediately obvious.

These two takeovers were a tipping point for Rogers.

One was relatively friendly, the other intensely bitter and hostile. Humour found a place as part of one; dirty tricks found a home in the other. One succeeded thanks to our respect for the CRTC, the other because our opponent misread the regulator and overstepped the bounds.

It's a David and Goliath story: scrappy, highly-in-debt Rogers with 203,000 subscribers versus CCL with 430,000 and Premier with 650,000. Combined, the two were more than five times our size. And yet we emerged victorious to claim the title of the largest cable company in Canada.

How Ted strung together the business deals with bank loans and bubble gum is well documented elsewhere, so I'll limit my commentary mostly to behind-the-scenes campaign manoeuvres and other lesser-known aspects of the two events.

It must be reiterated that at the time, Canada was a world leader in cable. We were the most wired nation on earth. Sure, there were differing points of view on how the broadcasting system should evolve, but given consumers' thirst for hit American programming delivered via cable, the Canadian cable industry was well ahead of its U.S. counterpart. The over-the-air television services and bunny-ears antennas were fine for most Americans, but not for Canadians having trouble picking up faraway U.S. signals. (It wasn't until U.S. cable channels like HBO, ESPN, and my friend Ted Turner's TBS and CNN became popular that the U.S. cable industry really took off.)

Here is where the genius and vision of Ted Rogers emerges. He was early to the cable industry in 1967, but certainly not a pioneer like Ed Jarmain in southern Ontario and Syd Welsh in British Columbia. And yet it was Ted's business savvy that led him to exploit the concept of "clustering"—that is, creating economies of scale by building or buying cable networks in key geographical areas in order to share expenses and increase monthly recurring revenues.

Nearing the end of the 1970s, Canada was already seeing its internationally leading role in cable slip: its many small cable companies couldn't keep up with the innovation and advancements coming from the U.S. We needed big, healthy cable companies.

Indeed, tough choices and policies steering us to the correct path became the linchpin of our campaigns to acquire CCL and Premier. Cable companies had three possible ways to go. One, uphold the status quo in the face of ever-decreasing investment in new plant and R&D, hoping new technologies like satellite TV from the U.S. wouldn't cripple Canada's broadcasting system. Two, sell out to the telephone companies, which were finally realizing that cable customers were willing to pay for quality programming. This would be an attractive option to everyone *but* consumers, who, in the absence of competition, would face higher prices. Three, establish big, strong cable companies to compete with satellite companies and local phone companies like Bell Canada. In my mind, the choice was clear. We just had to convince the various audiences: regulators, bankers, investors, media, and the public.

Business campaigns are similar to political campaigns, but there are distinct differences.

First, consider the team. In business, your campaign team doesn't include any hangers-on, as it often does in politics: no relatives who were given a job even if they weren't qualified, no old bagmen to whom the party owes favours but whose only real skill is pulling money out of like-minded political donors. In business, it's all hands on deck all the time with qualified people. If they can't do the job they're off the team, just as in professional sports. To lead a successful business campaign, you have to be focused and near ruthless.

Next is the story you're selling. Business campaigns have to sell their story to more audiences than do political campaigns, which really have only one audience—the voter. So with business campaigns the story has to be substantially the same, but tailored to specific audiences. This means you stick to two or three key themes over and over, but you express them differently depending on the audience. For example, the CRTC must understand that strong, innovative cable companies help protect and preserve the broadcasting system; bankers and investors must appreciate that industry consolidation leads to increased cash flow; and the public and media must recognize that healthy cable companies will mean increased consumer choice and fair pricing. It can be a delicate balance. And like a winning political campaign, the messaging for a business campaign must be very simple, even when you're dealing with often complicated concepts and the sophisticated minds at the CRTC or in the financial community.

Then there's research. Here's where the difference between business and political campaigns is more subtle. You have to do your research and lock it down tight for both, of course, but because business campaigns have to reach more audiences, you must focus your research not just on the electorate in general but on various specified targets. For example, in the 1970s, the CRTC's policy toward cable was that locally owned operators were best. But we knew that the new CRTC chairman at the time, Pierre Camu, was a disciple of former U of T professor Harold Innis, an economics historian and communications scholar. Innis believed that networks shape culture, build countries, and further economic development—whether they're the networks of rivers for fur traders, the networks of railway lines, or the networks of telegraph, telephone, and airwave signals. Innis died in 1952 at age 58, before cable, but he would have backed national cable networks, too. So we wrote our application—and had consultants write their reports—to reflect Innis's views. And it was effective, spurring many questions and comments from Camu and ultimately convincing the CRTC to change its local, small-cable policy and approve our deal. Know your audience.

As I mentioned, details of these takeovers have been laid out elsewhere—from Ted Rogers's memoir *Relentless* to CCL chairman Tony Griffiths's *Corporate Catalyst* (in which he accuses Ted of duplicitous behaviour and me of walking a delicate line between friendship with CCL peers and not getting caught up in the trickery) to Caroline Van Hasselt's in-depth biography of Ted entitled *High Wire Act*.

I'll focus on the acrimonious campaign in this chapter (and will talk about Premier in the next). Suffice it to say that with the CCL battle there was a lot of "he said, she said" stuff, and of course I wasn't privy to every conversation, handshake, and acknowledgment. The absolute truth may be unattainable. I can only report what I believe to be true and what I know as fact.

Here's a fact: the lion's share of the two companies' sub-scribers lay in Toronto, and our business relationship was, for the most part, amicable. We even shared a cable Channel 10 show called *Ask Us*, where Colin Watson, CCL's vice-president of operations, and I would take live calls over the air from viewers. That monthly show continued for 30 years, well after Rogers had taken over CCL, and Colin, one of my best friends and closest business associates, became the longest-serving president of Rogers Cable. He answered technical questions and I took the programming queries.

We had a lot of fun with *Ask Us*, even if the fun was at our expense sometimes. Over the years, friends—the likes of pranksters Jim McCoubrey and Al Marr—would disguise their voices and phone in with such embarrassing questions as "How much are you paid?" and "What type of fancy car do you own?" Or Al, who does a perfect East Indian accent, would ask us to explain the rules of hockey to new Canadians. Remember, this wasn't prerecorded; it was live TV.

The Commission loved the show because it displayed our commitment to customer service and local programming. As Colin Watson puts it, "The CRTC was over the moon that two dopes like us would sit in front of the camera and take shit from customers."

One time, we had an important guest: Michael Shoemaker, the CRTC's executive director. Very early in this particular show, a man phoned in with a terrible stutter. He had a question for Shoemaker that took at least a minute to get out. Colin and I were sure the caller was one of our friends, probably McCoubrey, play-ing a prank. We were dissolving in our chairs, doing everything we could not to start laughing out loud, so the cameraman had to focus on Shoemaker. Shoemaker looked at us with a startled expression, and once the questioner had finished, he answered him politely. And thank goodness—because it wasn't a friend, it really was a stammering subscriber with a serious question. Fortunately, Shoemaker overlooked our mistake: after all, the show was popular, and we made sure to answer all our callers' questions and concerns, either immediately or within a day or two when our staff would get back to them.

To return to the CCL battle: in early 1977, Ted Rogers received a call from someone at Brascan Ltd., the conglomerate then headed by my dad's friend Jake Moore, asking if he'd be interested in its 25.6 percent of CCL. Things went back and forth for months, and Rogers ultimately bought one-quarter of CCL for $17.2 million. Ted Jarmain, who was CCL president despite his family's owning only 8 percent, and chairman Tony Griffiths were not pleased, to say the least, and fired off accusations of having been torpedoed. But Ted Rogers maintained that he'd spoken to Jarmain and Griffiths about it beforehand and there had been no surprises. I've always believed Ted, but I wasn't there. In his memoir, he recounted having told Ted Jarmain that if his family wanted to buy the shares Rogers would step aside, but that Jarmain didn't take him up on the offer.

So was Ted a predator, which could impact the CRTC's views, or was he an opportunist who acted only when CCL declined to step up to the plate? I don't know the absolute truth, but it may lie somewhere in the middle. Over the years I've discussed this with Bob Buchan, and neither of us can say for sure.

Anyway, soon after Ted bought the shares, one of his law school buddies, Trevor Eyton, told him that Edper Investments Ltd., where he worked for Edward and Peter Bronfman, was diversifying into cable and planned to buy CCL stock, too. Edper quickly accumulated 24.2 percent of CCL and struck a shotgun deal with Ted Rogers—if either was about to sell its CCL bloc, the other would have first right of refusal.

Things got really messy now, with CCL flinging accusations at Rogers and Edper of trickery and underhandedness, using words like "predatory" and "raiders." In his book, Griffiths calls the Bronfmans "barbarians."

The CRTC held a hearing in January 1978 and determined that there had been a change in control, with Rogers-Edper now possessing effective control with 49.8 percent of the stock. The Commission then ordered another hearing to determine whether the change of control was in the public interest.

Before that hearing, Ted and I met with Peter Bronfman and his two closest advisers, Eyton and Jack Cockwell. They wanted to be either in or out—either Ted would buy their shares or they would buy the Rogers bloc and let Jarmain and Griffiths run CCL for them. And they let Ted decide.

Rogers finagled a bank loan and bought Edper's bloc for $17 million. To their credit, they told us that if the CRTC denied the takeover, they'd buy the entire 49.8 percent back from Rogers. In effect, they hedged Rogers: we wouldn't lose money and risk defaulting on the $34.1 million loans even if the CRTC turned us down.

Brascan did a heck of a lot for us when we weren't much of a company at all. It was a tremendous gesture. Not only was it gracious, but it represented an inflection point in the development of our company. And Edper really helped Rogers propel itself into a communications behemoth. Back then Rogers had a market cap of $79 million; today, in 2018, it hovers around $30 billion. It's a story not widely known, but I've never forgotten their help.

It's interesting how things turn out. The very next year, 1979, Edper gained control of Brascan, and in 1994 I was invited to sit on the board. In 2017 I stepped down after serving 23 years. And I can unequivocally say that Brascan—which became Brookfield Asset Management Inc.—was the best board I ever served on, for its independence, its intellectual rigour, and its overall corporate governance. And chief executive Bruce Flatt is the finest CEO in Canada today.

Returning to 1978, the CRTC hearing to determine whether Rogers's control of CCL was in the public interest was set to begin in September. Beyond nasty missives in the press, there were dirty tricks on both sides. It would be an acrimonious hearing, but the campaign that led up to it was just as bad.

CCL began a letter-writing campaign to the CRTC from people who either didn't exist or who were put up to it. In essence, CCL was trying to stuff the ballot box. While we submitted only 90 letters, CCL produced 1200, but how many were legitimate? As Caroline Van Hasselt wrote in *High Wire Act*, "CCL mounted a smear campaign against Rogers, flooding the regulator with anonymous letters of complaint." We countered by hiring tough-looking private detectives to track down the letter writers and question whether they'd actually written them. But these "detectives" went a bit too far in their questioning, and after the wife of one man said her husband was scared to death after being threatened, I cancelled the program.

On the positive side, though, there was one aspect of our campaign that changed CRTC hearings going forward. We commissioned serious third-party research: polling data, economic studies, and policy papers. We also hired expert witnesses—such as David Wilson, a Bay Street banker and future chairman of the Ontario Securities Commission—to crunch numbers and to testify that Rogers's borrowing for the deal wouldn't lead to higher cable rates. In the late 1970s, the CRTC didn't have a formal research department, and so the commissioners really appreciated being given so much hard data to lean on when making a decision. This altered future hearings in two ways: every applicant worth its salt would now present independent research to back its arguments, and in 1983 the CRTC would create its own internal research department by hiring Stephen Armstrong as director general of research.

We also introduced what would become known as a "benefits package" to the broadcasting industry and Canadians in general. The $3 million in this package was outside the purchase price, and would be given to people like independent producers to make quality Canadian programming and to offset the costs associated with broadcasting House of Commons proceedings on TV, the forerunner of today's CPAC channel. I called this promissory money a "social dividend," since in helping to repatriate viewers away from American programming to Canadian programming, it would strengthen the overall broadcasting system.

But back to those dirty tricks. During the course of our CCL campaign, we came across a University of Toronto economics professor who'd worked in the Department of Finance and had published policy papers that aligned with our arguments. We thought of hiring him as an expert witness, but decided against it after discovering that he had a drinking problem. But CCL also found this same economics professor, and hired him to support their arguments. Then it came time for the three-day hearing, which was held at L'Auberge de la Chaudière, across the river from Ottawa. On the day of this professor's testimony, a bottle of whisky was sent to his room "compliments of hotel management." By the time he testified for CCL, his reasoning was somewhat incoherent. We'd since hired a different economics professor, and the CRTC commissioners much preferred his testimony.

What likely won the day for us, though, were mistakes by the other side. Before the earlier "change of control" hearing, Jarmain had written to Ted Rogers saying that the CRTC wouldn't rule against CCL management, who opposed Rogers's predatory moves. To assume what the CRTC will do can be a death knell.

Then, at this hearing, Tony Griffiths said that Ted Rogers had promised to call them before entering face-to-face negotiations with Brascan's Jake Moore to see whether they wanted to buy the bloc instead of Rogers. Griffiths and Jarmain said he didn't call, as I recounted earlier. Rogers testified that he did. After a grilling by vice-chairman Charles Dalfen, Ted Rogers's version was deemed much more believable.

As I said, it was both a nasty campaign and a nasty Commission hearing, but in the end all's well that ends well. Much of the time I was in a precarious position, walking a fine line between my friendship with CCL's VP Operations Colin Watson and my loyalty to Ted Rogers. Colin had told me about several talented people at CCL, and I counselled him to keep his head down and their heads down during the struggle.

Even after all the acrimony, most key CCL players would stay on and help Rogers immensely, from Watson and the brilliant lawyer Albert Gnat to Graham Savage, a future Rogers CFO who would pioneer the high-yield bond market in Canada, and engineer Nick Hamilton-Piercy, the godfather of fibre optics in the cable industry.

There was very little humour during the CCL battle, but I do remember one funny exchange between Ted Rogers and Albert Gnat. Now, I can't say this enough: Albert was incredibly sharp, and a damn good lawyer. But as outside counsel for CCL he was on the other side, and he was giving us a hard time. So at one point Ted said to him during a break, "Why don't we go up to the top of the TD Centre so I can show you our headend?" (Cable headends are where TV signals are grabbed from satellites.) What Ted was implying was that he'd like to push Albert off the top of the building. Albert immediately got the joke, and said something like he wouldn't go up there without a bodyguard.

It's a credit to Ted—and to so many of the senior people at CCL—that they stayed on with Rogers and played such significant roles in building the company. (Although Albert was outside counsel, his services moved to Rogers, and he would be critical in forging many future deals, especially in acquiring the Blue Jays.)

Whenever Ted took over a company, he always welcomed the senior executives who wanted to stay. I think that's a tribute to his character. He simply never wanted to gas all the senior executives in the practice that's so common in business takeovers. Even Tony Griffiths, who was offered a senior role but left, wrote in his memoir that he "takes his hat off to Rogers for retaining management and winning their respect."

7

Cable, the Constitution, and a Cheshire Cat Grin

hortly after the CRTC granted approval for the CCL take-over, I was in Ottawa with Ted Rogers meeting with lawyer Bob Buchan. One evening, as we were coming out of the National Arts Centre after an industry event, I said, "Tell Bob. Tell him, Ted."

"Tell me what?" Bob asked.

"We finally got it. We're buying Premier," Ted said, referring to four different courtships with Premier's owners and management over the last five years.

The look on Bob's face was priceless. He even dropped his briefcase on the ground. He's a wonderful man, and someone I'd describe as loquacious, but that may have been the only time I've seen him tongue-tied. He's a lawyer, after all.

"But the CRTC just approved CCL," Bob protested. "I know they changed their policy that favoured small, locally owned cable companies, but I don't know if they'll go for this."

"I think they will. Phil's got a plan for selling it to the commissioners," Ted said.

Although it was based in Vancouver, Premier also had significant cable holdings in Toronto. It would fit perfectly with our "clustering" strategy, and would also give us a toehold in Vancouver to build a western Canadian cluster. I love British Columbia, and Colin Watson, though born in England during the war, had moved with his family to Vancouver in 1947, so we'd both enjoy our times working out West.

At that point I told Bob another "typical Ted" story about the latest round in trying to reach a deal with Premier. Ted had made three other unsuccessful attempts in the previous five years, so he figured he had to get more creative. While we were flying to Vancouver to make the pitch, he happened to strike up a conversation with a couple across the aisle who were orchestrating a cross-Canada tour of a Hawaiian band to promote travel there. Ted turned to me and remarked that it would be fun to have the band perform at the next day's meeting with Premier management, just to break the ice. After all, Premier founder Syd Welsh and some of his management owned the cable system in Honolulu (which was separate, and not part of the proposed deal). I thought it was a great idea, and so we hired them for $200. The next day in the Premier boardroom, Ted raised his voice and bellowed out theatrically, "What about Hawaii?" Right on cue, the doors burst open and in came two hula dancers in grass skirts and a bare-chested fellow banging away on the bongo drums. Needless to say, there were some surprised faces around the boardroom table, including chairman Syd Welsh's. In the end, the manoeuvre may or may not have helped us get a deal. But it was very funny.

The deal came later—after Welsh, who was then 66 years old, shuffled his management team and Ted's longtime friend and Sigma Chi fraternity brother, George Fierheller, became president in April 1979. George was able to convince Welsh to consider selling to a younger generation, thereby reaping the spoils of his 35 years of hard work as a pioneer in cable and building a terrific company.

We filed a 365-page application, complete with hard data and expert opinions about the future of cable and how Rogers's takeover of Premier made sense. In places I intentionally used florid language to outline what the future could hold for ubiquitous advanced communications networks. Unlike Marshall McLuhan I had no idea where we'd be today, but I knew in my bones that, given the programming bombardment coming from the south and the might of the local telephone companies once they made their moves, bigger would be better for cable.

In the application, I quoted the CRTC's decision a year earlier on CCL:

> In the Commission's view, the Canadian cable television industry should have as its objective the achievement of a dominant position—both nationally and internationally—in the development of cable television technology and services. This will not only permit it to survive as an effective participant in the Canadian telecommunications sector, but also to regain for Canada an international reputation as an innovative force in cable television.

Owing to the relatively friendly nature of the takeover, the Premier campaign would be tame compared to CCL's. But there would be land mines, especially with provincial governments flexing their muscles.

This was late in 1979, and there was plenty of constitutional debate going on around that time. We were in the lead-up to the first Quebec referendum, set for the following year, and provincial governments were clamouring for more rights. The newly elected federal government of Progressive Conservative Joe Clark was itself leaning toward decentralization by giving provinces more powers and more influence over their regional economies.

Likewise, there was a raging debate in the communications industry and at government levels over whether cable companies, given their supposed local characteristics, should be regulated by the provinces, just as hydro and gas utilities were. This was the antithesis of our plans to grow cable companies nationally and strengthen Canada's broadcast system.

Our first land mine was Ontario. Even there, a federalist-first province, bureaucrats in the Ministry of Transportation and Communications were working behind the scenes to move cable regulation away from the CRTC and into the hands of provincial regulators. I had to make sure we stayed under the jurisdiction of the national CRTC.

And I got my chance when I heard that Premier Bill Davis was about to give a major speech in which he'd lay out Ontario's position on various constitutional issues, especially provincial powers. Ontario bureaucrats were pumped to regulate cable, and they'd even gotten a paragraph into the speech in which the premier would call for just that.

As it happened, I knew Davis through my friendship with Darcy McKeough. So I found out the time of Davis's speech at a downtown hotel and when he'd be leaving Queen's Park. Instead of going to the hotel, I headed to Queen's Park and met the premier by his limousine, parked beside the Legislature. I asked if I could ride with him. He obliged, as long as I didn't object to his pipe smoking. Of course I didn't. And for the next few minutes, I explained the importance of a robust cable industry and broadcasting system for the future of Canadian culture and national unity.

Davis was one of the strongest federalists of his day, certainly among premiers. He was receptive to my argument, and with his pen struck out the paragraph calling for cable regulation moving to the provinces.

"My bosses went down to hear the speech and, magically, the paragraph they were waiting to hear wasn't there," says Stephen Armstrong, then a junior bureaucrat at the Ontario Ministry of Transportation and Communications. "They came back to the office and were still talking about it in disbelief—they had no idea why the premier didn't mention cable."

Some 15 years later, Stephen and I were telling war stories from the olden days in the cable industry. (Stephen left the ministry in 1983 to head up the CRTC's research department, and is now a crackerjack independent consultant who's worked for us over the years.) He mentioned the mystery that had become lore in the ministry: What happened to the disappearing words about cable in the premier's constitutional speech? No one in his ministry, even the bosses, seemed to know the answer. "As I was telling Phil about this mystery of the missing words, a Cheshire cat grin came across his face and he somewhat reluctantly told me the story of the limousine ride," Stephen Armstrong recalls. "Phil is a real student of public policy and politics, and he's so aware of how extensive your network of contacts has to be."

Paul Temple, a former colleague in Rogers regulatory, gives me credit for understanding how politics and commerce intersect: "Phil's a great politician who never got into politics." Perhaps. But it also has a lot to do with my background as a sociologist.

I was always a different cat in the industry. Virtually everyone in its top echelons has come from engineering, business, or legal backgrounds, whereas I came from politics and the art of the possible—and an understanding of where people are in the world and why they do the things they do. Why do they buy this, or why do they feel this way about a product or service? Public attitudes are very important. At times, I think this has given me a real advantage. I remember former CRTC chairwoman Françoise Bertrand once lamenting the fact that she was the only sociologist in the industry. To her surprise I responded, "Except me." She went on to say that she found it frustrating at times. I told her I found that my master's in sociology gave me a perspective the engineers and MBAs just didn't have.

That part of my personality is something Ted Rogers didn't get about me for the longest time. He kept urging me to go operate one of our cable systems so that I'd get a real understanding of how the business works: the nuts and bolts, the nodes and the wires, the "tree and branch" architecture of cable. For 10, maybe 20, years he continued saying that such operational experience could help groom me to be his possible successor. But I insisted over and over that running things didn't interest me. People interest me. Working out strategic moves fascinates me. If I was out operating some cable system in the boonies, he'd lose me as his right hand man, the one to bounce ideas off and to give him objective counsel. You can't fill both roles, I kept telling him.

It took him the longest time to understand, but I think it was when he named me vice-chairman in 1991 that he truly got it. In a sea of engineers and MBAs, my value lay in my sociology background. "For an engineering-dominated company, it was essential to have Phil around when it came to programming," says Tony Viner, the former president of Rogers Media. "The team who ran Rogers Radio for me—Gary Miles, Chuck McCoy, and Sandy Sanderson—would say Phil was deep down a programmer and the only guy who wasn't about wires. I knew that, too, and never really thought of Phil as a regulatory guy either, more as a strategist."

Returning to our campaign for Premier, the second land mine came in 1980 with B.C.'s Social Credit. Right in the midst of our takeover, two Montreal companies—Canadian Pacific Investments Ltd. and Domtar—each tried to take over Vancouver-based forestry giant MacMillan Bloedel, the biggest force in B.C. But the year before, Premier Bill Bennett had made headlines across the country by announcing that B.C. wasn't for sale. And like CP and Domtar, we weren't local either.

So it was critical that we get Bennett to support our takeover of Premier, or at least not actively oppose us. His "B.C. is not for sale" comments were disconcerting to say the least.

My great friend Peter Hyndman, whom I'd known from our Progressive Conservative Youth Federation and UBC days, was an MLA in Bennett's Social Credit government, and it was with Hyndman's help that we won Bennett's neutrality. But the NDP party in B.C. and its leader, Dave Barrett, rabidly opposed us, so we had to neutralize their opposition, too. Luckily, the CRTC accepted our proposal to hold the hearing simultaneously in both Vancouver and Toronto. The two sites were hooked up via satellite. We had Davis's government on board already, and when we got former Ontario NDP leader Donald MacDonald to support us, that offset NDP opposition in B.C.

Speaking of the live satellite feed, it reminds me of a story. Rogers's Channel 10 was broadcasting the hearing in Toronto, and so we controlled the feed at our end—things like monitoring audio levels and flashing the names of witnesses on the screen when they began to testify. There was one witness in Vancouver named Herschel Hardin, a political activist, journalist, and often-unsuccessful candidate for the federal NDP. At the time of our hearing, he was also a Vancouver-based editorial page columnist for the *Toronto Star*. Hardin hated Rogers; he held a deep grudge against us for some reason, and would hurl insults at us in his Toronto column even though he'd never been a Rogers subscriber. He was tremendously annoying and always digging at Rogers. I joked that, for all the grief Hardin had been giving Rogers in his testimony, our tech guys back in Toronto should misspell his name on screen as "Hard-on." Over the years, that story has been told and retold so many times that some versions have me actually ordering the switch. But just like a game of Telephone, the story has been embellished: it was always just a joking comment about Herschel Hardin's name.

The fact that I'd lived in B.C., knew something about the culture, and had political and corporate contacts there was essential in us getting Premier. That's because in many ways, the Premier campaign aptly turned into very much a political campaign—and our experience with political campaigns and politicians really came in handy.

A note about Peter Hyndman. With his effervescent personality and wit, Peter was always the most impressive guy in the room, and yet he had not a whiff of arrogance or hauteur. He held three university degrees, including being a Knox Fellow in Economics at Harvard. He was a true friend who helped us on more than one occasion, especially if his intervention would benefit B.C. And like me, Peter loved the outdoors, particularly the rivers and streams where he enjoyed his passion for fly fishing. I have many wonderful memories of fly fishing with Peter. He was a founding director of the Pacific Salmon Foundation and the Steelhead Society of B.C. and helped in the fight to save the Skagit River, a popular destination for fly fishing and whitewater rafting in B.C. and Washington state. Unfortunately, Peter's political career came crashing down in a tempest-in-a-teapot scandal over expenses claimed at a dinner with me, mutual friend Peter Brown, and our wives.

Here's how it came about. Besides my work with Rogers, I was on the board of Ontario Hydro at the time of our dinner on February 20, 1981. Peter was B.C.'s consumer and corporate affairs minister. We both worked extremely long hours and rarely saw our wives. And so that Friday-evening dinner was the proverbial killing of two birds with one stone: talking business and spending time with our wives. We talked about communications, things like cable services and consumer rates, and energy and hydro costs for consumers.

The cheque came—it was for $374—and Peter insisted on picking it up. Both Peter Brown and I tried to grab it but Peter stood his ground, saying it wouldn't look good if a senior minister was taking free dinners from executives. "It's a legitimate business dinner and I can expense it," he said. But once the media got hold of the expense claim they ran with it, calling it the "Pouilly-Fuissé dinner" because four bottles of the $37.50 wine were consumed along with our red snapper and pasta for six. The media kept the pressure up until Peter's friend and provincial premier had to accept his resignation.

Fate sometimes plays a large role in politics, and it's sometimes cruel and unfair. But it happened, and like so many other events in his life, Peter just dealt with it and moved on. I never heard him complain—it wasn't in his nature. There were lots of other ways to be involved in politics, he told me. But to lose an important job and a career over a dinner was a shame, a damn shame.

I'm not one to live with regrets; they waste energy and steer focus away from the tasks at hand, what we have in our control today. But, oh, how I wish I'd just taken that cheque, or at least split it three ways. Years later, in 2006, Peter died of cancer. I've wondered how much the "Pouilly-Fuissé dinner" haunted him over the years.

In the end, the CRTC did approve the Premier Cablevision deal—but with one caveat: the Commission made it clear that Rogers was forbidden from buying up other Canadian cable systems for at least a decade.

With that CRTC order and Ted's riverboat-gambling personality, I knew it could mean only one thing: there would be no more mere dabbling in America. We would soon be all in, and as the 1980s began I was heading toward some of the most exhilarating times of my life.

8

Southward Ho

I first met Colin Watson at the 1974 cable industry convention in Chicago. At the time he was CCL's vice-president of operations and I was Rogers's vice-president of programming and planning. Our bosses, Tony Griffiths and Ted Rogers, wanted us to meet, so we had dinner in Chicago.

We liked each other right away. And apart from being a couple of cable heads, we had many other things in common as well: we were both in our early thirties, we'd both graduated from UBC, and we'd both earned master's degrees at other universities, his in engineering and mine in political sociology. We also enjoyed fishing—Colin not as passionately as me—and would go on numerous fishing trips, particularly to the northern part of B.C.'s Haida Gwaii, formerly known as the Queen Charlotte Islands. Often these trips were with my friend Steve McDonald, whose family owned Western Cablevision Ltd. in Surrey, which Rogers bought in 1990. Colin, too, became good friends with Steve.

One of the first conversations Colin and I had in Chicago was about the vast, largely untapped cable market in the United States. Cable was more advanced in Canada, and it didn't take a genius to see all the potential for cable in the U.S. Until 1977, American cable was restricted to suburban markets, with local systems limited to between 5000 and 10,000 subscribers. Lucrative urban markets were closed for several reasons, one being that U.S. television networks were delivering their programming over the air and, fearing competition, were pressuring the FCC (Federal Communications Commission) to keep cable out.

But the writing was on the wall. Founded in 1972, Home Box Office Inc., or HBO, arguably became the leading premium cable station for its mix of movies and innovative original programming. It changed the programming universe in 1975 when it broadcast via satellite back to North America the famous "Thrilla in Manila" heavyweight title fight between Muhammad Ali and Joe Frazier. HBO became the first network to deliver its programming by satellite and thus became the first U.S. cable channel. Rival cable channels soon followed.

Ted Rogers and I had had many discussions about potential opportunities south of the border, and now I was having similar talks with Colin from CCL, then a rival cable company. And within five years of that first meeting, things would change immensely for Colin and me. Not only would we both be working for Ted Rogers, but important new rules would transform the industry in the U.S.

Once the 100 largest U.S. cities began calling for tenders for cable licences, several Canadian cable operators headed south to make bids for franchises. Initially, given our involvement in things like the CCL and Premier takeovers, we were just too busy in Canada to dive headfirst into U.S. waters. We did target Minneapolis, though, and won the cable licence there in 1979. Then, for suspect reasons, Minneapolis city council rescinded it and gave the franchise to our bitter rival Storer. We took the city to court for breaking the binding contract. The whole Minneapolis venture was a story in itself, so I'll return to it in the next chapter.

Anyway, the wheels of justice grind slowly, and it wasn't until the following year, 1980, that Ted Rogers decided to really break into the U.S. cable market. No holds barred. If we wanted to grow—and Ted always wanted to grow—we had to head south. After the CRTC had approved the Premier takeover, Rogers held 28 percent of all cable subscribers in Canada, and as I mentioned earlier, the regulator had let it be known that it would look darkly upon any more takeovers here.

Our American venture would be a two-pronged strategy, the main thrust being to win as many U.S. cable franchises as possible and then build them out. We would literally travel from city to city trying to win franchises from local councils. The secondary push would be to acquire existing cable systems.

Both Colin Watson and I were gung-ho on U.S. expansion and delighted with Ted's decision. He named me chairman of Rogers's U.S. cable systems and Colin Watson president, with both of us reporting directly to Ted.

My first job as head of the franchising team was to assemble a team of lawyers, lobbyists, and political operatives to persuade politicians, recruit local investors, and win U.S. cable franchises. I was already working with Minneapolis lawyers David Jones and Lee Sheehy of Popham Haik. I convinced Vernon Achber from CUC Broadcasting in Scarborough, Ontario, to join the team as my lieutenant after Rogers colleague Kevin Shea highly recommended him. Wes Heppler and Missy Goerner would soon follow, as well as others, but these folks were the core of my intrepid "U.S. Road Warriors" who were always ready and able for the many challenges we faced. (Though the Road Warriors were integral throughout the 1980s, the nickname was coined later for those who travelled from city to city seeking approval before Rogers could close the sale of our U.S. assets to Houston Industries in 1989.)

Along with the Road Warriors, the franchising team included a host of others, including Colin Watson, Nick Hamilton-Piercy, Graham Savage, Michael Allen, Bob Clasen, and my crew, among them Lyn Wickwire, Vernon Achber, Steven Moss, Liane Langevin, Bill Craig, Skip Cerio, Linda Moulton-Patterson, and Mitzi Scott. But it's the Road Warriors, and Colin, with whom I've stayed in close touch, remaining lifelong friends.

Even before we landed any deals, Colin's job was to compile a team of technicians and systems managers who would build and operate systems after we won the franchises. He already had Nick Hamilton-Piercy, the exceptional engineer who stayed with Rogers after the CCL takeover. Nick's engineering ideas, especially when it came to fibre optic rings, revolutionized how cable systems were built.

These were exciting days, and I was still in my thirties. The U.S. had just seen the launch of the first pay TV network, HBO, and what became known as the first "superstation," Ted Turner's WTBS. CNN (Cable News Network) and so many others would soon follow. Indeed, throughout the 1980s, infrastructure and programming investment boomed. From 1980 (when we arrived in the U.S.) to 1989 (when we left), the number of cable program networks increased from 28 to 79, and by the end of the decade nearly 53 million households had subscribed to cable.

What follows is the story of a Canadian company that went south and really succeeded. Americans tend to be brasher, bolder, and more willing to take business risks than Canadians. But we proved we could go toe to toe with the Americans—and on their home court, too. And here's something else that was unexpected: in the franchise wars, competing cable companies were bitter enemies—but as we built the cable industry across America, and as the franchising wars subsided, many became allies and friends.

By the time Ted gave us our U.S. marching orders, we actually already owned and operated a cable system in Syracuse, New York. Canadian Cablesystems (CCL) had been awarded that franchise in April 1978 in the midst of our bitter takeover battle. And with tiers for programming and non-programming services like fire and burglar alarm protection, Syracuse was just the advanced type of system we envisioned for Canada, as outlined in our Premier Cablevision takeover application to the CRTC. And so for us, the Syracuse system became the template for the advanced systems we'd build and improve upon.

Later, while serving on America's NCTA board (National Cable Television Association), I remember discussing with fellow board member John Malone of TCI (Tele-Communications Inc.) some of our new two-way capabilities, which, at the time, signalled the dawn of the interactive age. Every six seconds, for example, our control centre could sweep through the network and see how many homes were tuned to HBO, TBS, CNN, or traditional TV. We were beginning to transmit voice and data traffic to local bank branches and supermarkets more cheaply than what phone companies were charging. Malone was fascinated to hear that the cable network was attracting viewers to newer programming services in record numbers. As I said, these were fast-paced, riveting times to be in the cable business. How things have changed. Time marches on, but I wouldn't have missed the excitement of the U.S. cable industry in the 1980s.

Like Ted, Colin and I were kindred spirits when it came to going up against bigger foes in David-and-Goliath struggles. I'm an Americophile who relishes the politics of persuasion and political dogfights, and Colin loved to build state-of-the-art cable systems—real futuristic stuff in the 1980s. And Ted—well, Ted loved the art of the deal, the thrill of victory, and the relentless push forward. Always pushing forward.

And now one big U.S. city after another was issuing RFPs (Requests for Franchise Proposals), setting off a gold rush. Franchises were awarded by city councils after applicants made various promises on service, rates, and programming, especially local community programming. And the more an applicant promised, the higher its chances of getting the franchise. Then, once a franchise was awarded, it would take roughly 18 months to build the system and begin serving the first customers. And yes, we made some pretty enthusiastic public promises to pay for local enhancements, like funding art galleries, museums, libraries, and drug treatment facilities. We even promised to plant 10,000 urban trees to improve our bids' chances in politicians' eyes, but there was nothing shady about it (beyond the park benches under those trees).

Still, in winning U.S. cable franchises, we had three major obstacles.

First, we were going head to head against much larger companies like Time Inc., Westinghouse, TCI, Warner Communications, TelePrompTer Corp., Storer Broadcasting, Cox Broadcasting, and American Express, which all had cable divisions.

Second, with what were then double-digit interest rates, the cost of money was skyrocketing, and we had to borrow to build. In cable, you need monthly recurring revenue to pay debt and invest in infrastructure, but it could take months to win a franchise and months more before you had paying customers.

Third, we were foreigners in the U.S., and the ramifications of that fact cannot be understated. After the CCL takeover, we'd kept the name Canadian Cablesystems since it was already a publicly traded company and Ted had used it to turn us into a public company. But now we changed the company's brand name back to Rogers Cablesystems and dropped the "Canadian," in part to make us more palatable to Americans. Still, being "aliens" put us at a distinct disadvantage. Prime Minister Pierre Trudeau's flamboyant antics vis-à-vis the United States were extremely tough on us, too. (The Canadian ambassador at the time, Allan Gotlieb, describes these problems in his book *The Washington Diaries: 1981–1989*.)

There were other impediments, but those three were formidable.

Yet we had definite advantages, too. We'd already built cable systems in large urban areas, something our American friends hadn't done, so we had experience running these urban systems. And we had a solid strategic plan, an experienced team, and local business partners who were helping us not only with cash but with adding a red-white-and-blue feel to our applications for franchise.

By this time I'd convinced Ted that the best use of our limited resources would be to target a limited number of places. Applying in a hundred places with hopes of winning a few franchises would have yielded us nothing. So, where would we have the best chance of winning?

First off, I ruled out virtually every state where they were unfriendly to foreign cable companies or where elected officials had expressed anti-Canadian feelings in the media.

Next, we looked for cities that were like us: culturally similar or holding similar values as Canadians, near us geographically perhaps, and open-minded when it came to getting the best service, regardless of whether it was provided by a perceived foreigner. This phase pointed to cities in border states like New York, Minnesota, Michigan, Montana, Washington, and Oregon. I also looked at states with lots of Canadian residents, like California and Florida.

Then we drilled down into these states, looking at their demographics and the likelihood of viable local business people who could partner with us and lend an American feel to our applications.

Last, I'd study individual city councils and the personalities of the politicians. Sometimes when a city council was in session I'd sit and listen for hours—even a couple of days—finding out who were the leaders, the followers, the types who would buy our story to possibly win the franchise. I'll let my Rogers colleague Vernon Achber say it: "Phil's greatest strength is that he understands people's strengths and their weaknesses. And he will exploit both, which is good leadership."

Everyone on my team would be parachuted into a town knowing no one. Within months, they'd have contacts on every road leading to city hall, every office that had anything to do with the awarding of cable franchises. The franchising team was simply terrific, and did an outstanding job.

As you read along, you'll encounter more details about our strategies—and where they worked and didn't work and why—but those are the fundamentals.

I'd be lying if I said I had it all worked out going in, because I didn't. We learned so much, and we honed strategies as we went.

For example, there was one tough councillor in Portland, Oregon, who asked hard-hitting, penetrating questions over and over, one after the other. Now, I think I'm reasonably tough; I'd even survived that grilling from Dante Fascell on Capitol Hill back in 1974. But this councillor, Mildred Schwab, scared the crap out of me. I remember going to the washroom several times and throwing up before facing her questions at council. And Schwab was not only tough, she was smart. (It must have been in her genes: her brother Herbert was a justice on the Oregon Supreme Court, and one of the brightest legal minds in the Pacific Northwest.)

After I underwent a particularly rough grilling from Mildred, our local partner, Larry Black, said, "Congratulations, Phil. It looks like you're going to win."

I looked at him in bewilderment: "What? What are you talking about? She tore me apart."

"She only does that to people who come to council who she's serious about," he said. "If she takes it easy on you then you have no chance."

Larry Black was right. Mildred Schwab and I actually got along famously in the end. There's even a photograph of Mildred and me signing the cable franchise together with Larry, smiles all around. You just never know in life, and you just never stop learning.

I'm going to take a moment here to briefly point out the differences between American and Canadian cable regulations, since if we were to succeed in the U.S., it was very important that we master the variances. Still, these can get incredibly complicated, nuanced, and rife with legalese. I mean, you'd be bored to tears if I detailed all the differences. Instead, just keep in mind the one fundamental distinction: Canadian regulation is centralized at the CRTC while the U.S. system is a hybrid of the FCC and local governments. And it was the local authorities who awarded the cable franchises.

The reason for this essential difference is pretty simple. The U.S. has 10 times more people than Canada, so if the FCC had to handle all the local issues related to the cable industry, it would be swamped. And since cable uses streets, poles, and public rights of way, local governments want to be intimately involved.

Here's a fun story that underlines another jurisdictional difference in federal and local regulations.

In 1984, when the U.S. federal government was bringing in the first cable act, one of the sections included preventing alien ownership of U.S. cable: that is, foreign companies like us. The proposal was similar to what they had for the broadcasting industry. Because we were already established in the U.S., we probably would have been grandfathered. Regardless, I could not get behind that alien ownership provision, even though it was supported by the NCTA, of which I was a board member.

To help get the act through Congress, the NCTA's head, Tom Wheeler, wanted to hire a Tennessee lobbyist by the name of Fred Thompson, who was a good friend of Howard Baker, one of President Reagan's key allies and soon to become Senate majority leader. Thompson himself would later serve in the U.S. Senate and have a stellar acting career in movies and hit TV series like *Law & Order*.

Thompson politely turned Wheeler down. He already had a cable client: Phil Lind and Rogers. Wheeler was astounded— he couldn't believe I'd already identified Thompson as a key Republican operative, since he was largely unknown at that time. But Wheeler did ask me if I'd release Thompson from our exclusive contract so that he could work for the NCTA to help get this important bill passed to the benefit of the cable industry.

Sure, I said, so long as the NCTA publicly endorses the removal of the alien ownership proviso in the act. Wheeler dropped his head and agreed. The cable bill passed, and to this day it has allowed foreign companies to remain U.S. cable owners.

Thompson, a Republican and a terrific guy, died in 2015 of cancer. Wheeler, a Democrat who went on to be the chairman of the FCC from 2013 to 2017, turned out to be no friend of the cable industry, spearheading things like putting cable under utility-like oversight. But since FCC chairs are appointed by the president, I always blamed that on his bosses in the White House.

When we entered the U.S., Colin Watson had the unenviable assignment of building the franchises we'd won—an almost impossible task when you think of the nature of the commitments made and the amount of money required. In Minneapolis, for example, it took so long to close a big loan with one of the banks that by the time we finally managed to ink the deal, we were already in default. Colin just smiled, shook everyone's hand, and moved on to get the job done.

Our friendship and business partnership broke all the rules for business management and conventional wisdom. I mean, what manager (Colin) permits another manager (Phil) to direct his people on fundamentally important matters? For example, I'd make promises to win franchises, then I'd tell Colin's people to do it by a certain date or in a certain way. But it all worked out. Against many odds we survived and thrived, and Colin deserves tons of credit.

We started with one small, inherited cable system of 25,000 homes in Syracuse, and nine years later we departed leaving 550,000 subscribers in 69 communities in California, Texas, Minnesota, and Oregon.

I'm proud to call Rogers's American cable sojourn one of the great Canadian business stories about entering the U.S., competing really hard, and leaving as a financial winner. Back in those days particularly, most Canadian companies found only misery when they tried to expand south of the border. The United States has been the graveyard of broken dreams for many Canadian businesses—businesses that have failed to recognize the toughness of the competition on so many levels. Canadian Tire lost $300 million during its 1980s U.S. venture. RBC has written off more than that south of the border, as have other Canadian banks. There are many other examples.

And yet we came home with more than $1 billion profit in Ted Rogers's pocket. I'm biased, but our story is one that our business students should absorb. Canadians going south have to be bold, smart, and tough. In other words, to succeed you've got to out-American the Americans.

9

Minnesota

Back in 1979, lawyers David Jones and Lee Sheehy of Popham Haik wrote me a memo estimating that the legal fees associated with our run at obtaining the Minneapolis cable franchise would be approximately $50,000. In the end, the tab was well over $1 million—and worth every cent.

The Minneapolis saga has so many twists and turns it could be a made-for-TV movie. There were allegations of municipal corruption and lawsuits filed; there was Ted Rogers going off-script with comments about President Ronald Reagan's Star Wars missile defence; there was American jingoism at its finest and anti-Canadian sentiment galore; there was even a link to the U.S. hostages in Iran. During our decade in the United States, Minneapolis provided some of the highest highs and lowest lows.

In the early autumn of 1979, after intensive rounds of campaigning and presentations, we narrowly won the right to negotiate a contract with the city. The Minneapolis *Star Tribune* reported that "despite several months of intensive lobbying efforts, an array of four impressive systems proposals, two evenings of formal multi-media presentations, a public hearing and an inch-and-a-half-thick consultant's report chock full of more inconclusive findings than anyone could possibly digest, none of the four applicants had secured the seven votes necessary to win the franchise." With 13 members on the council, those seven votes would represent the majority. Under a complicated formula, though, we were the clear-cut winner when councillors' second choices were taken into account. It was our political and operational experience, and our commitment to local community programming, that carried the day. The city's two largest community groups were delighted with our win. In the months ahead, their support would become even more crucial.

That's because the losing companies claimed that "the Canadians" were illegitimate winners—and somehow convinced the council to vote again after the fall election. We narrowly lost that vote. It was one of the most depressing moments in my business life. We'd worked so hard, and now all that work was in jeopardy.

Make no mistake, this was a tough battle. Our competitors played up the "foreigners" angle big time against us. They took out newspaper ads illustrated with storks carrying bags of money and flying to Canada. The three losing bidders even teamed up to publish a full-page "open letter to the citizens of Minneapolis" in the local newspaper. Here's an excerpt:

At a time when the U.S. is already too dependent on foreign resources, including Canadian oil, why must we import services that American companies can provide? At a time when much of downtown Minneapolis is already owned or managed by foreign interests, including Canadian firms, why would we also turn over control of our future entertainment, communications and data transmissions network to foreign control when American firms are available?

The letter hammered home the point that Canada did not itself allow foreign control of its cable companies, and urged citizens to put heat on their councillors to block the interlopers.

And this hard-hitting "anti-Canadian" campaign would be repeated over and over in city after city where we applied for cable franchises. These were tough, tough campaigns. But Minneapolis was particularly stinging.

There was also a wild card by the name of Ted Rogers, who came to Minneapolis to meet local investors and councillors at a cocktail reception. His speech started off fine; he talked about the similarities between Toronto and Minneapolis: climate, hospitable people, cleanliness, and such. But then he began denigrating one of our competitors from Florida, making jokes about them stringing wires from palm trees and not having experience delivering cable in a cold climate. "Ted always seemed a bit of a duck out of water in the U.S.," says Minneapolis lawyer and Road Warrior David Jones. "Minneapolis is a city that loves process, and some didn't take kindly to his comments." Ted was also singing the praises of Ronald Reagan's Star Wars missile defence plan. That didn't go over well either, especially with the Democratic councillors. Minnesota was one of only six states that Reagan didn't win in the 1980 election, and in 1984, it was the only state he lost.

Meanwhile, plenty of monkey business was going on in Minneapolis. Before a second cable vote was called, all sorts of whispers were circulating about bribes and corruption. A copy of our application with detailed financials and commitments even went mysteriously missing from city hall.

We lost the second vote after councillor Zollie Green switched his earlier yes to a no, swinging the count to Storer Broadcasting. Word was that Storer had paid Green $30,000 to change his vote.

Making things even more illegitimate, the vote occurred after the council's election but before the new council took over. Green lost his seat and wouldn't even be on the new council. Nothing was proven, but it's worth noting that a few years later Zollie Green, who died in 1999, was indicted on bribery charges related to a city bus shelter contract.

After losing the second vote, we took the matter to court. Here's what our year-end 1979 corporate annual report said: "Although the award of the franchise was subsequently rescinded by [Minneapolis] City Council, Cablesystems considers it has a binding contract with the City and is continuing to press its case in the courts." When new mayor Don Fraser took office on January 1, 1980, he vetoed moving the contract to Storer until things could be sorted out. Although that was very good news, it didn't solve our problem: we'd won the franchise fair and square and wanted to move forward building the system—and collecting much-needed recurring revenue from subscribers.

Unbeknownst to us and the entire world, as this was going on, Canadian ambassador Ken Taylor was providing safe haven to six American citizens trapped in Iran in the aftermath of the seizure of the American embassy in Tehran on November 4, 1979. Fifty-two Americans remained hostage, but these six had managed to escape to the Canadian embassy. They had to be moved elsewhere, and many Canadians, not the least of whom was Ambassador Taylor, put their lives on the line for their American friends.

The "Canadian Caper" was a success when the six Americans got out of Iran on January 27, 1980. Hailed as a hero, Ken Taylor became a beloved figure in the U.S.—and the glow spread to all Canadians, who couldn't buy a drink in the U.S. for days, maybe weeks, after news of the story broke.

That gave me an idea to use the newspapers to our advantage: we took out full-page ads with the message "Thank You, Canada!" and had them "signed" by a fictional local Minneapolis group in support of the best cable system available, regardless of nationality.

Meanwhile, the lawsuits and counter lawsuits piled up. Private investigators were hired to dig up dirt on Zollie Green and others. Several councillors publicly stated that they'd been offered $30,000 to change their votes, too, but had declined. It was a mess. We were all in limbo: us, Storer, local politicians, and the citizens wanting cable TV.

Financing was always an issue for us during these franchise wars, and now hefty bills were stacking up. We needed a solution. Then one day I got a call from my counterpart at Storer asking if we'd be interested in splitting Minneapolis in two. What a great compromise, I thought. Storer could have the northern area where they had political support, and we'd take the southern where we had the same. Of course, this created a whole new set of problems. Namely, would we be violating U.S. antitrust laws?

I contacted Philip Verveer, a brilliant young antitrust lawyer in Washington who'd just left the Justice Department to begin private practice. As with Bob Buchan in Ottawa, I became Verveer's first client after he left government service. And talk about hiring the best talent: between 1973 and 1977, Verveer was the Antitrust Division's lead counsel in the investigation and prosecution of *United States v. American Tel. & Tel. Co.*—a landmark case that led to the breakup of the AT&T colossus. It had more than one million employees; only the U.S. federal government employed more. Indeed, no commercial enterprise had more employees, more customers, or more shareholders. Philip Verveer is currently the senior counselor to FCC chairman Ajit Pai. He was very important to us on several files, but especially in Minneapolis.

We negotiated the deal with Storer at a Las Vegas hotel. To make sure we weren't violating any antitrust laws, Verveer would sit beside me and confer; he would allow no note-taking. Across the table was a Storer executive and his lawyer. Here's how it went: I'd say something to Phil, then he'd repeat it to the other lawyer, who would repeat it to the Storer executive. That executive would respond, then his lawyer would talk to Verveer, and then Verveer would talk to me. Needless to say, it was awkward. And yet it was all strictly by the book: Rogers and Storer never spoke directly to each other about dividing the Minneapolis cable territory, and we were never challenged on any antitrust laws.

As it turned out, we began winning many of the franchises in the suburbs around Minneapolis—Minnetonka, Edina, St. Louis Park—in large part due to the terrific work of Bill Craig, a Rogers employee from Toronto who'd left programming to move stateside and be our man on the ground. It was apparent that Rogers was there to stay, so just six months later Storer offered us their half of Minneapolis in exchange for expenses rung up. We took the deal, and Verveer again made sure we didn't violate any antitrust laws when reassembling the city's cable franchise.

There's a funny story about how we represented ourselves in the press during the whole Minneapolis episode. Now, in those days, newspapers were very important when it came to local politics and politicians. At that time we had a public relations man named D.J. Leary, a local legend, and when we agreed to the Storer-Rogers division of territory, I asked Leary to set up a meeting with the *Star Tribune*'s editorial board so that we could explain the wonderful benefits of having two cable systems in Minneapolis. Then, six months later, I asked Leary to set up another meeting with the board, this time to explain the wonderful benefits of having only one cable system. Leary pulled it off. We had the *Star Tribune*'s endorsement of the original split and six months later its endorsement of a sole cable system. Leary was a real spin doctor.

Lee Sheehy and David Jones, my first legal hires in the U.S., were both integral to our American strategy throughout the 1980s and even later in the 1990s. The three of us have often pondered what Ted Rogers would have done if we'd lost Minneapolis: would he have pulled the chute on U.S. expansion altogether? After all, before the first paying subscriber was even hooked up, we'd spent millions of dollars that Ted didn't have.

Rogers's debt was soaring during the U.S. franchise years. So were interest rates, which were reaching 15 to 18 percent levels—and all our growth was financed with bank loans. It's here that Ted Rogers showed his brilliance and his sheer guts. Very few, perhaps no other, Canadian CEOs would have had the stomach to do what he did. Whereas other CEOs would have said "Let's cut our losses and move on," Ted was always supportive of us, even during the darkest hours.

10

Texas

_____

Although franchising was our main thrust, Rogers also moved into the U.S. market through acquisition. This created a different set of problems, among them reconfiguring network architecture, reworking programming agreements, and partnership issues involving Ted Rogers and the other owners. For those reasons, I'll delve a bit into that part of the story.

In May 1981, Ted figured out a way to supercharge our U.S. expansion. At that time UA/Columbia Cablevision Inc., the country's tenth-largest major system operator (MSO), was looking to ward off a hostile takeover from Dow Jones/Knight Ridder. So UA, led by Robert Rosencrans and controlled by the Naify family, placed a full-page ad in *The Wall Street Journal* opposing the takeover and seeking a white knight. Ted saw the ad while we were in Quebec City on business, and was immediately intrigued—this was a cable company that had almost half a million paying subscribers scattered in 15 states.

Ted was a lot of things, but I doubt any of his business partners over the years would describe him as a white knight. Nonetheless, the Naify brothers were desperate. When Ted came up with $185 million, he got 51 percent and Marshall and Robert Naify retained 49 percent, trading one hostile takeover for a more indirect one.

This transaction put Rogers on even more precarious financial footing. Ted had borrowed from the banks for the Naify deal, and by the time the deal closed later in 1981, the prime rate had shot up from 14 to 19 percent. All told, in a single year Rogers's debt jumped a whopping $400 million, from $163.6 million in 1981 to $566.7 million in 1982. Much of that was attributable to construction costs associated with the U.S. franchises and the loan to buy UA/ Columbia Cablevision. But from September 1981 to August 1982, interest charges alone amounted to $65 million.

The good news is that by August 1982 we were approaching 100,000 paying customers from our U.S. franchises, but the bad news was that we had lots more building to do. There were always cash problems.

The Texas part of the story isn't directly related to the franchise wars, but it's important on several levels. First, some of my favourite Ted Rogers stories occurred in the Lone Star state. Second, our eventual breakup with the Naify brothers is integral to the overall U.S. story. Third, this episode introduced us to Missy Goerner, who would become a longtime business associate, Road Warrior, and close friend.

For decades, the Naify family had been at the helm of UA Communications, the parent of the cable company. Marshall and Robert, both in their late fifties at the time, were sons of company founder Mike Naify. In addition to cable TV, UA had movie theatres across the country and a movie sound studio in Los Angeles.

Of Middle Eastern descent, the Naify brothers were fiery, hot-tempered Hollywood types who would go around yelling and screaming at themselves and others. With my work experience, I was comfortable with that, but others thought them strange.

Anyway, Ted had no intention of being equal partners. He wanted to roll his cable franchise division into the existing cable company, which he now controlled with 51 percent; its recurring revenues could help him raise the money he needed to build the franchise cable systems. But the Naify brothers and their team fought this at every turn. Just one year into the deal, they pulled the shotgun clause to end the partnership (or as we referred to it, "the marriage") with Rogers. Everyone had seen it coming.

Under the terms of our agreement, one side would split the company assets in two and the other side would choose which pile they wanted. The UA side created the two piles and we chose.

In dividing the systems, the UA team had a clear idea of which pile they wanted Rogers to take, and so they studded that pile with the personal likes of the Rogers senior executives. For example, they included smaller cable systems in skiing areas for Colin and in fishing areas for me, and Florida cable systems for Ted, who they knew had a home in the Bahamas. As well, they anchored the pile with the company's mature cash-cow system in New Jersey and with a slightly higher number of paying customers (about 325,000). Here they were betting on our need for cash flow to help pay for all the under-construction U.S. franchises we held.

The other pile contained smaller cable systems in high-growth areas in the south and western parts of the U.S. It had fewer paying customers (about 300,000) and higher costs for new construction, but greater long-term potential. The crown jewel of this pile was San Antonio, which had only 53,000 customers but a potential of about 350,000 subscribers.

UA wanted to keep San Antonio, but it underestimated our Rogers team. We based our decision not on vacation spots but rather on trends, extensive research, and modelling. Vernon

Achber and Michael Allen, my director of programming in Toronto at the time, were invaluable in analyzing the two piles.

Armed with solid logic to back us up, Colin and I suggested to Ted that we take the pile with fewer subscribers because it had more potential for growth. With no hesitation, he agreed. We never looked back. We added about 175,000 customers in San Antonio within five years.

"The UA team was shocked and devastated that you didn't take the other pile," says Missy Goerner, who'd been one of the first employees hired by UA at its cable company in San Antonio.

Which leads me to two fabulous Ted Rogers stories.

The first is his well-known meeting with Angelo Drossos, then the owner of the NBA San Antonio Spurs basketball team. The cable system owed Drossos lots of money because of promises made by our predecessor, UA Columbia, when bidding to get the cable franchise. And since we were bleeding money everywhere, Ted needed to renegotiate the deal. Under the Spurs-UA deal, we were paying Drossos a million dollars a year for the right to telecast the San Antonio Spurs on pay per view, and we hadn't even built enough of our system to carry one game. But Angelo, a tall, imposing, second-generation Greek American, was a San Antonio business giant—and one of the toughest, most litigious team owners in the NBA. He had no interest in or legal reason to give Ted a better deal.

Missy, who managed the Spurs file for our local cable system, prepared a dossier on Angelo for Ted. The background info was extensive, but two anecdotes, one verified and one urban legend, gave Ted an idea. He'd go on to craft a brilliant, ballsy plan that would help keep us afloat in the U.S.

The first anecdote was that Angelo, in the fledgling years of building his team, bet another team owner that if he could beat him in a game of tennis, he could take a player of his choice. The owner, having been a ranked junior tennis player, took the bet. Angelo beat him and grabbed a player who'd go on to become one of the best the Spurs franchise ever had. The second anecdote—likely apocryphal—was that Angelo, in a heated dispute with then–NBA commissioner Mike Storen, sent a telegram to Storen that read: "Fuck You. Stronger message to follow."

After Ted called Missy and asked her to set up a meeting with Angelo, he and I flew down to San Antonio. Two big-personality entrepreneurs like Ted and Angelo appeared ill-suited and ready to clash at this first meeting, which was set for lunch in Angelo's office. But Ted had taken from these anecdotes that Angelo was much like him: an entrepreneur and a gambler, someone for whom the art of a deal was part of the thrill of doing business, someone willing to put everything on the line to win.

Ted and I were late for the lunch, and Angelo was all about punctuality. So when we finally arrived, Angelo was steaming. He and Missy had already eaten their lunches while ours, prepared by Angelo's personal chef, were sitting on the table, uncovered and cold.

Ted, in full charm mode, moved to shake Angelo's hand. "You're late," Angelo said, "and you owe me a million dollars!"

This story has been recounted countless times, including in Ted's memoir, so I'll skip to the punch line.

"Angelo, I know," Ted responded. "And because I want to be a good partner, I brought the money with me." Just then, on cue, two burly Brinks guards wheeled in $1 million cash in 5-, 10-, and 20-dollar bills.

Angelo loved it. And he went on to repeat that story so many times that it was told at his funeral in 1997.

And yes, thanks to Ted's creativity and charm, Angelo eased up on the terms. We got a much better deal, one that saved us millions over our remaining time in the U.S. I've included a photograph that was taken that day, and that Angelo later hung in his office. Have a look at it, and remember that just moments before this picture was taken, Angelo was a very angry man.

The second Ted-in-Texas story took place before we ever met Angelo—when Ted first came to San Antonio for what he described as a "charm offensive" to meet key politicians, among them the city's mayor, Henry Cisneros. He even taped an interview for our local cable channel about how thrilled he was to be there. Actually, San Antonio is one of the States' most unique cities; among its attractions is a stunning downtown River Walk. One night Ted hosted a Rogers board of directors dinner on a barge floating on the beautiful San Antonio River, and the next night dinner was at a historic downtown building near the Alamo with Mayor Cisneros and his wife, Mary Alice, in attendance. It was a fun evening for all, and we were honoured to have the mayor and his wife stay with us long past the time they had allotted.

I was a big admirer of Henry, who was the first Latino mayor of a major U.S. city and one of the most recognizable mayors in America. He held office the entire time we owned the cable system there, and went on to serve as President Bill Clinton's secretary of housing and urban development. Unfortunately, he shared certain habits with the president, and those peccadilloes cost him his political career, just as Clinton's almost cost him the White House.

Anyway, after that dinner with the mayor, Ted asked us to organize a separate meet-and-greet cocktail reception for all the suburban cities we served; it would be a good way to chat with as many local politicians as possible. Problem was, most of these city council members had day jobs, so it was difficult to get many to travel downtown in the evening. And yet Ted was insistent, so dozens of invitations were duly extended.

When it became apparent that only a handful were going to attend, I roamed the halls of our San Antonio cable offices, rounding up any staff who looked like they could pass for politicians—that is, professionally dressed men and women in their late thirties and forties. We even had fake name tags made up with politicians' names from nearby towns like Selma, Garden Ridge, and Converse. When Ted arrived at the party it was nearly overflowing the room; he was delighted by the turnout, and began greeting people with his trademark style. Unlike at most events, where we'd split up and cover a room, I never left his side that night, making sure to introduce him to real councillors along with anyone else whom he thought were politicians but were really his employees.

Ted had a great time, and the San Antonio staff loved it, too: after all, Ted had been so gregarious, and they felt they were giving their new owner just what he wanted. It was only years later, at one of our Road Warrior dinners, that I finally fessed up. Ted laughed heartily.

He always enjoyed those dinners, where we'd tell him other stories like this. He'd always be a good sport about it, too: "I knew it all the time," he'd say. "I just wasn't going to let on because you thought you were so clever, Philip."

I don't believe he did know it, but he wasn't going to let me get one up on him. Besides, Ted was a real prankster himself, and these subterfuges were never mean-spirited. He knew that.

11

Oregon

One day in 1980, I walked into Black & Co. retail brokerage offices in downtown Portland, Oregon. Rogers's vice-president of finance, Graham Savage, had heard that if we wanted to find local investors for our Pacific Cablesystems in Oregon, owner Larry Black was where I should start.

We instantly hit it off, especially when we discovered our mutual passion for fly fishing. Larry introduced me to such Oregon fishing spots as the Rogue and McKenzie rivers, as well as spots near Portland itself. This picturesque city is eco-friendly and not particularly industrial, so there's very little pollution—even within city limits you can fish for salmon in the Columbia River or steelhead in the Willamette River. I enjoyed all the cities we operated in across the U.S., but I'd have to pick Portland as my absolute favourite.

Larry and I have remained friends ever since, and have fished many rivers in the Pacific Northwest, both in Canada and the U.S. We also share a fascination with politics and politicians. ("Phil has always had this magnetic personality that makes people feel comfortable," Larry says. "To use a baseball analogy, Phil is like someone in the major leagues as opposed to the rest of us toiling in the minor leagues. I could tell that immediately.")

Now approaching 90, Larry knew everybody in Portland. He was valuable to Rogers, not only in making connections for us but also educating us as to where the bodies were buried, so to

speak. He was also key to my dealings with the steely-tough councillor Mildred Schwab. And it was Larry's advice—to be truthful,
straightforward, and confident under Schwab's questioning—that
really helped at one pivotal moment.

At the final council meeting, the one where the franchise
vote would be taken, Ted Rogers had flown in and was sitting
with us in the first row of the council chambers. Mildred looked
at me and asked if we'd freeze our rates for 10 years. Holy shit,
I thought, we can't do that. Then I looked down the row at Ted
and he nodded subtly. I turned to Mildred and replied, "Yeah,
we can do that. We'll freeze our rates on tier three." That satisfied
her, and we never did raise our rates on tier three. (Basic cable was
tier one, enhanced programming was tier two, and both of these,
along with more expensive specialty channels, were tier three,
and the "all-in" package was tier four, which was the only one
we advertised.) Over the years we never had more than a handful
of subscribers on tier three.

Larry was also able to pull together a wealthy and influential investor syndicate for Pacific Cablesystems—and both CFO
Bob Francis and Graham Savage were appreciative of that, since
it meant they wouldn't need to work as hard in Oregon as they
did in other franchising areas.

One time, though, the normally unflappable Bob Francis lost
it on the side of the road in Oregon. As Ted, Vernon Achber, and
I were studying a map on the hood of our rental car, Bob was
pacing like a panther and taking drags on his du Maurier cigarette.
Then suddenly, and uncharacteristically, he ignited into a tirade.
He was beside himself. Stop winning franchises! he told me. Bob
knew that the company was on the edge of bankruptcy, and that
we just couldn't afford to keep building systems. By this point

we'd won Portland in May 1981 and were building it rapidly, which increased costs. (On the plus side, paying subscribers were getting service in only seven months.) And now we were battling for several franchises in nearby Multnomah County.

The funny thing is, Bob always mispronounced Multnomah, calling it "Malta-nomah," like the Mediterranean island of Malta. His arms were flailing and he was yelling, "I don't know what I'm going to do if you get Maltanomah! We can't do it, we can't do it!"

The image of this poor guy figuratively pulling his hair out while mispronouncing Multnomah struck me as funny. And when we all started to laugh, that got him even hotter. It took him a while to cool down.

We lost the Multnomah County franchises to Viacom, which had promised what was, back then, the impossible task of delivering 160 channels. Bob Francis was relieved. Even though our presentation was better, our commitment to local programming was second to none, and our overall quality topped our American competitors, we weren't ready to promise 160 channels to suburban systems. But as luck would have it—and much to Bob's chagrin—we ended up with Multnomah six months later when Viacom broke off negotiations with the county, probably because they knew they couldn't deliver 160 channels and still be viable.

Bob Francis was, in fact, pivotal to the franchising business. Although he'd always say we couldn't do this and we couldn't do that, he would always manage to find a way to come up with the money. He was a really great guy. Sadly, in February 1986, at the age of 50, Bob died of a heart attack at Ted's house in Nassau when we were all there for a company meeting.

There are two other things to recount about our Oregon adventures.

The first is what occurred when we were applying for the Portland franchise and the anti-foreigner, anti-Canadian issue rose again. It wasn't as heated as it had been the year before in Minneapolis, but it was certainly there. Rival bidder Monford Orloff, a prominent and highly respected businessman, arts patron, and director of Liberty Cable, not only urged councillors to keep the Portland cable company in American hands but also slandered all Canadians, calling us "untrustworthy."

It was powerful testimony, and particularly damning for us because Orloff's words carried tremendous weight in the community. But Orloff had an Achilles heel: his Canadian connection. The company he'd built, Evans Products, was among the state's largest publicly traded conglomerates, with holdings that ranged from home finance and equipment leasing to hardware stores and forestry products. Our research indicated that Orloff's businesses had extensive ties to British Columbia, including forestry and timber rights. And these "rights" were held at the pleasure of the government. Indeed, Orloff's company was one of the top 10 producers of timber and plywood in B.C.

I knew I couldn't let his unfounded accusations stand. So immediately after his attack I phoned my friend Peter Hyndman, then consumer and corporate affairs minister in the B.C. government, and reported what Orloff had said about Canada and Canadians. I don't know exactly what transpired after that, but I'm told Orloff received a phone call from Thomas Waterland, B.C.'s minister of forests.

The next day, Orloff asked council if he could say a few words. He recanted everything he'd said about Canadians, apologized, and left with his tail between his legs.

The second notable thing about our time in Oregon began, ironically enough, when we won the Portland franchise. In our proposal it turned out that we'd overestimated both our annual revenue and our subscriber penetration in Portland. We believed that by 1983 we'd be in 48 percent of the homes, but we got to only 35 percent, which made us fall way short of making our $12 million annual revenue targets.

Portland was the beginning when it came to breaking promises, but virtually every cable franchise would soon follow. It was a perfect storm: soaring construction costs, interest rates approaching 20 percent, slower subscriber sign-ups due to the recession, and having overpromised to win the franchises in the first place. We needed to negotiate relief packages with the cities by revamping our franchise contracts. Otherwise, we'd be toast.

So from 1984 to 1987 Vernon Achber and I criss-crossed the U.S., grovelling. (Ted called such reneging on our promises "get backs.") We needed concessions to survive, but it wasn't a pleasant job. These city managers were tough; they wouldn't just roll over. "It was humiliating at times," says Vernon (who had to do most of the grovelling). "It was hell on wheels. But it had to be done, and we got it done."

In a macabre sort of way, the only good news was that the cable industry overall was in a downturn—so if a city did consider pulling the franchise from us, it wasn't as if they'd have other operators lining up to take over the system. And we weren't the only operators seeking relief. But not all operators had the positive outcome we ultimately achieved in our efforts. For example, Drew Lewis, president of Warner Communications at the time and Reagan's former secretary of transportation, went to Pittsburgh and tried to play hardball.

The city kicked Warner out, likely costing the company four or five hundred million dollars.

Our strategy was different. We figured the soft-shoe approach would work better: after all, if we demanded concessions, we'd risk losing the system and having banks call our loans. So our strategy was to ask politely. "Plead" might be more accurate.

Vernon dreamt up the idea that, whenever we went to a city seeking relief, we should negotiate the insertion of the following clause in our revised franchise terms: "Where economically and technically feasible, the cable operator will ..." I thought it a wonderful idea. Ted most certainly approved, too. If we could get this clause in our franchise amendments, it would really give us an out, and boy did we need some outs.

So armed with that strategy and cap in hand, we set out on our arduous three-year "eco-techo" tour.

Most cities were tough but could be reasonable. They knew we were good cable operators and in dire straits, partly for having overpromised, but mostly due to the difficult economic conditions during the severe global recession of the early 1980s. And the councillors, many of whom had pushed so hard for the promises in the first place, felt some responsibility.

In the case of Portland, it was a good thing we'd cultivated a good relationship with Mildred Schwab by inviting her to tour our facilities in other cities whenever she was nearby on out-of-town business. One time, when Mildred was attending a conference in San Antonio, Missy Goerner picked her up at the airport and showed her around our showcase cable system and state-of-the-art production facility. "She was very appreciative and said she understood the difficulties of building cable systems in this tough economic climate," Missy says. "But she did notice many BMWs, including mine, in the staff parking lot and asked why we didn't drive more American-made vehicles." Luckily for us, Mildred knew I'd instructed that all our company service vehicles in the U.S., of which there were many, had to be American brands like Ford and GM.

Meanwhile, there were two nationally prominent Oregon politicians who were important to us, but both eventually fell from grace hard, the first in sinister fashion.

Neil Goldschmidt was Portland's mayor from 1973 to 1979. He was also a young man in a hurry: at the age of 37 he moved on to became President Jimmy Carter's transportation secretary, then governor of Oregon. Goldschmidt was a wunderkind politician. His ideas and legislation revitalized both the city of Portland when he was its mayor and the state when he was its governor. After leaving the governor's mansion in 1991 he worked as an executive at Nike, but remained a powerful force in Oregon politics as a lobbyist, dealmaker, and kingmaker.

Indeed, according to local historians and Oregon media, he was one of the most influential—yet controversial—figures in Oregon history. Sadly, we didn't see the whole picture when it came to Neil Goldschmidt. Behind the scenes lay a wicked part of his personality. When he was mayor—and 35 years old— he sexually abused the daughter of one of his aides, who was also the Goldschmidts' babysitter. The girl was underage when it began, and the abuse lasted for months.

The story came to light in 2004, as did allegations from other alleged victims. Owing to the statute of limitations (which has since been changed), Goldschmidt was never charged. His portrait was removed from the state capitol, however, and he lives in isolation and disgrace.

The story gets even worse. The poor girl, once a bright teen from an exclusive Portland neighbourhood, went on to struggle with drugs and alcohol for the rest of her life, which ended in January 2011 at age 48.

The other Oregon politician was Senator Bob Packwood, who from 1981 to 1985 was chairman of the Senate Committee on Commerce, Science and Transportation in Washington, D.C. That committee was critically important to the cable industry when it came to such issues as rate hikes, rate freezes, and the overall first U.S. cable bill.

Unfortunately, the senator had a penchant for grabbing women and forcing himself upon them. His downfall came in the mid-1990s—long before the #MeToo movement—when numerous women came forward. There were so many allegations that Packwood received the nickname "Senator Peckerwood."

Though his end story is deplorable, there is a humorous anecdote involving me and Packwood in the early 1980s, when he was still a powerful U.S. senator. At some fancy cocktail reception, I was telling him about a terrific fishing trip in Oregon I'd recently been on, and how I'd had this one steelhead hooked that was fighting like mad. I tugged hard on my jacket sleeve to mimic what the fish was doing to my line—and then somehow tore my sleeve right off from the shoulder. Packwood laughed and laughed.

In a backhanded way, that embarrassing moment was quite beneficial. That's because senators from the states where we operated were enormously important to us in Washington, so we always did our best to get to know them. And I can tell you, after that encounter, Packwood never forgot who I was.

12

California

When its cities and towns began issuing cable franchises, California experienced another gold rush 130 years after its original one. The *Los Angeles Times* and other media used words like "bedlam," "pandemonium," and "mayhem" to describe the mad grabs for franchises up and down the Golden State.

Rogers had targeted Orange County, just south of L.A., and was on a hot streak, winning more than losing. We picked up more than a dozen California franchises—and this despite all the anti-Canadian rhetoric.

Many U.S. companies were fed up with Pierre Trudeau's early-1980s National Energy Program that had chased so many from western Canada. And they and others weren't afraid to shout about it, especially at cable franchise hearings. The anti-foreigner NEP in Canada, coupled with the fact that American companies were prohibited from owning Canadian cable companies, really worked against us. But we won franchises by sticking to our political experience, our technical expertise in building advanced cable systems, and our commitment to local programming—in short, by being both savvy and reliable.

In presenting before city councils, we relied heavily on engineer Nick Hamilton-Piercy. Nick was especially important when we faced councils that, like many in California, included city managers and politicians who had an interest in the technological aspects. Nick knew what could be done in reality and what could probably be done in theory. He was also honest as the day is long. So whenever he was asked tough questions—like when we'd be able to deliver 60 or 80 channels—he'd get a little uncomfortable. But he also knew how pivotal his technical testimony could be in winning or losing. So he'd stand at the podium before the council and, while always avoiding outright lies, he'd theorize and stretch the truth as to what we could do. We'd be sitting right behind him, and would always know when this was happening because Nick would cross his legs, an unconscious habit he had. Thankfully, none of the councils seemed to notice.

Meanwhile, I didn't get every intricacy and nuance of California Republicans, so I relied on Stuart Spencer, an extremely bright and influential political operative with a tremendous sense of humour. He was a close friend of President Ronald Reagan—back when Reagan was California's governor, Stuart had been his campaign manager—and his consulting-business partner was Dennis Carpenter, a former state senator. Stuart also advised us on the best strategies to kill cable's alien ownership bill. He knew every Republican in California and beyond, it seemed, and would steer us to the right ones as required.

At the time, the Cable Communications Policy Act of 1984—the most important piece of legislation to date for the industry—was before Congress. We'd already stripped it of alien ownership provisions thanks to Fred Thompson, but now something new and dangerous had emerged: lawmakers were planning to freeze basic cable rates for almost three years until deregulation kicked in on January 1, 1987. And with our mounting debt, that would have been absolutely disastrous for Rogers.

Luckily, we found a procedural loophole in the law's passing that would give us exactly one day to notify cities of rate hikes. Even though our local franchises didn't allow for rate increases at that time, if they were properly notified, the hikes could go through.

So we put everyone on high alert at every Rogers cable system: get the rate hike notices ready and delivered when the time came. And every one of our systems pulled it off flawlessly. The San Antonio system, which covered a 100-mile area, had the most municipal cities to notify. They went so far as to hire pizza runners, and had them sitting at the office for several hours just waiting for the call to come from me to deliver the letters.

Chuck Dolan's Cablevision was the only other cable operator to use the loophole to get price hikes in before the freeze. We had some of the best minds in Washington, and it paid off. With so many banks breathing down our necks, if we hadn't been able to raise our basic cable rates, we would have been snookered.

Our time in California had its share of construction problems, too. For example, the contractors for Dickinson Pacific Cablesystems, Rogers's California partnership, had trouble finding the underground conduit where the cable was to be buried—and it had to be buried. This cost millions of dollars more. Dickinson Pacific started with a bank loan of $18 million. Then it increased to $27 million, and again to $35 million. At that point, the banks said no more. RCI in Toronto had to kick in an additional $20 million before the system was completed.

Despite those challenges, California was a fun part of our U.S. excursion. Although it wasn't always fun for the local managers and staff of each cable system as they built and then began operations. Whereas we were moving around the country, these local people were stuck with the more mundane, but necessary, tasks.

Meanwhile, my U.S. team always seemed to enjoy themselves (and work hard). One time, when a large group of us—Vernon Achber, Missy Goerner, Mitzi Scott, Linda Moulton-Patterson, Wes Heppler, Lee Sheehy, and David Jones—had gathered for a strategy meeting in La Jolla, there happened to be a Barenaked Ladies and Sarah McLachlan concert at the University of California San Diego that night, and we just had to go see these terrific Canadian artists. I drove one car and Vernon drove the other. Now, when Colin Watson and I began making our trips to the U.S., we'd play a game with our rental cars at red lights, bumping the other team member's rental car ahead of us. The number of bumps and level of intensity depended on the length of the light. That night, on La Jolla's poorly lit, winding roads, we got separated for a minute, until I saw what I believed to be Vernon's car in front of us. As we pulled up behind them at the light, I bumped the car. And since the light was long I bumped the car again, nudging it forward. "I knew it wasn't Vernon's car and I told Phil this, but he was convinced it was Vernon," Wes says. As I bumped the car a third time, it ran the red light to get away from me—and just then, up pulled Vernon and his crew. Shit. Everyone in my car started howling. Fortunately this was before cell phones; otherwise, the nice old couple we saw pulling away would surely have called the police on me.

Later that weekend, when Linda had to get back to her family in Orange County, Vernon volunteered to drive her to the train station. They were late, of course; it was dark, and Vernon was trying to find a shortcut to the station's drop-off area. He made a wrong turn and got stuck on the Amtrak line. Only Vernon could literally get a car stuck on a track. Luckily some railroaders at the station saw them and came over to guide the car off the line. Poor Linda was a bit rattled, but she made her train.

At that time there were so many cities in Southern California up for grabs, but here's how we won just one of them: La Mirada. Our California team was headed by Liane Langevin, a smart, highly capable young woman from Ottawa who'd worked for the CBC before joining us. She was tremendously persuasive. And once she hit California, you knew she'd never be living in Canada again. Liane was and still is very attractive, and she had a wonderful manner with people that made them feel special. The politicians and bureaucrats in La Mirada were absolutely charmed. The city manager in particular fell head over heels for her—and to our great benefit, he really pushed our application. If someone began espousing anti-Canadian rhetoric at a hearing, for example, that city manager would look over at Liane and then interrupt the speaker, saying things like, "If you can't stick to the facts about who can build La Mirada the best cable system, then I'll have to ask you to wrap it up." (Liane Langevin married another Rogers U.S. team member, Bob Clasen, who went on to become chairman and CEO of Starz cable channel. Now retired, they're prominent wealthy philanthropists in Colorado.)

Skip Cerio also deserves mention. We first got to know him through our cable system in Syracuse, where he'd been the mayor's executive assistant. With his passion for politics and the political process, Skip jumped at the chance to join our franchise team. He was a key player in Oregon for us, landing franchises there, and once they'd been secured he moved to our California team, where he worked with Liane. Skip just loved the excitement of our campaigns, as we all did. But, given his background, he especially revelled in them, once comparing every minute of the franchise wars to the frenetic pace of the last two weeks of a political campaign.

It's an apt analogy: we were high-octane, energetic teams moving like a political campaign with a business focus. Whether it was Minnesota, Oregon, California, or Texas, we hit pay dirt time and again. As I said before, we out-Americaned the Americans with smart, bold ideas coming from every part of our franchise teams.

I really enjoyed all the states, but my favourite two were Oregon and California. I loved Oregon because of its progressive nature and its fantastic beauty, not to mention the fly fishing. And California—well, what isn't there to love about it (except maybe the traffic)? Doing business there was different from what we'd experienced in any other state: the municipalities were smaller, meaning that we operated in a number of different cities. And the victories just kept on coming, which was exhilarating for me and for our entire crack team of franchisers led by Liane and then bolstered by Skip. The two had entirely different styles but achieved remarkably similar results.

During my time in the States, besides winning franchises and building a substantial U.S. cable business for Rogers, I learned the Pledge of Allegiance by heart! That's because it's recited before every council meeting across the country: "I pledge allegiance to the flag of the United States of America, and to the Republic for which it stands, one nation under God, indivisible, with liberty and justice for all."

Like me, its author, Francis Bellamy, was a graduate of the University of Rochester. Unlike me, Bellamy was a self-proclaimed socialist. He wrote the Pledge of Allegiance in 1892, and those were certainly different times, but it always struck me as ironic that so many Americans daily recite a pledge that was written by a socialist.

13

Exit Stage Left

W hen Ted summoned Colin and me to his house on Sunday, April 10, 1988, we knew what he was about to tell us: that it was time to sell our American cable properties, pay down our whopping $1 billion-plus debt (due in large part to our U.S. expansion), and retrench in Canada.

In his memoir, Ted says that he asked our opinion that day, but the reality is that he'd already made the decision. "As soon as they sat down, I posed a question," Ted wrote. "Should we sell the U.S. cable operations? They each had a hunch I was thinking this way, but their jaws still dropped with that bombshell."

To suggest that we were shocked is just not accurate. We could read the balance sheets. We could read the tea leaves as far back as 1985, when we began offering up several smaller stand-alone cable systems, like Syracuse to Craig McCaw and the Laredo, Texas, system on the Mexican border. And during our eco-techo tours, Ted always wanted Vernon to ask councils to rejig the cities' buy-back clauses. In short, many things had already pointed to grooming the assets for sale.

Indeed, a couple years earlier, as Ted was selling off the smaller systems, Colin and I had seriously thought about leaving Rogers and starting our own cable company. And maybe buying those very systems from Ted, if possible. As Colin puts it, "We could have gone to the banks and said, 'We know all about regulations with Lind, and we're pretty good on operations with Watson. We could put together a team in a flash. And we're going to go buy small cable companies in Canada and the U.S., if you lend us the money.'" And Ted, who by this time was getting more and more focused on the emerging wireless telephone business, had employed the same cable model a decade earlier. It was risky, but we had the know-how and the connections to make it work.

Yet we didn't pull the plug and go for it. To this day, neither Colin nor I is totally sure why we didn't. Was it our loyalty to Ted? Was it that we couldn't stomach the risk as Ted could? Risk fuelled Ted, but we weren't Ted. Few are. As well, my kids were still young—Sarah was born November 22, 1975, and Jed came along February 28, 1978, and they weren't even in high school at that point.

I suspect that Colin and I abandoned our plan for a combination of those reasons, along with other factors. Interest rates had peaked back in 1981, but they were still in the double digits. And maybe I was simply destined to be a right hand man, like my mentor, Darcy McKeough. Which ain't that bad, as Darcy can attest.

Hindsight is 20/20, of course, but looking back, Colin and I would have made a lot more money together on our own. Regardless, we're not asking anyone to hold bake sales for us. Colin and I have both done fine financially. "I don't say we should look back and say it's something we should have done, because you shouldn't be critical of your life," Colin says. "I'm profoundly happy, and Phil is, too. But in perfect hindsight, we could have done extremely well."

We never discussed this with Ted, and I don't believe he ever knew how close we were to breaking away and starting our own cable company. We've never discussed this publicly before, either; only a very small circle of friends know the story.

But back to that spring day and Rogers's U.S. cable operations. Even though it was a lost cause, Colin and I put up the argument for retaining our American holdings.

First, we'd built so much so quickly, and had one of the finest reputations of any cable operator in the States. (My former colleague Ken Engelhart kindly says this: "I remember being in Washington with Phil at least 10 or 15 years after we exited the U.S., and everyone in the cable industry still held him in such reverence.") Second, we reminded Ted that the U.S. cable market was exploding, and that new rate hikes were in the offing. Third, we were friendly with the likes of Ted Turner, John Malone, Craig McCaw, the Roberts family of Comcast, and every other major American cable operator—and if we remained in the U.S. we could share ideas and technology with these powerful allies more formally.

Ted Turner was especially critical to the industry: his programming had really helped launch cable in the U.S., which made the value of our systems go up, up, up. In fact, the year before, 1987, Turner's importance was one of the reasons I talked Ted Rogers—with a lot of help from Peter Barton, John Malone's right hand man—into ponying up $5 million to join the cable titan's investment cabal to bail out Turner Broadcasting. Ted Rogers was the first to get out because he needed the money (we always needed the money back then). Those who hung around made hundreds of millions from their investment in Ted Turner.

Another intriguing example of our desperate need for money was the case of USA Network. Shortly after it was founded in 1977, one-third of it was acquired by Rogers as part of our UA transaction. But in the late 1980s, at a time when cash was extremely tight, Rogers sold our stake for under $100 million. Several years ago, USA Network was valued at $6 billion. But back then, Ted really had no choice. Because USA Network was a "non-core asset," he had to sell our stake just to keep the bankers at bay.

As for selling our U.S. cable operations, Colin and I argued that many more opportunities would lie ahead if we didn't sell. Ted Rogers listened on that spring day, but that debt was hanging over the company like the sword of Damocles. And he knew it. So did we.

In Ted's last few years, after wireless boomed and generated 70 percent of company revenue, he would often say that selling the U.S. assets had allowed him to achieve his dream of making Rogers Communications an investment-grade powerhouse. But it's not quite fair to say that the profit from the U.S. sale went directly into wireless: if anything, it went into upgrading our Canadian cable network to make it Internet-ready for the digital economy, which of course was also a very good thing. And yet the fact is that we all underestimated the colossal investments required for wireless infrastructure—investments that, in the late 1990s, pushed Rogers Communications to the brink for one last time. The $1 billion profit from U.S. cable couldn't possibly have been enough when we were spending $1.5 to $2 billion on wireless capital expenditures every year.

But I'm getting ahead of myself here, since this is the story about the final hectic months of Rogers in America.

Seven suitors were interested in our U.S. cable operations. But in August 1988, we agreed to sell the entire thing to Houston Industries Inc., the parent company of Houston Light & Power, the eighth-largest American power utility. The initial price was US$1.26 billion, or a whopping US$2400 per subscriber—a record at the time, and triple the per-subscriber price only three years earlier.

There were two important caveats to the deal, though. First, the buyers made the mistake of insisting that the price go down by $2400 for each subscriber who left before the deal closed in six months. Second, they insisted on our gaining local council approval for all the major cable systems—like San Antonio, Portland, Orange County, and Minneapolis—before the deal could close.

The first point ticked Ted off: it implied that after reaching a tentative deal we'd abandon the quality of our service, which he took as a personal slight. The second point put the pressure squarely on me and the Road Warriors to get all those difficult approvals from local councils and the FCC.

But Ted came up with a brilliant idea for dealing with that first caveat. He'd agree to an adjustment clause, but the number of subscribers had to work both ways, up or down. Houston Industries said okay.

This meant that it was in our interest to up our subscribers. So back at the office we brainstormed furiously—and came up with the idea of targeting the fast-growing Latino population around San Antonio, where our subscriber penetration levels were lower than in English-speaking homes. We launched an advertising campaign that featured a Mexican-American actor and that promised $100 grocery vouchers to new subscribers if Rogers couldn't hook

up the cable service within 24 hours. We all knew that this was
an impossible pledge—back then, Rogers had never connected
anyone in 24 hours—but we didn't care. The phones started
ringing off the hook. And for every new order and $100 grocery
voucher, we received $2400 extra on the cable deal sale, so it was
well worth it. In the end, a total of 42,000 people ordered Rogers
cable over the six months leading up to the February 1989 close.
That added $101 million to the deal, for a total of $1.37 billion—
and after subtracting our investments in the U.S. over the decade
we spent there, we gained a profit of about $1 billion. It was vin-
tage Ted at his creative best.

Meanwhile, as Rogers was handing out all those grocery
vouchers in San Antonio, the Road Warriors were racking
up frequent flyer miles as they went about meeting with city
managers, cable commissioners, and councillors. (Wes Heppler
was quarterbacking our discussions with the FCC, with occa-
sional appearances from me and Vernon in Washington.) But
when you're dealing with 69 different municipalities, it's never
going to be easy to get them all on board. Each wants something in exchange for their approval. And for a deal this big,
we were willing to grease the wheels.

Progress was inching forward in most of the cities until
a big problem surfaced in San Antonio. And this would have its
knock-on effects, since, not wanting to miss an opportunity, three
of our biggest franchises—Portland, Minneapolis, and several
others in California—started slow-rolling their approvals as they
waited to see whether San Antonio would agree to the transfer.

San Antonio's city manager at the time was a bright guy
by the name of Lou Fox. While we were making progress with
that city, Lou flagged an overlooked clause in their original UA/

Columbia franchise contract—a clause that, frankly, we hoped the city wouldn't focus on. But Lou saw it as a major bargaining chip to get maximum benefit from the sale.

The clause stipulated that the municipality could buy back the cable TV system at 5 percent below market value after 10 years. As I said, Lou was as dumb as a fox. A decade earlier, when negotiating the original deal with UA/Columbia, he'd inserted this highly unusual buyout provision. And now, 10 years later and right in the middle of closing the deal with Houston Industries, Fox told his council that they should buy the system at a discount and either operate it through the city's electric utility company or resell it.

Ted Rogers thought it was all bullshit and bluster. In his view, city government didn't know anything about operating a cable company, nor would it want to. Then, to make matters worse, Fox was quoted in the industry press as having said on a radio program, "We have Ted Rogers by the balls." Ted was incensed. The San Antonio franchise was the jewel of the deal, representing almost half the entire Rogers U.S. subscriber base, with 250,000 customers and counting. But Fox and the others weren't budging.

That's when Ted and I flew down to San Antonio to meet Lou Fox and the city's consultants on the project. After Ted told Lou that his "by the balls" comment had offended him, he launched into his charm offensive, trying his best to convince the city to abandon the ridiculous buyback concept. But at the end of the meeting, Lou remained unpersuaded. (There was one funny moment, though: as we were walking out of the room, Lou held back from the group and whispered in my ear, "Well, Phil, at least I didn't say we had him by the 'fucking' balls." I laughed, and I still laugh today thinking about it.)

Flying back to Toronto, Ted was still seething. He said, "Lind, I don't know how you're going to do it, but fix it."

My opportunity to fix it came through Missy Goerner, who'd worked with Lou for years at the city before she joined the cable system. She knew him well, and he trusted her. On her own initiative, she called Lou and asked him to speak to me directly one more time about the situation. He told her that in the next few days the consultants would be submitting their report recommending the city take over the cable system. And that he was heading to the airport to catch a flight for a city managers' meeting in Raleigh-Durham, North Carolina, and didn't have time for a call. "If Phil Lind wants to talk to me he can meet me there," he said. To that Missy responded, "He'll be there tomorrow." Then she called me. I grabbed Vernon Achber, and we literally raced to the Toronto airport to grab whatever plane would get us to North Carolina that night.

Early the next morning, Lou and I met for breakfast. He was impressed that I'd made the trip, but shit, this was a $1.37 billion deal at risk, and Ted Rogers was breathing fire—I would have been there even if I'd had to walk. Lou was cordial enough, and we talked for some time. When I told him that no city wants to run a cable company, he said his consultants had told him the city could do it easily, especially if they kept the well-qualified Rogers employees in San Antonio to run it. On went our verbal joust, back and forth, until I picked up a paper napkin and handed it to him: "How much? Write it down. How much do you need to drop this matter and approve the sale?"

He wrote down $25 million and handed it back to me. We signed the napkin and had a deal. I didn't have Ted's approval at that price, and I knew that Lou would have to get his council's approval. But he was one of the best city managers in the country, and I felt certain they'd follow his lead.

Directly after that I approached Houston Industries: would they cover a $15 million construction overrun in California if I could deliver San Antonio? They readily agreed. Now, Houston had seen Lou Fox's "by the balls" quote. And they had no idea I had a napkin agreement in my pocket, let alone how much we'd offered. So I'm convinced that they agreed only because they doubted we'd be able to close San Antonio. And with their $15 million in the pot, my $25 million offer netted out to $10 million for Rogers.

When I gave Ted the news, a big smile came over his face. He lifted his right arm in his electric-blue suit, shook hands, and said, "Philip, you did it!"

He even stopped being pissed off at Lou Fox. Not long after we left San Antonio, Lou left as well—with a big bonus based on that $25 million deal—for another city gig. A few years later, he hung out his shingle as a municipal affairs consultant. In 1994 I hired him to help us get city approvals for transferring the Maclean Hunter U.S. cable assets, which you'll read about later. As I've said, when you hire the best talent, it pays off.

As for that $25 million napkin? "Lou told me he framed it, and that it hung in his office for many years," Missy says.

Leaving the U.S. was one of the biggest disappointments of my life—along with swapping our British Columbia cable properties with Shaw and leaving that fabulous province in exchange for lesser systems in Ontario and New Brunswick.

During our 40 years together, Ted and I had four really, really big disagreements. Those two cable deals were among them. The other two battles involved Ted's plan to change the Rogers brand name and selecting a U.S. partner for our long-distance company. I lost two and won two, which is a terrific batting average and speaks well of Ted's business acumen. When it came to Ted, if your arguments were solid, well researched, and convincingly presented, he was not afraid to change his mind.

I'll return in more detail to those other battles, but first I'd like to elaborate on the U.S. cable sale from a hypothetical perspective. Was it the right or wrong thing to do?

A strong argument can be made for each option. (I can even imagine the decision someday being used as an MBA case study.) But simply put, Rogers couldn't do both U.S. cable and Canadian wireless. The company was just too stretched and loaded with debt. And Ted's ultimate choice led to the world's first truly multidimensional communications company, with wireless voice and data, cable TV, high-speed Internet, home phone service, radio, television, print media, online media, professional sports franchises, home security, and more.

Ted Rogers was a true entrepreneurial visionary—and the most successful, I believe, that Canada has ever produced. We started with nothing. In 2018, Rogers is a blue-chip investment, paying healthy dividends with a market cap of around $30 billion, or US$23 billion.

During our time in the U.S., for a while there, in 1981 and 1982, we were the world's largest cable company. And when we exited, we were still one of the biggest. Back then, powerhouse U.S. cable companies like Comcast were small by comparison. Comcast's market cap today is around $200 billion, or US$155 billion. I'm not suggesting that Rogers would have hit similar home runs in the U.S. as Comcast has, but I'm sure we would have succeeded. I'm also not suggesting that Rogers is in any way not an amazing Canadian success story.

What I'm saying is that we came to a fork in the road in the late 1980s, and that Ted was far more comfortable in Canada than in the U.S. He chose one way over another, but either way he would have succeeded. Our success in the United States meant that whichever road he took, Rogers Communications was going to win.

In early 2001, the U.S. Cable Center came to Toronto and recorded an hour-long discussion with Ted and me (it's still available on YouTube). When the topic turned to U.S. cable, Ted was gracious and laudatory, both about my team's work and about the wonderful experiences we had with Americans. He also addressed our fork in the road between U.S. cable and wireless. "Financially, we couldn't do both," Ted said. "Was it the right decision? Actually, probably not. We probably should have stayed in the States and not done wireless, except we were convinced you had to be a certain size in the States, and I couldn't figure out how to put these things together with the limited resources we had."

Would Ted have said the same thing even five years later, after wireless in his home country absolutely exploded with the iPhone and other devices? Would he say the same thing today, if he were still alive?

Who knows?

14

Be Careful What You Wish For

W e all know that paradoxical idiom: "Be careful what you wish for—you may just get it." And that was the case when it came to our early 1990s involvement with the long-distance phone company Unitel Communications Inc.

The story of the Unitel catastrophe has been diligently recorded elsewhere, in everything from newspaper and magazine pages to books and websites. In fact, a book called *Wire Wars*, by former telecom reporter Lawrence Surtees, is all about Unitel's battle to create long-distance competition. And in his memoir, Ted Rogers devoted an entire chapter to the "disaster, bloody disaster" that was our Unitel venture.

So there's not much sense in going over all the gory details, but a few things should be addressed, particularly events that have never been publicly disclosed and occurrences that only the passage of time has revealed to be funny. We weren't laughing at the time.

And lastly, the Unitel story is a perfect example of a well-run campaign by Rogers to win a major CRTC victory. And yet for

Rogers, it was a Pyrrhic victory. Most of our successful campaigns led to greater success. Not Unitel.

In Canada, I had a core team who supported my regulatory efforts over the years. Ken Engelhart, David Watt, Pam Dinsmore, Dawn Hunt, and Susan Wheeler were all regulatory specialists; Michael Allen, programming; Jan Innes handled communications and messaging; Heidi Bonnell was a government relations whiz with extensive experience and Parliament Hill connections; Colette Watson ran Rogers's community television and Cable Public Affairs Channel (CPAC) for many years; and Robin Mirsky runs the Rogers Group of Funds that are so important for the production industry and Rogers's government relations. Beginning in 1980, this core team—some members would join later—would meet regularly over the next 35 years to discuss and debate company positions on various regulatory files. Outside counsel Bob Buchan has been an invaluable and integral part of our team since the 1970s. And Stuart Langford who, after his time with the federal government, served for many years as a valuable consultant to the Rogers regulatory group.

But back to Unitel and the early 1990s: a full decade after telecom competition began in the United States, we kicked Bell Canada's butt and the CRTC broke the century-old phone monopoly. But for us, the CRTC decision was fool's gold. That's because after our victory, we started losing.

A little background is needed here. In 1985, Unitel (then called CNCP) botched its first attempt to get permission from the CRTC to offer long-distance phone service. Bell (which operated in Ontario and Quebec) and its monopoly allies across Canada (among them Alberta Government Telephone, BC Tel, and Newfoundland Telephone) had the $7-billion-a-year long-distance market all to themselves, and CNCP, owned by railways Canadian National and Canadian Pacific, wanted some of the cake. But in 1985 the telephone monopolists outflanked the railway duopolists in every corner. Bell was terrific at convincing people that artificially high long-distance rates subsidized local rates and thus kept monthly phone bills lower for ordinary Canadians—as long as you didn't make many expensive long-distance calls. In short, Bell lawyers and economists mercilessly stripped apart CNCP's business case—and the CRTC had no trouble denying its application.

Not long after the drubbing, CN had had enough and sold its stake in the company to CP. Still without approval to compete in the public long-distance market, CNCP was restricted to public data (telegrams and telexes) along with private data and voice-like, between-office networks for large corporations and governments. (It would be two more years before the name changed from CNCP to Unitel Communications Inc.)

Just as CN left CNCP, Ted Rogers sold our U.S. cable holdings for a tidy $1 billion profit after 10 years of building and operating south of the border.

A couple of things to understand about Ted. First, as I've said, he was one of Canada's greatest entrepreneurs and risk-takers. He truly believed that if you're standing still, you're falling behind—and so all that U.S. cable profit was burning a hole in his pocket. Second, he detested Bell and its allies in other provinces, often deriding them for their "Soviet-style" control of markets. Whereas we borrowed money to invest in Rogers networks, the phone companies lived on rate-of-return regulation, which meant that the more they spent, the more they could charge customers.

Yes, like other cable companies, Rogers had monopoly territories, but we never lived in a rate-of-return environment; we had
to argue before the CRTC for rate increases. And Ted really wanted
to go after Bell. He loved the David and Goliath imagery, and relished going into battle against the giant.

Quite frankly, so did I. To drive home this point, I'll let
my friend and longtime communications lawyer Bob Buchan
tell a story. (As with most campaigns and hearings, Bob was
our main outside counsel in our application to break the phone
company's long-distance monopoly.) "Phil has a 'don't take any
prisoners' attitude, and he didn't want to have anything to do
with the guys from Bell," Bob says. "The general counsel for Bell
was Bernard Courtois, who is a very polite, nice guy. [Before the
hearing] Bernard came over and I said, 'Oh, Bernard, I want you
to meet Phil Lind.' Phil looked at him and wouldn't shake his
hand because he was with Bell. That really pissed me off, but that
was Phil."

Now here's how our initial investment in Unitel happened.
John A. Tory (mayor John Tory's father), a Rogers board member,
set up a meeting between Ted and Bill Stinson, CP's chairman and
CEO. CP was a huge conglomerate back then—rail, aviation, ship-
ping, hotels, oil and gas, you name it—and Tory Sr. had convinced
Stinson that Ted would be a good partner: something that Stinson
never forgot, and probably won't until the day he dies.

After a few months of corporate dancing, in April 1989
CP agreed to sell Rogers 40 percent of Unitel for $288.7 million.
As part of the deal, Ted made sure that my regulatory team would
be in charge of the second application to the CRTC. That made
sense, given our experience not only with CRTC applications but
also in public campaigns leading up to crucial hearings.

Now, Ted was not the greatest equity partner at the best of times, except maybe with his old mentor John Bassett, but as a minority partner, let's just say Ted wouldn't act like a minority partner.

We knew that CNCP's president, George Harvey, might not like us coming in and exerting our regulatory authority, but that didn't concern me, especially after our first strategy session with the CNCP team in the summer of 1989. When we were ushered into this large boardroom on the twentieth floor of their downtown Toronto building, it was packed with people. Perhaps the CNCP executives were trying to impress us with numbers, but it was more like a muddling bureaucratic government meeting than anything else. Their crack downtown lawyer nodded off at one point and the officious technocrat chairing the meeting kept saying "Let the record show ..." The formality and the haughtiness were the direct opposite of Rogers's regulatory meetings, where opinions flowed freely and F-bombs were used for punctuation. After a few minutes in the CNCP meeting, I turned to Bob Buchan and whispered, "We're going to convince the Commission to break the Bell monopoly with these clowns?" He nodded ruefully.

Albert Einstein once said that the definition of insanity is doing the same thing over and over and expecting different results. Not a chance would I let that happen. The campaign to win over the CRTC had to be run with precision, putting legal work in the background and public relations and public opinion at the fore.

I'm not blaming George Harvey, who inherited the team when he took the job in 1987. Originally from Liverpool, U.K., George could really spin a yarn. He was a decent businessman who could tell stories and close deals, and he was smarter still to allow our Rogers team to run the campaign while he played the front-man role. Ever the showman, he even once played to the cameras by rolling up his sleeves and donning red boxing gloves, insisting he was serious about knocking out the mighty Bell.

Behind the scenes we worked our tails off, pulling together the application and cleaning out regulatory deadwood. Eventually we were able to move out all the CNCP regulatory folks, except the exceptional economist David Watt, who went on to become an invaluable member of Rogers's regulatory team for 25-plus years. He was a diamond in the middle of a rough bunch.

George Harvey, with my encouragement, hired Jan Innes, whom I'd met years earlier in Ottawa when she was a political aide for the Trudeau Liberals. Jan, who by then was back in Toronto working for the Ontario Liberals, became Unitel's vice-president of public affairs, handling issues management and media and government relations. Like Dave Watt, Jan eventually left Unitel for Rogers.

We went public at every opportunity to sell Canadians on the benefits of competition. We staged media events in cities across the country and would talk to any reporter at any news outlet. Initial data unearthed by our research consultant, Chris Kelly, found that barely a third of Canadians had even heard or read anything about long-distance competition. We needed to raise awareness.

On May 9, 1990, we announced the name change from CNCP to Unitel Communications Inc., and that we'd be filing the CRTC application within days. In June I hired Richard Stursberg, who was head of telecom policy at the federal government's department of communications, to become Unitel's senior vice-president of regulatory. This was a key hire: Richard understood both the landscape and the arguments.

Again, Bell was great at convincing people that artificially high long-distance rates subsidized local rates, making a phone in the home affordable. And Bell wasn't ashamed to play the scare card: namely, that local phone rates needed to stay low for the elderly, especially in the event of a medical emergency. Of course a phone is essential in a medical emergency—I later found this out firsthand—but Bell's cries about local rates rising because of long-distance competition were baloney. Richard Stursberg puts it this way: "Phil has this ability to distill an argument and come up with the essence of it with a simple message to illustrate it. Local rates do not go up. That was our message, and we repeated it over and over again."

Richard was instrumental in helping us convince the Unitel gang to stop buying Bell's arguments. Instead, Unitel would pay "contribution" money to Bell to keep local rates affordable. Should local rates rise, the real culprit would be rate-of-return regulation that inherently led to bloated, inefficient monopoly phone companies—which would have the effect of underlining our position.

I'll let Ken Engelhart, an expert in telecom law who worked for me, explain our filing: "The business plan must be on a knife's edge. The way the CRTC works is that if your business plan says you're going to lose a shitload of money, they'll say 'not approved' because they figure you'll be back in a year or two looking for breaks. They hate that. So, you need a business plan that makes economic sense so they feel they can approve it and it won't get revisited in two years. But you can't say you'll make bags of money because then they'll want you to pay more, and in the case of telecom, that means more contribution payments."

After working on several different models, we came up with what we thought made sense. Then one Sunday night Ken,

Michael Allen, and I went to Ted's Forest Hill home to present the plan. When Ted found what he considered mistakes in it, he got pissed off and started yelling at me (and not at my underlings, thankfully).

As Ken remembers it, "This was my first presentation to Ted in his home. And Ted is just dumping shit on Phil by the bucket load. It went on and on with no let-up. Finally, Phil gets up, grabs his briefcase, and starts shoving his papers in it, about to leave. And Ted says, 'Oh, Philip, oh, Philip, sit down. I'm sorry, I'm really sorry, please sit down.'"

It's easy to laugh now, but at the time I was seething. (There's a reason why Rogers executives called Ted's house on Frybrook Road the "Frying Pan.") "Phil sits back down, unpacks his brief-case, and Ted keeps apologizing. And then within seconds it starts all over again and Ted is dumping all over Phil," says Ken, tears of laughter streaming down his cheeks.

Somehow we did finalize the business plan, receiving approval from Ted and Canadian Pacific to submit it to the CRTC. Now the campaign could really start rolling.

The CRTC announced that, before the main hearing in Gatineau, it would hold regional hearings in every province. Normally these were more or less a public relations exercise: the CRTC would let members of the public speak, and their evidence wouldn't be particularly challenged. Lawyers them-selves didn't worry much about regional hearings, believing that the CRTC didn't put as much weight on the average per-son's opinion as they did on industry's expert testimony and legal minutiae.

But I'd studied the 1985 hearings and come to the conclu-sion that Bell's unions did play an important role at the regional hearings. And with our new application, we were about to take this tactic to the next level: I was betting the CRTC would definitely care what the public had to say—especially if we could stack each regional hearing with supporters of competition.

Leading up to the hearings, we set up offices in every province—"regional desks" we called them—with people on the ground in each one. These local agents—lawyers, consultants, lobbyists, sometimes simply friends—would monitor media, listen to local business and consumer groups, identify who were friends and foes in the battle. They contacted friends and asked them to make written submissions and volunteer as witnesses at the regional hearings to talk about how competition would benefit them.

Our campaign team was structured like an election campaign team, except that everyone was paddling together and there were no hangers-on. We had a government relations team and a public relations team, working on their own and in tandem, with both being coordinated by Jan Innes. And we had Liberals and Progressive Conservatives (even one New Democrat) all working together in all regions of Canada.

We had so many talented people on the ground: Cindy Grauer and Patrick Kinsella in B.C.; John Gormley in Alberta; Doug Richardson in Saskatchewan; Janis Johnson in Manitoba; Carleen Carroll, Martha Wilson, Paul Curley, and Amanda Walton in Ontario; Sharon Vance in Quebec; Greg Byrne in New Brunswick; Stewart McInnes in Nova Scotia and PEI; Gary Anstey in Newfoundland, and a host of others working with them.

We lobbied provincial governments, seeking their support. Richard Stursberg and Bill Stinson travelled the country in the CP corporate jet, meeting premiers. Alas, New Brunswick premier

Frank McKenna was the only premier anywhere in Canada to support us, and only after Richard promised to build a call centre in that province. (McKenna, coincidentally, would later become an excellent chairman of Brookfield, and our paths would cross once again.)

I met with many cabinet ministers in various provinces, either on my own or with Jan and Richard. One of the more colourful meetings happened in Toronto with a minister in Bob Rae's recently elected NDP government. It should be mentioned that, beyond Rae himself and a couple of ministers, most of the cabinet was made up of greenhorns. Anyway, this particular minister was all in favour of Bell's monopoly, even after I mentioned that the company's head office was in Montreal, not Ontario. I'll let Richard pick up the story. "Phil got very annoyed and said, 'Don't you understand what this is? Montreal is the capital of monopolies and Toronto is the capital of competition. And you're opposing stuff for Toronto?' Phil was really annoyed. Normally he's very placid about these sorts of things, but he was very angry with her."

History has shown that I was certainly not the only executive who was frustrated with Bob Rae's government. Nonetheless, after that meeting, Jan Innes, who'd worked a decade in government, put her foot down and forbade me from meeting any other officials from Ontario's NDP government! I reluctantly took her counsel.

Another avenue we followed was print ads. Our ad agency in Montreal was called Bos, led by Michel Ostiguy, and they were brilliant. One ad showed two cartoon babies, one wailing after the other had taken the phone away. The caption read, "It's tough when you've been an only child for all these years." Another beauty was a full-page ad featuring close-ups of two powerful men: Mikhail Gorbachev, who'd just ended communism in Russia, and Jean Monty, Bell's president. The caption said something like "Just one of these men believes in monopoly markets," implying that even Soviets supported competition more than Bell did. (We didn't need to run it, in the end, but it was certainly tempting.)

As for the regional hearings, as I mentioned, we were going to out work Bell and get our friends to pack the room. Now, technically, a letter submitted to a hearing had to be written by the person signing it. But in the real world, people are busy and often say things like "Sure, I'll support you, but could you write the letter and I'll put it on my letterhead?" So Ken Engelhart and others on the team wrote many such letters for various people and organizations. I seem to remember Bob Buchan deciding to use some of the best regional letters at the main hearing, and unbeknownst to him, almost every letter Bob selected had been written by members of our team.

"Our fingerprints were all over the regional hearings," Ken Engelhart says. "I thought we'd get called out by the CRTC for organizing the campaign, but a funny thing occurred. Telecom consultant Eamon Hoey had a group called the CCC (Communications Competition Coalition) that was taking loads of money from large companies, like the banks, that wanted phone competition, and this group took all the credit for the submissions. No one pointed a finger at Rogers."

I guess Hoey uttered such hooey about the letters as a way to justify to his clients what he was billing them. Or maybe he did organize a handful of letters. No matter. We were delighted with the deflection.

The hijinks even went beyond letter-writing to the testimonies themselves. At the Halifax hearing, a particularly good witness was urging the Commission to create a competitive marketplace for Canadians. This guy was both knowledgeable and convincing. Also at the hearing was Stewart McInnes, a high-profile Halifax lawyer and former federal cabinet minister who was in charge of our Nova Scotia regional office. He was sitting beside one of our lawyers, Laurence Dunbar, who said, "Stewart, this presentation is compelling ... really, really good." McInnes shot back: "Better be. He's my articling student."

At another hearing, Martha Wilson's elderly father was set to testify, and slowly made his way to the stand with the use of a cane. It was a wonderful image, given that Bell kept saying that seniors needed affordable local rates. Martha's dad talked about how he couldn't afford to call his children living far away from home as often as he'd like. He demanded long-distance competition and fairness. The CRTC commissioners listened with rapt attention.

The regional hearings proved to be a carefully engineered spontaneous outburst of support for competition—and this was more than a decade before the flash-mob phenomenon began. Still, Bell and its phone company allies fought rigorously and rather effectively. Of course, they spent a lot more money on lawyers and consultants than we ever could. At one of the regional hearings, Bell's union even had U.S. consumer activist Ralph Nader, then at the peak of his popularity, give a speech to rally the troops before testifying to the Commission.

We got wind of this because Nader's speech was to be in a ballroom in the same hotel where we were having a meeting. Having decided to check it out, I slipped in at the back of the room. Nader was on stage yammering on about how small, rural

communities could lose local phone service if long-distance competitors ate into Bell's margins. Complete bullshit.

I suddenly realized that I was leaning up against the
room's thermostat. Discreetly, I pushed it up to the maximum.
And within a few minutes the room was over 100 degrees
Fahrenheit. Ever the trooper, Nader carried on with drops
of sweat dripping from his forehead. With TV lights also heating the room, everyone was sweating profusely and getting
more and more irritable by the minute. Any tactic to inflict
discomfort on an enemy campaign!

On March 14, 1991, the regional hearings wrapped up after
a three-week cross-Canada tour. A month later, on April 15, the
main hearing began across the river from Ottawa; it would end
on July 5, after 53 days of testimony. The process was much more
intense than it had been regionally, with nitty-gritty legal details
and testimony from telecom experts and business leaders.

After nearly a year of deliberations, on June 12, 1992, the
CRTC issued its landmark decision. Numbered 92-78 (meaning
its seventy-eighth decision in 1992), it found in favour of long-
distance competition. Bell appealed the decision to the Federal
Court, but it was quickly tossed out.

The battle against Bell's monopoly was one of the hardest-fought
campaigns of my life, but within weeks we were losing buckets
of money. Eventually, Unitel would be losing $1 million per day.

Unitel would make a great business case study for the "what
can go wrong will go wrong" principle. The price of long distance
dropped from 15 cents or more a minute to virtually nothing,
and far more quickly than anyone had anticipated. Margins were

razor-thin overnight. And just as important was the corporate culture clash between Rogers and Canadian Pacific.

Rogers was entrepreneurial at the time, and Unitel was
slow-moving and bureaucratic. There was so much mistrust
on both sides. Unitel executives would often be telling their
masters at CP that Rogers was either ripping Unitel off (the
fibre optic deals, for example) or doing other dirty tricks
like using fees from Unitel to subsidize the construction
of Rogers's wireless networks.

Ted didn't help matters, either. He'd yell at Unitel-CP executives
Ron Gamey and Jacques Konig just like he'd yell at me or Rogers
Cable president Colin Watson or CFO Graham Savage. We expected
it, but they'd never been spoken to that way in their entire careers
with Canadian Pacific. He also criticized CP chairman Bill Stinson,
even after he'd lent Ted $135 million in 1991 when things got
really rough financially around Rogers. Ted did not like Stinson,
and I suspect the feeling was mutual.

I liked Stinson, but I think he was suspicious of me. One
meeting the two of us had tells the story. Shortly after winning
the CRTC ruling and without authority from Ted, I called Stinson
up and went to his Toronto office at the Royal York Hotel. I laid all
my cards on the table: Unitel was going over the cliff, I said, and the
only way to save it was to change everything and nearly everyone.
I wasn't making a play for more authority, but a complete overhaul
was essential. Indeed, in 1990 a so-called anonymous "disgruntled
former executive" had been quoted in *The Globe and Mail* saying
that Unitel "has to be burned to the ground and started over." But
when I said the same thing, Stinson just told me to go talk to Ron
Gamey; this, he said, was the way it was done at Canadian Pacific.
But that wouldn't work. Gamey was a close friend of George

Harvey and would surely tell him my plan, causing even more mistrust. Stinson probably thought I was a messenger boy for Ted, and that my goal in meeting him was to get Rogers to run Unitel, even though CP was the majority owner. I told him Ted didn't even know I was there. It didn't matter: he wouldn't move.

There were also some bad decisions made. I'll take some of the responsibility for agreeing to pay high "contribution rates" to Bell to offset local phone bills that were rising too much for consumers. We were paying Bell too much money, and so from our perspective, it wasn't fiscally sound.

But there were plenty of others. For example, Unitel aimed to push the timetable for interoperability—connecting our networks—from 12 months to only three months. When Bell said it would cost $30 million to speed up the work, the CRTC ruled that if Unitel wanted a faster timetable, it would have to pay the added costs. Unitel did pay the $30 million, but then wasn't even close to being ready in terms of its own systems and its marketing to attract new customers. Far too often, Unitel would just piss money away like that.

So in January 1995—after getting hit with $500 million in losses, or half the profit from the sale of our U.S. cable assets—Rogers walked away from Unitel with our tail between our legs.

After our exit, a consortium of banks and the U.S. phone giant AT&T came in to run Unitel. But even with all that financial might, Unitel was a lost cause. Its brand went the way of the dodo bird.

Some good was to come of it all, though. During the Unitel period, a Rogers subsidiary called Rogers Network Services (RNS) was laying fibre optic cables everywhere we could in what we thought would be Unitel's success. We leased some of this fibre to Unitel itself, and hoped to provide much more. Then a few years later, in 1998, with something called the Internet fast developing, Rogers sold RNS for $1.5 billion, thereby recouping our Unitel losses and then some. Or, as Ken Engelhart jokes, "The way Ted told the story was that Phil lost Unitel but Ted made the money back with RNS."

15

Whew!

With Unitel, Rogers had gone on the offensive and almost lost a burgeoning empire, and yet somehow we escaped. Even more intriguing, just as Unitel was burning up, Ted Rogers was already preparing for his next move: the colossal hostile takeover of Maclean Hunter Ltd., a rival cable and media company.

Like the Unitel saga, details of the MH takeover have been chronicled elsewhere many times over. There's no point in covering old ground. There are, however, some things that have been overlooked or not given the attention I feel is warranted—one being our campaign for CRTC approval, and another how close we came—within mere minutes— of losing the deal on the regulatory front. Indeed, Maclean Hunter's president and CEO Ron Osborne was so confident in wiggling off the hook that he was dumbfounded when he got final word of our Tom Brady–like victory.

The genius of Ted Rogers was that he could compartmentalize things like the huge Unitel stresses and problems and continue to develop strategies to retrench and expand his communications empire. While absorbing huge Unitel losses, and long before pulling out, Ted was planning a massive $3.1 billion offensive.

In his memoir he reveals that in early January 1994 I was the third person he told about this coming bold move—after his wife, Loretta, and Rogers Communications chairman Gar Emerson. (Five years earlier, Gar had designed Maclean Hunter's poison pill to ward off hostile takeovers, but then he worked with Ted to dissolve that pill.)

Ted was interested only in the cable assets, and specifically the Canadian cable—because he knew that, without selling Maclean Hunter's U.S. cable operations as part of the deal, he wouldn't be able to do the deal at all. (Indeed, he signed a $2 billion bridge loan with the banks on condition that he sell the U.S. cable to help pay it off.) From a cable operator's perspective, Ted's idea was a brilliant strategic strike.

Although I was helping with the business deal, my perspective was a little different. Back then, "convergence" had become a buzzword to describe the rapidly changing worldwide media and communications landscape. Phone and cable companies were merging with or buying up content producers; massive media companies like Time Warner, Disney, and Viacom were consolidating. These were exciting times, and few knew exactly where we were headed. One thing was easy to see: Canada, long bombarded by American media content, now faced an onslaught from elsewhere, too. There was grave concern that Canadian voices and culture could be drowned out by these mega content producers. And so I knew that, before we could sell the deal to the public and the CRTC, we'd need a compelling campaign story that would convey its benefits not just to Rogers and our shareholders, but to Canadians in general.

Since the business details of the takeover are well known, I'll do my best to keep the specifics brief. Throughout January

Top: Winning in the 1980s U.S. cable franchising wars. (L-R) My U.S. lieutenant Vernon Achber, Minneapolis mayor Donald Fraser, and me.

Right: With Mildred Schwab, Portland's city commissioner, who was the toughest regulator (Canadian or American) I ever had to appear before. She was known for her sharp tongue, colourful personality, and frugality with city funds.

Top: The City of San Antonio held the trump card to the US$1.4 billion sale of our American cable systems in 1989 (if no deal with the city, then no sale to Houston Industries). (L–R) City manager Lou Fox, me, and Mayor Henry Cisneros.

Left: Ted's favourite story from our U.S. days was delivering $1 million in $5, $10, and $20 U.S. dollar bills to Angelo Drossos, owner of the NBA's San Antonio Spurs.

Top: Downtime with my intrepid U.S. Road Warriors in La Jolla, California, 1989. (L–R) Me, Wes Heppler, Vernon Achber, and Lee Sheehy. David Jones. (Not pictured: Missy Goerner.)

Left: Our 2018 Road Warriors reunion. (Back row, L–R) Lee, Wes, Vernon; (front row, L–R) David, Missy, and me.

Bottom: 1999 Turner Broadcasting trip to Russia, with three extraordinary U.S. cable innovators. (L–R) Tim Nehr, Continental Cablevision; me; Terry McGuirk, Turner Broadcasting; Peter Barton, Liberty Cable.

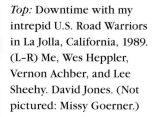

It's tough when you've been an only child for all these years.

Recently, the CRTC said "yes" to competition in long distance.
But some monopoly telephone companies are trying to block this decision.
Right now, the only thing standing between you
and lower prices is the telephone companies.
Why?

Competition brings out the best in us.

Top: At the podium with Ted, announcing our proposed $3.1 billion acquisition of Maclean Hunter Ltd. On my left is Ron Osborne, MH president.

Left: One of the ads from our successful campaign to open up long distance in Canada. (The old adage "Be careful what you wish for" proved true: we lost $500 million.)

Top: My superb go-to team in Canada. (Back row, L–R) Dave Watt, me, Susan Wheeler, Ken Engelhart; (front row, L–R) Jan Innes, Robin Mirsky, Pam Dinsmore, Dawn Hunt, and Heidi Bonnell. (Not pictured: Cindy Grauer.)

Top right: Bob Buchan, my brilliant outside counsel and regulatory compadre for nearly 50 years.

Middle right: With Ken Engelhart, my regulatory lieutenant, at one of the three fee-for-carriage CRTC hearings, among the most satisfying regulatory victories of my career.

Bottom right: With Nadir Mohamed, RCI's former president and CEO, and Alan Horn, RCI's former CFO and chairman of the board.

My mother, Susie, and father, Jed, instilled in their children the importance of a strong family bond.

One of our many extended family holidays together. (L–R) Me, my brother Geoff (kneeling), George Burbidge (my sister Jenny's husband), Susie, Jenny, and my brother Ron. (Not pictured: Geoff's wife, Jane.)

My son, Jed; my daughter, Sarah;
and my granddaughter, James.

A historic mill, built in 1856, sits on our family farm at the edge of the Rocky Saugeen River in Ontario. In 2005, after five long years of planning, approvals, and restoration, my lifelong dream to restore it was fulfilled (William Bennett, architect; David Powell, Powell & Bonnell, design; Dan and Jonathan Dresar, Twin Construction).

1994, Ted was buying as much Maclean Hunter stock as he could on the open market without drawing attention. Then on January 28 at seven-thirty a.m., before a regular MH board meeting, Ted and Gar Emerson went to Maclean Hunter to meet chairman Don Campbell and CEO Ron Osborne to tell them about Rogers's plans for a "strategic merger."

I was supposed to be there, but the night before an ice storm had closed Toronto's Pearson International Airport while I was at a black-tie event with Francis Fox in Montreal. (Francis, a former Trudeau cabinet minister, was then chairman of Rogers Cantel in Quebec.) I got on a bus before midnight, figuring I could still make the meeting, but the storm moved eastward and the bus, with me still in my tuxedo, was stuck near Kingston for the entire night. (Osborne, who was in Calgary, couldn't get to Toronto either, but he took part in the meeting via telephone.)

Maclean Hunter, it turned out, didn't want any part of a strategic merger with Rogers. And from that point forward, though still not in the public domain, the tactical moves and the jockeying for position would be intense.

On January 31, I flew to Ottawa to brief the CRTC, apprising chairman Keith Spicer and vice-chairman Fern Belisle of Ted's forthcoming move. It was only while flying home that the campaign strategy hit me like a ton of bricks: this takeover wasn't about cable; it was about creating Canada's first great communications company—one that would be big enough to battle not only Bell but foreigners, too. We need companies that can tell Canadian stories and paint Canadian dreams, I thought to myself as the plane circled above Pearson. Ted loved the idea (and for the most part, would stick to the script).

The next day, after Maclean Hunter issued a press release about its Friday meeting with Ted and Gar Emerson, the deal went public. That's when a war of words erupted in the press between Ted and Ron Osborne over Ted's true intentions: acquiring cable assets or creating that great Canadian defender of culture and broadcasting in the new age? I'll let Ted tell that story as he recalled it in his memoir, *Relentless*:

> ... there was also a tempest in the teapot when a *Globe and Mail* reporter called me and I told him we would walk away if we could simply buy the Maclean Hunter Canadian cable assets. This was in response to a question about Osborne threatening to break up the company and sell off pieces. I probably was too candid, but I was responding to questions about Osborne's sabre-rattling about his various defensive measures. I was not saying all I wanted was the Canadian cable systems of Maclean Hunter. Of course, Osborne went to town in the media, accusing me of all sorts of nasty things and me being untruthful about our intent to create a powerful multimedia company when it all boiled down to the Canadian cable systems. Not true.

Let's take him at his word, but remember: Ted himself acknowledged that the Maclean Hunter idea came to him while he studied a Canadian cable map, not while flipping through *Maclean's* magazine. And yet when the *Globe* article appeared, I went berserk. I thought the deal could very well be scuttled. Ron Osborne, as expected, responded to Ted's off-script comments in another *Globe* news article:

> We've gone a long way from creating the Time Warner of the north ... to the cheapest, schlockiest greenmail that I've ever come across. It's appalling. We've gone from the grandiose vision to this kind of green-mail or blackmail, whatever you want to call it. I'm just staggered.

But we managed to work past it by sticking to the "telling Canadian stories and painting Canadian dreams" message. And to Ted's credit, in subsequent years he bolstered many of Maclean Hunter's non-cable assets, especially the magazine division.

After more than a month of acrimonious back-and-forth and business wrangling, on March 8 Ted won the $3.1 billion takeover by offering a 50-cent-per-share bonus. Ron Osborne admitted defeat after getting the best possible value for shareholders he could.

Or so he thought, and so did we.

But it wasn't over. Not by a long shot. And the clock was ticking toward the most difficult day of my entire business life—March 31, 1994. That's when the deal was set to close, and it was a mere three weeks away.

Bear in mind that a public offer for a company must have a deadline, given that the longer the close, the more things can change. It's just like a closing date when buying or selling a home. And remember that when Osborne and the MH board agreed to our offer, they turned the takeover from "hostile" to "friendly"—which, ironically, meant that we had a major problem on our hands.

Here's why. To close the deal, we needed the FCC to transfer ownership of the U.S. microwave towers from Maclean Hunter to Rogers. Now, in hostile takeovers, the FCC expedites such matters because deals can die on the vine if things take too long. (The FCC established this practice after Ted Turner's 1985 hostile bid for CBS failed due to stall tactics.) But now that our takeover was friendly, it looked like the FCC would never sign off within three short weeks, given all the approvals we needed to get before they could sanction the transfer. The actual towers were under federal jurisdiction with the FCC, but the cable systems themselves needed local municipal councils to approve their change in ownership (Missy Goerner was leading the team completing that work). In short, we needed all approvals, both local and federal, for what was now a so-called "friendly" (i.e., non-expedited) takeover.

But to back up for a moment: it had been Wes Heppler, absolutely the finest FCC lawyer around, who alerted us to the problem in the first place. And it was thanks to the now-friendly status of the takeover that he was able to advise us at all: when the takeover was still hostile, Wes—my go-to guy on FCC matters during the Road Warrior years of Rogers U.S. cable—had been on the sidelines. That's because, as a partner at the law firm Cole, Raywid and Braverman, his firm had also done work for MH, meaning that as long as the takeover was hostile he'd be conflicted out and couldn't help us. (During this time Wes asked his friend Diane Killory, a former FCC general counsel, to take his place. Brilliant move. She would be a valuable asset in our moment of crisis.) But when we struck the deal, of course, Wes could return to us. As he recalls, "Phil called me at six-thirty in the morning, and without saying even hello, said 'You're back on the team. There's no conflict now.'"

Given our FCC challenges, Maclean Hunter's lawyers assured Osborne that the takeover just wouldn't happen, that the deal would collapse. Osborne had new life and a spring in his step. Meanwhile, as head of Rogers regulatory, my neck was on the block. It was not comfortable.

I've been asked if Ron Osborne submitted to the deal knowing he had a not so "faint hope" chance of thwarting us by turning it into a "friendly" takeover. I am convinced he didn't. He was an intelligent business leader and an honourable man. After getting that extra 50-cent premium for his shareholders, he signed the deal in good faith. I truly believe that.

But I will say this: when he was tossed the lifejacket, Ron put it on. And why wouldn't he?

To make matters worse for us, the FCC didn't like it that we had a trustee. (Our Ottawa lawyer, Bob Buchan, had convinced former CRTC chairman Pierre Juneau to come out of retirement and act as trustee to oversee Maclean Hunter operations leading up to the CRTC hearings.) Days after the deal turned friendly, Wes explained that problem to us, too. In a long, sombre, and depressing strategy meeting, he briefed Ted and me and the other Road Warriors managing the file (Missy Goerner, Lee Sheehy, and David Jones). In all too clear terms, he laid out how the FCC approved ownership changes from one entity to another, not through third parties like a trustee. And the FCC feared a precedent, Wes said. It had approved a special trust arrangement waiver only once before in a non-hostile situation, he told us, and that was only because the owner was dying of AIDS.

When we learned this, David Jones, with his signature deadpan delivery, turned to the boss and said, "Ted, are you willing to take one for the team?" We all burst out laughing. It broke the tension in the room, but only temporarily: our seemingly impossible hurdle remained.

After the meeting, Wes returned to Washington with only days to somehow find a solution. He and Diane kept working their sources at the FCC, explaining that the deal was technically friendly but not really friendly, and that it would collapse without the FCC-sanctioned transfer.

The temporary acting chairman of the FCC at the time was James Quello, who'd been a Michigan broadcast executive before serving as an FCC commissioner for 20 years. It turned out that, by a curious and fortunate stroke of luck, both he and Wes were graduates of Michigan State.

On March 30, only one day before the deadline, we had a breakthrough. Wes convinced Quello that our case was a "purple cow," meaning it wouldn't set a precedent because it had to do with a non-American jurisdiction and regulatory environment. Quello signed off, but we needed four more commissioner signatures.

"Once Quello was good with it," Wes recalls, "I left it in the hands of his chief of staff to get the other signatures, because she said that once the boss was good with it—they all called Quello 'The Boss'—the others would sign. So I returned to Toronto the day before the closing." There he briefed Ted, me, and the rest of the Rogers executives.

March 31 was a stress-filled day, to say the least. Everything hinged on the FCC. If it approved the waiver, our deal would go through; if it denied the waiver, our multibillion-dollar takeover of Maclean Hunter, set to expire at five p.m., would fail.

In late afternoon, with the deadline approaching, Osborne and his team of lawyers and executives showed up at our offices in the Scotia Plaza Tower on Adelaide Street. They were taken to the boardroom, looking confident as hell. I was sweating bullets.

Imagine the tension in the room. On one side of the long conference table sat Maclean Hunter executives while on the other side sat Ted Rogers, me, our in-house counsel David Miller, Wes Heppler, Missy Goerner, and other Rogers executives.

Wes had been calling Washington constantly all day long. But still no word. Finally, at ten minutes to five, a call came from the

FCC's general counsel. As they transferred it to the boardroom, the call got dropped. "Fuck," I mumbled.

Wes scrambled to an adjoining room, where we could all see him through the glass wall. He got the FCC on the line and then turned away from us, concentrating on what was being said.

He then turned and gave us a thumbs-up. Smiles immediately disappeared from the faces of all the MH folks. Then the entire Maclean Hunter team, led by Ron Osborne, a real gentleman, a tremendously disappointed gentleman, stood up, shook our hands, and promptly left the building.

Feeling exultant after such an incredibly tense day, David Miller and I went to the next room to congratulate Wes for a job well done. Wes was now on speakerphone with the FCC lawyer and taking notes. The caller was describing the conditions that the FCC had imposed on us in granting the waiver. David Miller, mistakenly thinking the caller was one of Heppler's assistants back in D.C., shouted, "Hell, no—that doesn't sound fuckin' right!" Wes leaped across the table and took the phone off speaker. "Yeah," Wes said into the receiver, "that's perfectly all right." Luckily, the FCC counsel hadn't caught exactly what David had said.

After Wes hung up and explained the situation, David went white as a ghost. "My life just flashed before my eyes," he said. "That's all right," I responded. "Today just took a few years off my own life."

Without Wes and Diane, there is no way we could have closed the Maclean Hunter deal. And if the deal *had* collapsed, who knows what would have happened between Ted and me? I think we'd have survived, but you never know. That was a $3.1 billion takeover, and Ted had made it clear leading up to the closing that,

after all his tactics and manoeuvres to land MH, it would be a hel-
luva shame if a U.S. regulatory snafu killed everything.

Years later, Wes Heppler paid me a compliment. I wish Ted
had lived long enough to hear it. "There was nobody else I would
have done that for, and it's not like Phil was my biggest client
anymore because TCI was," Wes said. "I cashed in all my political
chips at the FCC. But it was personal for me to help a loyal friend,
and I'm glad it all worked out."

Once that Whew! moment was over, next on the to-do list were our
two related campaigns: garnering public support across Canada
in preparation for the CRTC hearing, and lobbying local U.S.
politicians to approve the sale of Maclean Hunter cable systems
to emerging giant Comcast, owned by our friends the Roberts
family of Philadelphia. Both would be less stressful than what
had happened on March 31, but neither would be exactly easy.

I immediately went on the rubber chicken circuit, speaking
at lunches and dinners about the benefits of the Rogers–Maclean
Hunter strategic merger, as Ted liked to call it.

On July 22, 1994, we released our application to the CRTC
for the merger, which included a $101.9 million public-benefits
package. In my opening statement at the press conference, I stuck
to our familiar messages: "The merger of Rogers and Maclean
Hunter will create a new, strong Canadian multimedia company
with the resources to compete with huge, integrated foreign media
companies like Time Warner. We have the opportunity to create
a company which can ensure that there is a place for Canadian
stories, Canadian ideas and Canadian values on the Information
Highway."

Getting CRTC approval would be a significant task, given that the regulator looks upon big-time mergers with skepticism. But I knew that chairman Keith Spicer fancied himself a true reader of the public pulse, so I figured that if we could convince the public that the deal was okay, Spicer would follow.

Things went fine until September 16, 1994, the day before the CRTC hearing began. Now, Ted was a pioneer in rehearsing for hearings, and had done it for 25 years. He believed in preparation. Unfortunately, though, he always had so many things on his mind that he wouldn't focus until the last minute. So we'd have six or seven versions of our presentation speeches done, with no input from Ted, and then he'd come on board and crap on everything, wanting to change it all. It was like clockwork.

But now we were facing arguably the most important CRTC hearing of our lives—and I've presented to every CRTC chairman over the last 50 years or so. After our long cross-Canada campaign we were confident of getting approved, but I wasn't in the mood to take any chances. Ted, on the other hand, had other last-minute ideas. Fuck that, I said—and we got into a huge row. "Oh, they really got into it," Bob Buchan says. "It was like a dog fight. One said, 'Fuck you, you can't say that' and the other shot back, 'No, fuck you.' I tried to settle them down, but to no avail. Ron Osborne turned to me and said, 'Do you have to do this sort of thing very often?' He couldn't believe his eyes."

Yup, it was one of our biggest jousts, maybe our biggest ever. I was so pissed off, thinking we could blow everything in the morning if Ted went rogue and started reading out something different from what we'd written. I couldn't sleep, so I went for a walk along the Rideau Canal. Surprisingly, Ted was out walking too, which wasn't normal for him. By that time my anger had subsided, and we stopped and talked. We made up. No apologies, but he agreed to read the opening remarks we'd prepared for him. "Ted never let us down," says Ken Engelhart. "We'd often be shitting Twinkies at these hearings because he'd start saying stuff we'd never heard before. But with Maclean Hunter, he threw us a curve the night before, but he was on script when we needed him."

The only time I remember getting nervous during the hearing was when chairman Keith Spicer asked Ted if he'd lower rates given the economies of scale and scope that we kept saying the merger would achieve.

"No," Ted responded forcefully. Spicer simply moved on to another topic.

The CRTC granted its approval on December 19, 1994. We held our customary celebratory dinner, this time at Toronto's Park Plaza Hotel, to which Maclean Hunter folks were cordially invited.

Now, another custom of Rogers dinners in those days were bun fights. I've always believed that an army marches on its stomach, and that dinners were important—and that campaign victory dinners should be especially fun, a time to let off steam after a lot of hard work. This particular dinner got a little out of hand, though. Some Rogers people loaded up with buns and started hurling them, and the MH people, who had no idea what was coming, had nothing to defend themselves with. "I could tell by the looks on their faces that they were thinking, 'How could we let these barbarians buy us?'" Ken Engelhart says.

Ken's observation was prescient, because very few of the MH executives hung around at Rogers for very long.

Once the deal was approved, Maclean Hunter's U.S. assets were duly sold to Comcast. This had our Road Warriors regulatory team fanning out across the U.S. to secure municipal consent from more than 100 communities, both large and small, wherever MH had systems. They did an excellent job in record time.

Like our Unitel campaign, our bid for Maclean Hunter was one of the most exhilarating, hard-fought Canadian operations of my career. Although there would be more to come, none could match the scope and scale of those two. But as we marched through these arduous campaigns, trouble was brewing on the home front.

16

Farm and Family

I'd like to talk about some family history here, beginning with our farm, which has been an oasis my entire life. My grandfather, John Grieve Lind, started it all in 1932 when he bought the property on the Rocky Saugeen River, south of Owen Sound, Ontario, and later built a fishing camp there.

Over the years it morphed into two distinct family compounds—one for my uncle Jenny's descendants and the other for those of his brother, my dad. While Uncle Jenny's family occupies 98 acres around the original fishing camp, our family has 135 acres upriver. Between the two properties are about 500 acres of bush, which are jointly owned. The two sides have grown so much over the generations that interaction between them is uncommon.

On our side, we operate under a condominium format where we share expenses and communal amenities like tennis courts, a baseball diamond, and a swimming pool. My sister, Jenifer, and her family occupy the original homestead, built in 1865, where I have so many fond childhood memories. My brothers, Ron and Geoff, have each built homes for their families. And I renovated the mill, which dates back to 1856, so that I could use it as my living space. (Architect William Bennett and designer David Powell did tremendous work, and the refurbished mill—a unique, historic riverside property with the original stone and wood-beam exterior and all the modern amenities—has even been featured in leading U.S. and Canadian architectural and home decor magazines.) My children, Sarah and Jed, and Jed's family share a nearby cottage known as the stable (since it actually had been an old stable; in 1967, shortly after I married Anne, my dad converted it into living quarters and we've occupied it ever since).

The farm—Aberdeen Farms Ltd., named for a little nineteenth-century village that was on the property—makes some money through leasing agricultural land, selling wood, and producing maple syrup, which my brother Geoff spearheads on our side of the property. He's branded it Rocky Run Maple Syrup, and it's delicious. "Just like Scotch whisky, you can have higher-quality malts than others," Geoff says, "and our trees produce the best maple syrup I've ever tasted."

For me, the farm is simply a special place filled with so many wonderful memories. It's where Dad taught me to fish. It's where I can still envision Mom working in the garden, producing beautiful flowers and herbs. It's where I escaped from work and really relaxed. It's where my wife and children visited almost every weekend, the kids mixing with their cousins so much that they were like siblings. It's where we've played family baseball games and tennis matches, enjoyed hikes and river rafting, and have had fabulous barbecues and picnics. It has always been the focal point of the Lind family.

My mother was an avid gardener. She was president of the Garden Club of Toronto in 1974–75, which was a pretty big deal, and a club member for more than 30 years. Among her many accomplishments were getting the government to grant the club official charitable status and organizing a Royal Ontario Museum show called *Flowers Through the Ages* that drew 34,000 people over four days.

She was also one tough, resilient lady. She learned how to speak German just because; that's the type of person she was.

At the age of 60, a scary thing happened to my mom: while on a cruise with lady friends, a fire broke out on board and they were dumped into the sea, in the dark, off the coast of the Bahamas. She and her four friends, along with the captain of the 19-metre boat, spent several hours in the shark-infested water before being rescued. According to the Canadian Press report, on February 1, 1979, the boat "sank so quickly there was no time to release the cruiser's life rafts, a spokesman for the United States Coast Guard said." It was a terrifying experience for everyone: bobbing around in lifejackets, so far from land, all the while worrying about sharks.

My sister Jenny read somewhere that severe trauma in life can later ignite Alzheimer's. It's a complex disease, but one school of thought holds that trauma can negatively impact the brain years down the road. I don't know, but about 15 years after that 1979 accident, my mother had the disease.

At her funeral in May 2002, my brother Ron summed her up succinctly: "My mom was my hero; she was beautiful, she was smart, she was talented, she was loving, she was ambitious. In short, she was perfect. She was our real American Beauty."

My dad was more complicated. He loved our mother dearly, but he could be difficult, which I didn't like. I'll say this about his genuine love for his wife: despite his own declining health he looked after her, and had help come in near the end to keep her from being put in a facility. He died two years before her, in 2000. By that time my mother was totally out of it, but an odd thing occurred the day he died. In an unexpected moment of coherence, Mom said to my sister Jenny: "Your father is dead." Life is a mystery, that's for sure.

Dad was a lawyer who suffered terribly from ulcers, and as a result he lost more than half his stomach. He was also a vice-president of a large trust company, although ill health prevented him from working through much of his forties. He returned to work at another trust company in his fifties, and served on a provincial government commercial tribunal.

I used to love talking business with Dad. He was smart, and he knew a lot of well-known business people, including P.J. Phelan, the mastermind behind Cara Operations Ltd., which owns Swiss Chalet, Harvey's, and airline catering firms; George Gardiner, a Bay Street whiz; Jake Moore, who ran Labatts for many years (and from whom Ted Rogers bought that CCL stock); and Jack Devlin, president of Rothmans.

Dad was not effusive in his compliments, even as Ted and I kept growing Rogers to greater heights. My father had been raised in a home where praise was rare. His mother, Gertrude Heming Lind, was a woman who believed children should be seen, not heard. "Dad was not a person to lay on accolades," says my brother Geoff. "But I do know he was very proud of Phil's business success, especially in his later years." So I suppose I come by it honestly, because over the years those who reported to me directly would always tease me about the lack of praise I gave them. "One time, my performance review from Phil was a piece of foolscap paper with the words 'Good job this year,'" says Ken Engelhart. Adds Jan Innes, "You knew when he wasn't happy, so when Phil did offer praise it meant a lot."

Speaking of my grandmother, she didn't much care for the farm, and rarely went. But she's central to one of the funniest incidents to ever occur there, a story my dad and Uncle Jenny would tell often.

Grandmother, whom we used to call Mio, had a warm side to her, but she was strict and I lived in fear of her. She was also rather humourless, which just adds to the story. Mio was a widow by this point, and one day she decided to take a group of ladies up to the farm. They were all sitting near the dam on the river, enjoying the idyllic summer day and having a picnic. Just then a gargantuan 200-pound Great Dane arrived on the scene and started gobbling up as many sandwiches as it could. The ladies were terrified, all of them screaming and running for safety. Now, this giant dog belonged to the farm manager, Jim McLaughlin, who knew that it wouldn't hurt a fly. McLaughlin was hiding nearby, bent over in a fit of laughter. My, oh my, Mio was mad, and embarrassed. Her sons would tell that story for years and years.

No wonder Mio preferred to stay in her huge St. Marys home rather than spend time at the farm, even if it was (and still is) one of the most peaceful and picturesque places anywhere.

This family history would not be complete without Anne Rankin, the mother of my children, who died of an aneurysm in 2004, a decade after our marriage dissolved. Anne was beautiful, smart, had a terrific personality, and got along with everyone.

She'd grown up in British Columbia, after her dad was transferred there by E.P. Taylor to sort out one of his forestry companies in turmoil. I met her when I returned to UBC for summer school to pick up my English and French credits. It was six weeks of intense schoolwork, so when it was done I headed to the Kelowna Regatta with Jake Kerr and David "Barney" Barnhill to blow off some steam. Late one afternoon a beer-hall fight broke out, and that's where I met Anne. I didn't start the beer-hall battle, but Anne and I began talking while the shenanigans were going on about us. Turns out she was Kappa Kappa Gamma at UBC, a sorority I was familiar with, being in the Zeta Psi fraternity myself.

We dated for a couple of years, and then I told her I was going to Rochester to get my master's. Although it was only a one-year program, she said the cross-country thing wouldn't work, just as Martha Nixon had told me. But this time I wouldn't let her walk away: when I returned at Christmas, I proposed. We got married on August 19, 1967 (the same day as my grandfather Bridgman's death in 1936), the day before my twenty-fourth birthday.

After my Rochester studies were complete, as newlyweds we moved to Ottawa, where I was working for the Progressive Conservative party. Then, in 1969, we moved to Toronto, where we bought our first home on Rathnelly Avenue, north of the train tracks and west of Avenue Road. It was a modest, semi-detached house that cost $37,500, and I had two mortgages on it. It was in this house that an extraordinary and frightening thing occurred one night.

Our next-door neighbours were John Craig Eaton, then chairman of the giant department store chain, and his lovely wife Sherry. Their fully detached house was far nicer than ours, but they were wonderful neighbours nonetheless. On June 15, 1976, around midnight, Anne and I were going to bed when I happened to look out the window—and saw a man cut across our front lawn and then go between our house and the Eaton house. I thought that was unusual, but maybe he was picking worms, which sometimes happened on our street during the summer. Anne, though, thought he might be trying to break into our house or, more likely, John Eaton's house, and asked me to go out and check. I looked around and saw nothing. When I returned Anne decided to call the Eatons, which she did several times and got no answer.

She sent me out to check again. That's when I went into the Eaton backyard and saw a very unusual thing: a flashlight was shining on the ceiling of a second-floor room in the Eaton house. That seemed strange, considering no one was answering the phone. So Anne called the police, who came very quickly. I'd waited outside for them, so I walked into the backyard with one police officer while the other officer entered the Eaton house through the side door.

All of a sudden I heard *bang, bang, bang* and then some yelling and people running.

It turned out that the guy had tied up John and Sherry Eaton and was trying to kidnap John's 14-year-old daughter from his first marriage when they ran into Constable Sean Clarke, only 24 years old, according to the *Toronto Star* report on the crime. The kidnapper, armed with a high-powered rifle, "ordered Clarke to drop his service revolver, but Clarke ducked back behind the house," the *Star* said. "When the girl saw her kidnapper's attention diverted, she scrambled back into the house."

After firing the shots, the kidnapper went into our backyard and jumped the fence. Clarke and Constable David Linney, who was with me, gave chase. In no time dozens of police, including the emergency task force, surrounded the neighbourhood, shutting off the power in the entire area. An hour or so later they found the would-be kidnapper lurking behind a nearby bush.

That was one night I'll never forget, especially because we'd recently adopted Sarah, who was only seven months old at the time and sleeping not far from where the gunshots were fired.

Over the years, Anne and I would own two other homes in the area, one on Cottingham Street and the other on Warren Road, which is now owned by my friend Jan Innes. Only one other night, during the summer of 1988, would compare to the chaos and danger of that night on Rathnelly. Sarah was hanging out with a couple of friends on the roof on Warren Road when she stumbled—and then fell two storeys, breaking her jaw in two places. Just as in the Rathnelly incident, things could have been far, far worse. I was definitely not pleased that the 12-year-olds were out on the roof in the first place, but thankful she wasn't hurt really badly.

Returning to Anne's personality and our marriage. She not only had a marvellous manner; she also had an overriding affection for all living beings. It was something she came by naturally (and interestingly, her sorority, Kappa Kappa Gamma, prides itself on encouraging women to strive for excellence in academics and community service, according to its website). This empathy and compassion are what made Anne a tremendously effective social worker. She saw goodness everywhere and conveyed hope to others always. When we had trouble having children, she got to work on adoption. No wallowing, just get the job done.

I wasn't the easiest husband. I was constantly working, often with two breakfast meetings in the morning, a full day's work, and then two or three evening events to attend. Or I'd be travelling: when the children were young, I was often on the road in the U.S. for 20 days a month or more. "One day I came home from school around four o'clock and Dad was home," Sarah remembers. "I literally thought I was in the wrong house."

When I was away I'd phone home every night and mail postcards to the kids. I tried to get to all their recitals, concerts, and sporting events. And during the two-week spring break every year we'd take the children on at least one big trip—to places like China, South Africa, Australia, Thailand, Alaska, England, and Costa Rica.

But it wasn't enough, and Anne and I inevitably drifted apart. The Kennedys were my political heroes, but I also loved the glitzy Camelot lifestyle and could behave like a Kennedy man, too. Such behaviour caused pain for my family and friends. It probably wasn't the smartest thing to do. One can't allow one's regret to elbow out the fond memories and good times, but as I look back, there are some things I wish I'd known then that I know now.

What I said at Anne's funeral remains true: "Though we caused each other pain, we always remained loving, respectful, and determined to make our children happy and productive."

A few years after my stroke, I met Ellen Roland at a dinner party hosted by my friend Alix Hoy, now the associate chief justice to the Court of Appeal for Ontario, and her husband Mark Feldman. Ellen and I have been together for 16 years now. We share a love for and interest in contemporary art, and have travelled together to many shows in Europe and North America. I'm very close to her terrific daughters, Signy and Alexa, and their partners Connar Walik and Rob Yelavich.

Ellen and I are patrons and members of Art Toronto's Host Committee. Founded in 2000, Art Toronto is an international contemporary art fair that's held at the Metro Toronto Convention Centre each October. Providing unique access to the Canadian art market, the fair is one of the most important annual art events in Canada.

Some of my happiest family memories involve fishing, especially with my son, Jed, and my brothers and father. Sarah never enjoyed fishing, but Jed loves it—and he's a real angler, far better than me. He studies the river, turns over rocks, assesses what the fish are eating, and other things I never do. Every year since the early 1990s, Jed and I have gone to Big Timber, Montana, to fish. (We also fish at the farm, and have taken fishing trips to British Columbia, Oregon, Atlantic Canada, and elsewhere.) Big Timber is a rustic place, with a population of only 1700. The real trendy spot in Montana is Livingston, about 30 miles away. But we like the much less yuppiefied places, and we've met and fished with some great guys there: people like Michael Keaton and his son, Sean Douglas; Tom Brokaw; and Skip Herman, a prominent Chicago lawyer. They are really fine people. (By the way, Michael Keaton's real last name is Douglas, so it's pretty easy to see why he changed it for the screen.) They all own property in Montana, especially Skip, who has thousands of acres. (Skip is a passionate Chicago Cubs fan, another way that connects us.)

Jed and I got hooked up with a terrific guide named Steve Pauli, who has become a great friend; we see him every year. "I consider Steve a mentor in some respects," Jed says, "but he's one of the most intense fishing guides you're ever going to meet." On our first trip to Montana, when Jed was about 14, Steve was lecturing him about always protecting the tip of the rods. Now, Jed is a quick study when it comes to gags. He listened intently, but when Steve got out of the truck to check on something, Jed reached over and slammed the door. Then he hollered, "Oh no, look what happened!" and bent down to pick up a broken tip of a rod from the floorboard. Steve became deathly quiet. His face reddened, and he was clearly struggling to control his anger. And as Jed puts it, "My dad was killing himself laughing inside." After a moment of silence in the truck, Jed started laughing himself. He showed Steve that all the rods were intact, and that the tip was one he'd found earlier and saved for the right moment. "Steve went almost to eruption before I told him the truth, and it took him a day to cool down," Jed says.

Unquestionably, the happiest two days of my life were when Sarah and then later Jed entered our family home.

By far the saddest day was when I left our home in 1994 and began my separation. I fell into a totally depressed state. I'd never anticipated that this would happen, and nothing had prepared me for it. One thing that lifted me up was when my good friend Michael Leranbaum took me to an Eagles concert—my all-time favourite band—at Toronto's Ontario Place. Just soaking that in raised my spirits. Eventually the cloud lifted completely, and fishing was a tonic that helped me. It's been an integral part of my life, not only for relaxation but also for quality time with my son and other relatives and friends—especially going to Montana with Jed after my new life of separation began, and maintaining that common bond with him to this day.

Despite some bumps along the road of family life, I've always striven to be the best father I could be. And I've been fortunate with my children and our relationships. Says Sarah, "Jed and I won the adoption lottery, no contest."

17

CPAC Man

For 30 years, beginning in 1970, the CRTC maintained a church-and-state approach to Canada's broadcasting industry. Cable operators essentially played the role of hewers of wood and drawers of water by delivering programming into homes for broadcasters, who bought popular U.S. programming and aired Canadian content (Cancon) to fill out their schedules. For the most part, cable was shut out from programming.

Today, with streaming applications to myriad devices, including phones and tablets and so much more, this all sounds archaic. Consumers can get content anytime from anywhere.

But from 1970 to 2000 the CRTC maintained the policy, which, as I've argued already, did a great disservice to Canadians by limiting choice and innovative services. American viewers received things in the areas of news, sports, and movie specialty channels far sooner than Canadians did. And it didn't need to be that way. Canadians deserved better than *The Trouble with Tracy* and *The Beachcombers* surrounded by hit U.S. shows like *All in the Family* and *Mary Tyler Moore*. Choice was possible, but denied.

During this time period, every CRTC chairman came down on the side of broadcasters. Each seemed to adhere to the broadcasters' distorted view that they were the guardians of Canadian culture and those in cable were the barbarians at the gate, threatening to choke them out of the limited bandwidth available. But as I said earlier, the CRTC could easily have limited the cable companies' amount of profitable programming without restricting them to programming that couldn't make money.

Indeed, this CRTC table-scraps policy limited cable to things that the networks, and later specialty-channel operators like Alliance Atlantis Communications Inc., weren't much interested in doing. That is, cable could do local community programs and alphanumeric services. The only full-motion video programming cable could own were things the networks deemed to be insufficiently profitable, like foreign-language ethnic programming, parliamentary proceedings, and a children's specialty channel.

The CRTC even did its best to kill off home shopping in Canada throughout its first 10 years by limiting it to still pictures and graphics with voiceovers. Meanwhile, it was a phenomenon in the U.S.: the Home Shopping Network (HSN) had begun in 1982 on a couple of Florida cable systems, and by 1985 it had gone national and was raking in mega dollars. Since Rogers already owned a piece of Cable Value Network Inc. (CVN), a rival to HSN, we knew how the industry worked, and so we acquired the Canadian Home Shopping Network (CHSN) in January 1988, one year after it went on the air.

But Canadian broadcasters convinced the CRTC that if TV shopping took off here it would drain advertising dollars away from them. In the States, both HSN and CVN were hot commodities, with attractive men and women modelling wares and hosts talking up items, all inducing spur-of-the-moment purchases. We just couldn't do that with still photographs, meaning that Rogers suffered a decade of mounting losses. We rode it out, though, and today's Shopping Channel is a valuable piece of Rogers Media.

I won't keep banging the drum about how consumers would have been better served if the CRTC policy had been more like the FCC policy of enhanced competition in programming. Instead, let's look at a few interesting things cable did with what it could.

The first involves CPAC, the Cable Public Affairs Channel— Canada's only privately owned, commercial-free, not-for-profit, bilingual licensed television service. It was founded in 1992 and is owned by a consortium of cable companies, with Rogers owning the largest piece. CPAC is strictly neutral when it comes to party politics. It is scrupulously non-partisan. (The most political view CPAC has is this: it likes majority governments because covering elections costs it a lot of money and blows its budgets.) It receives no government funding, nor is it affiliated with any government department or agency. Funded through Canada's cable and satellite companies with a 12-cent-a-month subscriber levy, CPAC is delivered to about nine million homes daily. Its goal is to inform as many Canadians as possible about current affairs and public policy and to thereby strengthen our democracy.

For me, it was something Rogers should do; it was never about making money. "Without Phil driving it, CPAC would not have happened," says communications lawyer Bob Buchan. "Ted was supportive, but he didn't much care one way or the other." Bob tells a story about the time he was preparing our application for CPAC's CRTC licence. He was working late in our Rogers offices when Ted poked his head in to say hello and ask Bob what he was doing. "I'm working on the CPAC application," Bob said. "Come back and see me when you're working on something that will make me some money," Ted replied.

CPAC provides a window into Parliament, politics, and public affairs both in Canada and around the world. I've been on the board since its beginning, and have also served as chairman. Over the years we've gotten tremendous support from JR Shaw and Louis Audet at Cogeco cable. Ken Stein, a Shaw Communications executive, has been CPAC's longest-serving chairman.

From its broadcast centre two blocks from Parliament Hill, CPAC's talented and well-connected editorial staff stay on top of events as they happen—and have direct access to the politicians. The channel provides insight and analysis that takes the viewer beyond headlines. During election campaigns it does some really interesting work, like going into various regions of the country to knock on doors and ask voters what's important to them. It's the only bilingual network in Canada. It also covers various public hearings, from the CRTC to commissions of inquiry into things like performance-enhancing drugs in sport. (Our research has shown that there's a small portion of viewers, around 2 to 3 percent, who just love quasi-judicial inquiries.)

Admittedly it's not for everyone, but CPAC contributes to the quality and choice of programming for Canadians. And when things turn political—federal budget time, elections, scandals—informed Canadians turn to CPAC.

The story of CPAC is a long and winding one. Rogers already had a long history of allowing politicians to use its networks—both cable and radio waves—to reach their constituents. Ted Rogers would invite politicians of all stripes to record messages, policy statements, and so forth, which we'd air on CHFI and CFTR radio in the 1960s and Rogers's Channel 10 in the 1970s and 80s. The difference between this practice and CPAC is that whereas Ted Rogers received goodwill from the public when these things were carried under the Rogers banner, CPAC offers limited benefits for the Rogers brand.

With TV converters and expanded bandwidth, cable enabled Canada to become the first country in the world to televise live parliamentary debates, beginning with Queen Elizabeth's Speech from the Throne on October 18, 1977. In those days, the CBC operated the Parliamentary Channel service. Then, in 1982, former CRTC chairman Pierre Juneau was appointed CBC president. A forward-thinking man, Juneau saw the benefit of the Parliamentary Channel and was interested in expanding its coverage to more events, similar to what CPAC does today. And as Bob Buchan says, "Phil and Pierre Juneau really got along and trusted each other." But there was a problem. Juneau, who was closely identified with the Liberal party, was viewed with hostility by the Progressive Conservative government of Brian Mulroney that came to power in September 1984. He would clash with the Mulroney government repeatedly, especially over CBC budget cuts.

It was around this time that Rogers Cable made its first attempt at getting a public-affairs-channel licence from the CRTC. We even had a blue-ribbon collection of journalists on board, among them Robert Fulford and Peter Desbarats, supporting our application. Nonetheless, the CRTC turned us down. But then, later in the 1980s, I came up with the idea of partnering with the CBC to enhance the Parliamentary Channel with cable funds to pay for more public affairs programming. Juneau liked the idea, and within months the first incarnation of the original CPAC (called the Canadian Parliamentary Channel) was born. It was half owned by the CBC and half by the cable industry.

There's an interesting story about CPAC and Pierre Juneau's successor, Gérard Veilleux. Although Veilleux had been a Mulroney appointee, he couldn't halt the government cutbacks to the CBC. And so, in December 1990, he announced in his opening statement to a House of Commons heritage committee that the CBC was pulling out of our partnership as of April 1, 1991. But Veilleux was speaking in French, and he made that announcement before I could get my earpiece to work. "I saw Phil fumbling around with his earpiece, so I started scribbling notes to him that the CBC was pulling out," Bob Buchan says, adding that the CBC even had a press release at the back of the room about it, saying that since it could no longer afford the $1.3 million in satellite costs, it was finished with CPAC.

What the hell, I thought.

The chairman of the heritage committee was a guy named Chuck Cook, an MP from British Columbia who used to be a private broadcaster and despised the government largesse handed to the CBC. When I was called to testify, Cook asked me about the CBC pulling out of CPAC. "First I've heard of it," I responded.

What a way to do business. You end your 50-50 partnership without even telling the other side before publicly announcing it. Over the years, Ted Rogers was often accused of not being a good partner, but he would never have pulled something like that.

The immediate aftermath was that, in place of the CBC, the House of Commons began paying for the satellite transmission of its proceedings—at an annual cost to taxpayers of $2 million. That was a little bit of "robbing Peter to pay Paul," given that the CBC is the public broadcaster and so is itself taxpayer funded. Under the agreement with the Speaker back then, the cable industry carried House proceedings live, then repeated the entire thing each day.

The CBC's unexpected withdrawal opened the door for us, though. In 1992, a consortium of 27 cable operators took over the operation and distribution of the House of Commons broadcasts, ensuring that millions of Canadian cable households would continue to receive them.

We also changed the name of the Canadian Parliamentary Channel to Cable Public Affairs Channel (while keeping CPAC) to reflect the greater diversity of programming and the cable industry's ownership. The original ownership structure continues today, with Rogers Communications (41.4 percent), Shaw Communications (25.05 percent), Vidéotron (21.71 percent), Cogeco (6.7 percent), Eastlink (3.76 percent), and several other cable companies (including Access Communications and Omineca Cablevision) owning a combined equity of 1.37 percent.

Ironically, CPAC broadcast the entire CRTC hearing into Rogers's takeover of Maclean Hunter in 1994. And each time CRTC chairman Keith Spicer announced that proceedings were being carried live over C-SPAN (Cable-Satellite Public Affairs Network, the terrific American equivalent of CPAC), it would absolutely drive me nuts, given all the work and effort cable had put into saving CPAC. So when the CRTC approval for the Rogers-MH deal was being made public in December 1994, what happened to Spicer served him right. He was flying back from Paris at the time, and ordered that a trailer be rented and parked at the Ottawa airport as a makeshift news conference facility to accommodate reporters and cameras. When his underlings suggested it wouldn't be necessary—the CRTC approval wasn't controversial, and so journalists were unlikely to trek out to the airport to talk to him—he overruled his staff and waited in the trailer for reporters. Alas, no one showed up, not even C-SPAN.

Today, CPAC produces 30 hours a week of original programming and 46 hours a week of long-form programming, which includes inquiries, hearings, conferences, speeches, and proceedings from federal and provincial legislatures.

It's worth mentioning Colette Watson, the president and general manager of CPAC from 2001 to 2016. She was sensational, not only in running the service but in never getting on the wrong side of any of the political parties, which is critical for CPAC. Colette still works at Rogers as senior vice-president of TV & Broadcast, and I can't stress enough how important she was to CPAC. The current CPAC president is Catherine Cano, and the chairman is Serge Sasseville of Vidéotron.

The cable industry has taken its knocks over the years from the public, the CRTC, and the broadcasters. And yes, we've made errors, and we've deserved some of the heat.

But the CPAC story is one that's not commonly known among Canadians, and I'm proud of the cable industry, not only for investing $50 million so far in CPAC but also for developing and growing a tool that enriches and strengthens our parliamentary democratic system in Canada.

The V-chip story is another tale that needs telling because it was one of the rare times we went toe to toe with a sitting CRTC chairman. The V-chip was intended as a tool that would allow parents to manage their children's television viewing based on a ratings category similar to what's used at movie theatres, but Keith Spicer overreached and we campaigned to stop him. Beginning with the term itself, much of the story is convoluted and confusing, so I'll keep it brief.

Some say V-chip stands for "violence" chip; others say it's a "viewer-control" chip; and still others claim that the V stands for

Jack Valenti, head of the Motion Picture Association of America at the time the V-chip debate took place in the mid-1990s. Simon Fraser University professor Tim Collings claims he invented the technology, yet at least two others claim the invention, too.

Anyway, in 1993, CRTC chairman Keith Spicer visited the U.S. to urge the FCC and TV executives to do something about violence on television. He promoted Collings's idea, and in Canada he used his CRTC platform to push the issue much further. He wasn't willing to wait for V-chip technology to be made mandatory for all new TV sets manufactured; he wanted immediate action. Getting violence out of television was going to be Spicer's legacy, come hell or high water.

Specifically, he wanted cable to start blacking out violent U.S. programming. (Typically, the onus was placed on cable, not broadcasters.) Not only was this nanny-state regulation at its finest, it was untenable and undeliverable—a logistical nightmare. In my opinion, it was also the thin edge of the wedge. If we were to black out supposedly violent cartoons and shows like *Power Rangers*, what would be next? Would hockey and football be deemed too violent for Canadian cable customers? But Spicer had a lot of wind in his sails, given that the public was concerned about the issue of violence on TV. I was concerned about it, too. Spicer's solution wasn't the right way to go, though.

Alison Clayton on my regulatory team and I led the charge, arguing before the Commission and in the court of public opinion that Spicer's plan was undoable. Alison was even invited to speak on major U.S. TV programs.

During one heated exchange at a CRTC hearing, I told Spicer that if we were forced to black out any programs a notice would appear in big, bold letters on the TV screen saying that this was being forced upon us by the CRTC. This threw him for a loop because normally we'd defer to the CRTC, even when we didn't like what it was doing. Spicer made some comment about my impertinence, and that I was usually "progressive" and willing to embrace new things. But I refused to back down, telling him in no uncertain terms that cable couldn't afford to be blacking out shows, unilaterally limiting programming choice, and ticking off customers. U.S. direct-to-home satellite services—which the CRTC could not control—were making inroads into Canada at the time, and cable was still smarting from the "negative option" fiasco.

Spicer's term ended without his imposing such stringent measures upon cable. The U.S. eventually made it mandatory for all manufacturers to build into every TV some sort of parental controls for all sets made after 2000. That was the right solution, even though our research indicates that few parents use such a tool and prefer to simply monitor what their young children watch.

Back in 1980, as part of our benefits package in the CCL takeover, Rogers Telefund began with a few million dollars to support television and film production. Through the 1980s we sprinkled money around in bridge financing and grants, but didn't give the fund the attention it required.

Then, in August 1989, I hired a bright young summer student intern named Robin Mirsky to run the fund. Almost 30 years later, Robin not only still runs it but has grown it beyond even what I had envisioned. The Rogers Group of Funds is now made up of four entities: Telefund, Documentary Fund, Cable Network Fund, and Theatrical Documentary Program.

And over the years, and with more money from other benefits packages, the Rogers Group of Funds has enabled us to allocate $600 million in grants and loans to 2000 independent productions—productions that have ranged from a fictional Toronto detective named William Murdoch to an impish red-headed Anne of Green Gables.

Our funds help Canadian storytellers excel. I'm proud of the part played by the Rogers Group of Funds in Canadian culture, and just as proud of what Robin has achieved.

Here's another little-known story—the tale of how Rogers acquired CFMT. This multilingual TV station in Toronto is now the anchor of OMNI Television, which consists of six multicultural TV stations—in Ontario (two stations), British Columbia and Alberta (two stations), and an affiliate in Quebec.

Back in 1977, three of Toronto's biggest names in its ethnic communities each applied to the CRTC for a TV licence. They were Leon Kossar, founder of Toronto's annual international Caravan festival; Johnny Lombardi, head of CHIN radio; and Dan Iannuzzi, publisher of *Corriere Canadese*, the largest daily Italian newspaper in the world outside of Italy.

By this point, Rogers knew there was a growing market for multilingual programming. Several years before, we'd bought as many foreign-language shows as possible (and as I mentioned earlier, even recorded some of these from hotel rooms in Brazil, Italy, and Greece to fill our Jerrold converters). We called it MCTV—Multicultural Television. In 1972, when the hip urban channel City TV launched, it too aired a smattering of multilingual programming by Toronto producers—and after securing rights from the individual local producers, Rogers would replay these shows on our MCTV channel.

But the CRTC turned down all three applicants in 1977, telling them to come back with better business models. In 1978, they did, and on December 27 of that year, Iannuzzi's MTV (Multilingual Television) won the licence.

The target date for MTV's launch was December 1979 or January 1980. Iannuzzi, who was also a minority owner of City TV, had pushed City TV honcho Moses Znaimer to broadcast multilingual programs since 1972, so everything was looking up for him now. Ahead of schedule, CFMT—no longer MCTV—signed on the air September 3, 1979. The call letters stood for Canada's First Multilingual Television. Dan Iannuzzi was president and executive producer.

Unfortunately for Dan, that was about all the good news he would experience with CFMT. Blown budgets and financial difficulties. Not having any hit U.S. programming to subsidize Canadian and foreign-language programming. Technical issues with its over-the-air channel 47 signal. You name it. One problem after another kept popping up. Like the proverbial boy plugging holes in the dike, Dan was running out of fingers to prevent CFMT from taking on water.

To make matters worse, CFMT's banker, Seaway Trust, had its assets seized by the Ontario government and all its borrowers put into receivership. CFMT had to operate under receivership for a couple of years while Iannuzzi tried to find a way out. He knocked on door after door looking for investors. Nor were Canadian broadcasters offering Dan any lifeline.

As Ted Rogers and I watched these events unfold, we knew this could be a way to get Rogers into television. If we could grab

CFMT, the CRTC would likely have to approve us—no one else was interested.

I kept in touch with Dan, and invited him to lunch on Friday, February 28, 1986, at the Albany Club in Toronto. It was at this lunch that Dan told me the jig was up: the receiver of Seaway Trust was calling his loan, and if he didn't pay up by 12:01 a.m. Monday, March 3, CFMT would be forced into bankruptcy. Since we'd been watching events from afar, it was no coincidence that I was having lunch with Dan, but it was totally a fluke that it was right when he heard about impending bankruptcy.

I returned to the office and met with Ted Rogers. Here Ted exhibited his business genius once more. He was usually incredibly impatient, but when necessary he could bide his time—and when it came to CFMT, he'd been biding his time for months, if not a couple of years. "Ted was the buyer of last resort, absolutely last resort," says Bob Buchan. "CFMT was going bankrupt and going dark, off the air. Ted and Phil knew this was their chance to get into the Toronto television market specifically, and get a toehold into Canadian television generally." Ted called in Albert Gnat, our corporate secretary and outside counsel for mergers and acquisitions. Along with Jim Sward, head of Rogers TV, the four of us worked all weekend on a deal, and were able to meet the midnight deadline.

Then, on June 19, 1986, the CRTC approved the transfer of CFMT's control from Iannuzzi to Rogers—although not without some misgivings.

"This was the first time I worked with Phil on a CRTC application," says Stephen Armstrong, "and Phil's work changed CRTC policy." One change was the CRTC's agreement to reduce multilingual programming to 60 percent so that CFMT could run some U.S. sitcoms to make advertising dollars that would subsidize the other programming. But the biggest change in CRTC policy was allowing a cable company—for the first time ever—to own a television station. Until then, as I've said, broadcasters had been able to convince the CRTC that cable was a pariah and must be restricted to local community television and alphanumeric services.

"Make no mistake, the CRTC was not overjoyed, and referred to the 'hygiene problems' of cable moving beyond local programming," Armstrong says. "But Phil ushered this through the regulatory process." Indeed, the CRTC did not like those hygiene problems one bit. We knew this because later Rogers had tried and failed three times to get a multilingual TV licence for the Vancouver market. Of course, in the end we did succeed when we bought it from the licence holder.

We've had some good people at OMNI—including Leslie Sole, Madeline Ziniak, and Jim Macdonald—who've really helped it grow and serve important audiences. And relative to all the deals I've been involved with at Rogers, the amount of money involved in buying CFMT was inconsequential—absolutely minuscule compared to our deals with CCL, Unitel, Maclean Hunter, U.S. cable franchises, Fido, NHL rights, and so many others.

In the years ahead, Rogers would get into many more programming endeavours—from sports to specialty channels to City TV—that have overshadowed CPAC and OMNI, but these two laid the groundwork for what was to come. And for very different reasons, each of them has played a role in Canadian broadcasting history and Canadian culture.

18

The Stroke and the Road Back

The late 1990s was a difficult period in many ways.

Rogers Communications, saddled with massive debt, fierce competition from satellite and telephone companies, and a still-seething customer base over the negative option fiasco, saw its stock dip to an all-time low of $2.80 on February 1, 1997.

With our plummeting market cap, the Toronto Stock Exchange removed RCI from the index, putting even more downward pressure on the stock. Beyond the personal financial implications of our now underwater stock options, this meant that the company had a much tougher time manoeuvring—including borrowing money, a key ingredient in such a capital-intensive business. We were all under so much pressure and stress, especially those of us in executive offices and at the board level.

And while this was happening, another, perhaps even worse crisis was developing: the impending sale of St. Marys Cement, the company founded in 1912 by my grandfather John Lind and several partners. Among them was Alfred Rogers, who, coincidentally, was a first cousin of Ted's father, Edward S. Rogers Sr., and whose family was in the coal, oil, and lumber business at the time. By the mid-1990s, and after many business deals and cash calls, three branches of the Alfred Rogers family owned 75 percent of St. Marys Cement, while the two branches of the John Grieve Lind family owned 25 percent. Early investors like the Gooderham family had all been bought out over the years. The board of the privately held St. Marys consisted of six Rogers seats and two Lind seats. I'd taken over my father's seat, and my cousin John had taken over Uncle Jenny's seat. (Sadly, John died in 2018.)

In 1996 it was reported to the St. Marys board that the Rogers family was being nudged by money managers at National Trust, led by Chris Wansbrough, to sell the cement company and diversify their holdings. When I heard this, I absolutely freaked out. I was vehemently opposed to any sale, and for months fought as hard as I could to stop the process. But the Rogers group—led by Jalynn Rogers Bennett—held the votes. Although I received lukewarm support from my cousin John, it was a fight I couldn't win. Assisted by my brilliant lawyer, Alix Hoy, we fought bravely on and even succeeded in getting the price raised, but we lost in the end.

On April 2, 1997 (April Fools' Day would have been more appropriate), it was announced that St. Marys had been sold to Georgia-based Blue Circle America Inc., a subsidiary of British Blue Circle Industries PLC, for US$266 million and an assumed debt of US$50 million. Ironically, when Blue Circle was taken over by Lafarge a couple of years later, the Canadian Competition Bureau ordered Lafarge to divest St. Marys. Then, four years after we sold, St. Marys was sold again, this time to the Brazilian conglomerate Votorantim for US$722 million—almost three times more than we got. In 2001, after that second sale was announced, I wrote to my sister Jenny and brothers Ron and Geoff: "It kind of sticks in my craw."

Kind of? That was an understatement. Today, looking back, that sale was the worst business move I've ever been associated with. St. Marys was going along just fine; it was a terrific business in a great industry, with a good management team in place. We didn't need to sell, and it's now worth at least six times what we received. Maybe a lot more.

I can understand what motivated Wansbrough, namely the fees for National Trust, and out of loyalty to that Rogers family, but to this day I don't get why Jalynn Bennett (who died on January 23, 2015) wanted out. I'm just not buying the diversification story. She may have believed it but I didn't buy it, and it turned out to be horribly wrong. One of her relatives on the board was ambivalent about the sale, but he buckled under her pressure. What hurts all the more is that Jalynn and I were very close: we were the same age and had grown up together; I thought of her as more than a friend, more like a first cousin. In the 1970s the two of us had started Sierra Club Ontario, where she was vice-chair of the environmental group and I was founding chairman. And I'm godfather to her eldest, Braden, while she was godmother to my daughter, Sarah (by the way, Ted Rogers was Sarah's godfather).

And Jalynn was no naïf, either, when it came to business. She knew her way around spreadsheets and financial statements. She was a director on the boards of many high-profile companies, including CIBC, Sears Canada, and Cadillac Fairview. She knew that St. Marys was performing well. We just didn't need to sell, a fact that echoes every time I think about St. Marys Cement.

Ted Rogers understood my point of view, and thought that that side of the Rogers family made a big mistake.

It ruined my relationship with Wansbrough, whom I had to work with at Rogers because he was also in charge of some of Ted's holding companies and sat on RCI's board. And it ruined my relationship with Jalynn. We barely spoke again, and never beyond pleasantries, until her death. The whole thing was a tragedy of the highest order.

Beyond these business pressures, personal issues were impacting me as well during this period. The cloud of depression that descended upon me after I left Anne and the family home had lifted, but my children were still very much upset with me. And it was at this time that we got the diagnosis of my mother's Alzheimer's. Susie, our beautiful, vivacious, free-wheeling, fun-loving mother, was leaving us mentally and finding periods of clarity less and less often.

The late 1990s were certainly rough, and things were about to get much worse.

In my life there have been many important dates, not the least of which were when my children Sarah and Jed arrived. Another important date was July 1, 1998, the day of my massive stroke at age 54.

The stroke may not have been the end, but it certainly was the beginning of a new and very different life. Earlier, in the prologue, I talked about what happened, so there's no need to go over it in detail again, except to say that I truly thought my life was ending as I slipped in and out of consciousness that day. During the arduous days, weeks, and months that followed, I was convinced that I had maybe five years left, ten at the outside.

Instead, through a combination of good fortune, hard work, and tremendous support from friends and family, I've had more than 20 years. And although these years have been a physical struggle much of the time, they've been productive. And I am very much thankful.

I don't say this often, and never in public until now, but these years have been different—very different—because I'm different in many ways. You can't help but be changed after a stroke. It's not like recovering from a broken leg, or even a heart attack.

Unless you've had a debilitating stroke, it's almost impossible to fully understand. The stroke changes your brain structure, with 20 to 40 percent of it finished and useless. I remember Ted Rogers—who had a slate of health issues, including a couple of aneurysms—telling me that he knew what I was going through. But he didn't, really. That's because his problems were fixed before they became real, incapacitating problems. Ultimately, heart failure killed him, and I'm certainly not minimizing his health challenges in life; I'm only saying that strokes aren't the same.

Unless you go through one yourself, you can never really appreciate the massive intervention it causes in a normal life. A stroke creates a total mental state change-out. To this day, I still can't move my toes. People see the obvious physical impairments, like dragging my right leg and not being able to use my right hand, but those things are minor compared to what went on in my head.

Sure, it takes longer to dress and I can't tie my shoelaces anymore, but those chores are nothing like overcoming the fear of not being able to pull out the right words in conversation. For months and months after the stroke I was absolutely terrified of public speaking, even with small groups of eight to ten friendly people, let alone with larger audiences or during potentially hostile business meetings. Some of my closest friends will be surprised to read this, but I'm betting I'm not unique, and that most people who've survived a stroke feel the same way.

Even today, after all these years, I'm quieter, less gregarious, more likely to fade into the background at social events. It is a tremendous effort to try to get back a normal life post-stroke. Many people don't do it; it's just too tough. They can't find the strength and the will to learn all over again—learn to interact fully with others, learn to talk and walk, learn to yearn to be as they once were. I can understand that, and why many just accept that "this is it" and play out the days.

Indeed, one of my closest friends, Colin Watson, jokes that the stroke changed me, but not in the way one might think. "The wonderful thing about Lind is that a lot of people would be softer after the stroke, but he's a bigger jerk than before," Watson says. "Seriously, I haven't seen any diminution of his facilities and his activities. It's hard as hell for him to go to airports as a physical activity, and he's in the air three-quarters of his life. Phil is simply not a guy to look back. Everybody has problems, and he doesn't dwell on his."

He's correct. I don't dwell on or talk much about my stroke. The candour here comes from a hope that perhaps my story can help someone else. I'm no better than the next guy, but I was bound and determined to break through and conquer the psychological aspects of the stroke.

And to be honest, I couldn't have done it without incredible support, especially in the early days, from Missy Goerner, Alison Clayton, Jan Innes, John Tory, Robin Mirsky, Bruce Philp and his

GWP team, David Barnhill, and my family, but particularly Missy and Alison, who did so much in those first dark days.

"Phil gives us credit, but the fact is, both Missy and I knew we were the ones with the most flexibility in our personal lives and work schedules," Alison says. "I didn't have children and Missy's were older, while Robin had two young ones and Jan had three. Missy and I pulled out our calendars and said we could pretty much divide up the days each week so that there'd always be a main person to orchestrate the comings and goings to help Phil get better."

Alison and Missy were both longtime Rogers consultants; they knew Ted well, and were paid a monthly retainer by Rogers Communications to manage files in specialty services and sports, respectively. Unbeknownst to me, Ted took each of them aside and told them that their retainers would be paid, but that while I was in hospital and rehab their priority was me, not their regular work. "I have to hand it to Ted," Missy says. "He looked me in the eye and said 'I want you to help my friend and not worry about the other stuff.' So for the next several weeks I worked from my laptop at the hospital and the rehab centre."

Ted was a highly emotional man, and our relationship would most definitely change over the coming months and years, but I have to tip my hat to him in those early days after my stroke. He had nothing but my best interests at heart.

Missy and Alison got to work on making me as comfortable as possible in hospital. Someone was there virtually every waking moment, from breakfast until nine p.m. They played traffic cop with visitors and phone calls. And when other close friends and family were there, they'd take breaks, run errands for me, or catch up on work files. They'd also talk to doctors

and nurses on my behalf. And each day, as new flower arrangements arrived from business contacts around North America
and even Europe, they'd take the flowers that had arrived the
day before and give them to other patients who weren't so fortunate as to receive flowers.

During those first days, as I was lying in that hospital bed,
it felt as though I was watching everyone from the outside, that
I wasn't part of things. I couldn't really talk, and I couldn't move
without help. The delirium had passed, but I was struggling
with what this new life would be like going forward. I needed
my friends, and am forever thankful.

Oftentimes, if your stroke affects the left side of your brain
as mine did, you'll have problems with the right side of your body.
In most people the left side of the brain also controls the abili-
ties to speak and understand language, and mine were definitely
affected. Left-side strokes can also often bring on severe depression, but fortunately that didn't happen to me.

"It was unsettling to see such a giant, such an alpha male
cut off at the knees," Alison Clayton says now. "It was disturbing. I don't voluntarily choose to go back to parts of my life that
were disturbing, but I know [Phil] wants me to talk about this."
Missy adds, "They were long days, and we did what we could
to help. We all knew Phil needed people around. It's who he is.
I remember a doctor telling us to give him more time alone, and
we called bullshit on that."

Looking back, there were humorous moments, but at the
time they weren't funny to me at all. One involved real, solid
food, which after a few days I was craving. They were afraid
I'd choke, though, so they sent me two or three times for "swallowing tests," which involved hooking me up to equipment and

monitoring whether I could manoeuvre the muscles needed
to swallow. They'd stare at the screen and not even look closely
at my neck, where I felt I could get the muscles in my throat
to perform swallowing actions. But each time they'd say "Nope,
the monitor is showing you can't swallow, so no solid food just
yet." Each time I failed one of those tests even though I knew
I was swallowing, it would piss me off so much. Today, Missy
can't help but laugh when that story comes up. "Wheeling you
back to your hospital room after those tests was difficult. You
were such a bear," she says.

Not only were my friends trying to lift my spirits, but they
were also protecting me from others who wanted to take advantage of my situation. The old gossip rag, *Frank* magazine, which
was in its heyday back then, tried to get a photographer in for
a picture of me in this weakened state. "That made me so angry,"
Alison says. "It made all of us mother lions so mad. We were
going to protect the cub, and we were vigilant enough to make
sure they never got a photograph."

There was also a broadcast executive from a different company who had an ulterior motive when he phoned me in hospital.
I'll let my good friend Bob Buchan pick up the story. "I remember
being in the room and Missy asking if I'd mind staying while
she went out for dinner. I told her to take her time; I'd stay
as long as necessary," Bob says. "Phil couldn't move anything.
That's how bad he was at that point. He could barely talk, and
certainly couldn't speak without incredible effort." The phone
rang and Bob answered it. The caller thought he was John Tory
at first, but after explaining who he was, Bob put the phone to my
ear. "After asking Phil how he was doing, [this broadcast executive and a partner in Sportsnet at the time] starts talking about

a problem with Sportsnet and how he could use Phil's help with Ted. The guy was calling to use Phil to get around Ted. I thought, Phil's in a dire situation right now, and that's about as bad as it gets in business."

The funny thing is that it was all about where Sportsnet would end up on the dial when it launched four months after my stroke. "Ted wanted it on a tier and [this guy] wanted it on basic cable," says Tony Viner, Rogers Media president at the time. "To be fair, he may not have known how bad a shape Phil was in at the time, but he definitely called just to get Phil's help with Ted." Rogers is the sole owner of Sportsnet now, but when it launched on October 9, 1998, CTV network owned 40 percent, with Rogers, Molson, and Fox Sports each owning 20 percent. Sportsnet is now on basic cable, so the caller to my room had been right.

After less than two weeks in hospital, on July 13 they moved me across the street to the Toronto Rehabilitation Institute's University Avenue centre. Rogers colleague Sandy Sanderson, our executive vice-president of Rogers Radio, was on the board of the rehab institute, and he ensured that I got in when I did. My new life was just beginning in earnest. I'd never shied away from long, gruelling hours and working hard, but I was about to be tested to the limits of my endurance.

According to the Heart and Stroke Foundation of Canada, in this country someone has a stroke every 10 minutes, on average. And one-quarter die as a result, which occurs when blood stops flowing to any part of the brain. The effects of a stroke depend on the part of the brain that was damaged and the amount of damage done.

Mine was severe, but within two weeks I could move my extremities and talk well enough to be transferred to rehab. That's where the really difficult work would begin, from learning to write with my left hand to taking the baby steps toward relearning how to walk. After a stroke it's very common to have communication problems, and this certainly happened to me. It's called aphasia, and it affects your ability to find the right words (even if you can imagine them) and to understand what others are saying at times.

It was on my first night at rehab, having finally passed the dreaded swallowing test, that I would get my first taste of real food. Toronto restaurateur and friend Al Carbone brought dinner to my room, complete with tablecloths, and fed me along with all my daily supporters. Al's food at Kit Kat restaurant is always terrific, but that night it was stupendous and, for me, unforgettable.

Alison, Missy, and others continued their support, bringing me some return to normalcy. They even brought in favourite artworks from my apartment and hung them on the walls of my room. And just as when I was still in hospital, someone was always there by breakfast and often past nine p.m.

Alison, who lives in Ottawa, stayed at the InterContinental Hotel on Bloor Street three to four days a week during my rehabilitation, as she did when she came to town for Rogers work. The hotel provided a free minibar to customers who stayed there 50 nights a year, and Alison certainly did that. So each morning she'd fill up a pillowcase with the contents of the minibar and bring it all down to my room. Though I don't drink and haven't since my university days, all my guests were treated to a fully stocked bar. "Almost every day by four p.m., captains of industry would drop by Phil's room for visits, chats, and cocktails," Alison says. "It quickly became a high-level and popular place to be."

Of course, up until that time each day I'd be spending punishing hours on rehab, but it was always great to have so many visitors. My son, Jed, would ride his bicycle over during his lunch break at our ad agency Garneau Wurstlin Philp, where he was interning that summer. "Seeing him so vulnerable and helpless was crazy," Jed says, almost 20 years later. "But watching him come back from that was very inspiring."

At the time of my stroke, Sarah was living in Vancouver. She admits that she was glad to be away, because when she flew in immediately after the stroke, it overwhelmed her to see me in that condition. "I had a way harder time dealing with it than Jed, seeing Dad that way, and I'm so glad Jed was there," Sarah says. "It was just deeply disturbing to me to see my father, whom I thought of as 'The Man,' in such a weakened state." And without realizing it, I inadvertently upset Sarah after she returned to Vancouver. "Dad would always send me postcards from wherever he was. I wish I'd saved them all; there would have been hundreds," she says. "The first one he sent me after he had his stroke and was learning to write with his left hand made me cry for days. But he still did it. Pretty cool."

My siblings and nieces and nephews also made trips in to visit. And Anne, the mother of my children, would visit once a week or more. I am a fortunate person in so many ways.

Speaking of which, the flower arrangements just kept coming from cable companies, TV producers, networks, and other industry folks. It was overwhelming. Then Ken Engelhart came up with a splendid idea: instead of sending flowers, companies could "sponsor dinners" for my room from local restaurants. Plenty of people leapt at the chance, and some were there to enjoy dinners others had sponsored! During my hours of tough, really tough, rehab, I looked forward to those dinners and conversations. "To be honest, Phil needed others around," says Jan Innes. "If he'd been left alone, I'm not sure he would have survived."

It's difficult to overstate the thanks for all the help I received. Jan did all my laundry and seemed to be around daily, even though that couldn't have been possible with three children under the age of 10. The same could be said of Robin, who also had two young children then.

John Tory was in my rehab room every Saturday, reading me all the newspapers; I still couldn't read or even properly hold a newspaper, for that matter. And as he read to me I remember him stretching out my coiled right hand, working it for hours like a therapist, trying to help me get some use from it again. Then, a month after the stroke, knowing how much I love movies, John loaded me and my wheelchair into a van and took me and a few others to see that summer's hit comedy, *There's Something About Mary*. It probably took longer getting me up and out of the room, into the van, and into the movie theatre than the entire length of the movie, but it was worth it.

Two weeks later, on August 19, friends took me out to Al and John Carbone's Kit Kat on King Street West for an early birthday dinner. Al was misty-eyed seeing me out from my rehab room, and they served me another extraordinary meal, but I must admit that the noise and tight surroundings were overwhelming for me that evening, only seven weeks after the stroke.

And two weeks after that, on September 4, I left rehab. My daily physiotherapy, however, would continue for more than two years. Indeed, my physiotherapist, Julie Vaughan-Graham, is someone I still see at least twice a month all these years later. Julie owns Physio-Logic; she's an expert on stroke recovery. For a rather petite woman, Julie can inflict a lot of pain, but if her work didn't benefit me I wouldn't still be seeing her after more than 20 years. She is probably more determined than me.

Meanwhile, around the time I left rehab, my sister Jenny had just leased a terrific two-bedroom apartment in uptown Toronto that was more spacious than my little apartment. And although she was excited about her new place and had just finished decorating it, she insisted that we swap places for the next several months so that my needed live-in help would have a place to sleep. All these years later, Jenny still reminds me that, while I enjoyed the luxury of her apartment, she could barely even turn around in my apartment's tiny bathroom.

But who was that live-in help to be? I couldn't leave rehab without someone to live with me. Fortunately, Missy had already cold-called my old university friend Barney (David Barnhill). "I'd never met or spoken to him before, but I explained the situation, and he immediately put his life on hold and flew from Vancouver to live with Phil for the next four or five months," Missy says. "Quite astonishing, and it speaks to Phil's deep and loyal friendships with many." Barney fed me, dressed me, drove me to my daily physio appointments, read to me, and watched and debated the Bill Clinton impeachment hearings with me.

A while later, when Barney needed a break, he returned to Vancouver for three weeks in October and November before coming back for three more months. And in his absence, I was able to take two trips.

On November 1, I attended a Buffalo Bills football game in Orchard Park, New York, with Missy, Alison, and her husband

Steve Clayton. That was my first lengthy drive since the stroke and it was frigid in the stadium, but I managed to walk from the car to the stands, watch the game, and make it home without any stumbles or setbacks.

Two weeks later I flew, for the first time since my stroke, to San Antonio, where Missy lives with her husband Herb and her kids Erin and Lee. Along with Jan and others, one of the spots we visited was former president Lyndon Johnson's birthplace, now a national historic park called LBJ Ranch. It's a couple of hours north of San Antonio, and Missy drove us there in her "Texas Town Car," a Chevrolet Suburban. That day, as we toured the beautiful Texas Hill Country, we laughed a lot—and got into mischief with park rangers for irreverently making fun of the name, calling out things like "the L ... BJ Ranch," emphasis on the BJ. At one point, while we were on a two-car tram in the park, friends Lenny Stern of New York, Richard Stursberg, and Bruce Philp were getting pretty loud, and some of the other tourists in our car were giving us dirty looks. Jan, Missy, and Nancy Jamieson were simultaneously amused and embarrassed. At our first stop everyone got off the tram to tour Lady Bird's house, where she spent much of her time after LBJ died in 1973. Then a funny thing happened: when we returned to the tram everyone else not in our party crammed into its second car, leaving our rowdy group to its own devices in the remaining car. "That trip was all about character," says Richard Stursberg. "Phil pushed himself so hard every day, and he was cheerful and friendly all the time. It was quite extraordinary."

Both excursions were meaningful because I've always loved to travel, and to do so five months after the stroke brought some normalcy back to me and made me think seriously about getting back to work, with all the travel it required. In fact, within the first year after the stroke I would also travel to California, Florida, Hawaii, Chicago, Oregon, Banff, and Vancouver. (Longer, more exotic trips, to places like Fiji and Africa, would soon follow; I am indebted to my friend and business partner Vernon Achber for his patience with and understanding of the challenges I faced, especially in travel.)

Meanwhile, shortly after the Texas trip, I experienced an "aha" moment when I realized that this was my new life, that things would never fully go back to the way they'd been. I'd gotten on an elevator in a downtown business office, and as I struggled everyone looked down at the floor, trying to be polite by silently signalling something like "no worries, take your time." But also in the elevator was a senior Toronto business executive whom I'd known for many years and who didn't acknowledge me. Like the others, he was politely looking away, and either didn't realize it was me or, more likely, didn't know what to say when he saw how much I'd changed. I've had many other such moments of sudden comprehension and clarity, but that one may have been the most profound.

The Chicago and Banff trips were both in June, and were notable for being annual industry events: the National Cable & Telecommunications Association conference and the Banff World Media Festival. In some ways, it was my post-stroke coming-out party for many industry colleagues who had yet to see me. To say I was nervous would be an understatement, but in less than a year I'd certainly come a long way.

I was about ready to return to work, so making these public appearances, with a right hand that didn't work and a right leg I had to drag along, were important next steps. I knew that returning to work would be difficult, but I didn't realize how much it would alter my relationship with Ted Rogers.

19

Changeup: The Jays Purchase and My Evolving Relationship with Ted

The purchase of the Toronto Blue Jays in September 2000 by Rogers Communications Inc. would prove to be one of our best investments, although few thought that way initially, or even for the next decade.

As a lifelong sports fan, I felt that live sports would be practically bulletproof for generating advertising revenue—especially in the emerging era of "free content" via the Internet and streaming. So for me, our ownership of the Jays combined a personal passion with a sound business proposition. Besides, people like Ted Turner, Rupert Murdoch, and the folks at Disney had all invested in professional sports teams, so it wasn't a novel idea for a communications company like ours. Still, we took heat from the financial community, and even from our own board of directors. Ted Rogers deserves a lot of credit because he was no sports fan—he wouldn't know the difference between Abner Doubleday and a double play—but he always defended the move and never wavered.

Along with Albert Gnat, a brilliant lawyer at Lang Michener who was also a Rogers board member, we hatched the plan to purchase the Blue Jays not long after I returned to work in the summer of 1999. The Blue Jays had been on the block for some time, ever since the multinational Interbrew SA bought the Jays' owner, Labatt Brewing Co. Ltd., in 1995.

Albert Gnat was ingenious in understanding what motivates people and gets business deals done. With Ted's approval and Albert's ability, I knew we'd be the frontrunner to land the Jays. We just needed the cash. Then it appeared, seemingly out of thin air. And it was all thanks to Vidéotron.

Indeed, getting the Jays took some, but not all, of the sting out of losing the fight against Quebec nationalists for control of Vidéotron, then the second-largest cable company behind Rogers. With Vidéotron, we'd had an opportunity to bridge the two solitudes and create a mammoth English-French communications company that could really give giant Bell Canada a run in the new century.

Here's how that fight unfolded. Under the terms of our friendly offer in February 2000, the Chagnon family, who controlled Vidéotron, would become Rogers's second-largest shareholder and receive seats on the board, with Ted Rogers retaining control through voting shares. But given the prospect of an Ontario company taking over a strategic company like Vidéotron, I told Ted that I was afraid the Quebec government wouldn't approve the deal. His response was that once Chagnon agreed, the government wouldn't interfere. I began to think that maybe Ted was right. But as it turned out, the government was indeed not happy, which led to the white-knight Quebecor getting the financial backing it needed from a Quebec government agency.

We'd been outflanked by Quebecor Inc. and its Quebec-first financial backers, the giant pension fund Caisse de dépôt et placement du Québec, with its $5.4 billion all-cash deal. Having been created by the Quebec government, the Caisse's mandate, according to section 4.1 of the Act respecting the Caisse de dépôt et placement du Québec, is to maximize returns while at the same time "contributing to Québec's economic development." The Caisse was already a minority shareholder in Vidéotron, and once it stepped up to back Quebecor—with its hundreds of billions of dollars in managed net assets—we knew that political forces wouldn't allow our friendly offer to stand.

What are you going to do? When you get a lemon, you make lemonade. Under the terms of our offer to Ted's old cable pal André Chagnon, if someone else trumped us, Rogers would receive a $241 million breakup fee—more than enough to buy the Jays, which cost us $165 million.

A genius at spinning publicity, Ted often said that it was Quebecor that bought the Blue Jays for us. He liked to think such comments would get under the skin of Pierre Karl Péladeau, CEO of Quebecor and a future leader of the separatist Parti Québécois. Indeed, Ted didn't limit such comments to the Blue Jays. He would go on to say, at various times, that Péladeau's breakup fee helped Rogers pay for acquiring radio stations, upgrading television networks, and buying wireless spectrum. Ever the showman, in Ted's mind that breakup fee grew to $1 billion or more in Rogers's spending.

Those jabs weren't entirely in jest; there was an underlying meaning. Ted was a dyed-in-the-wool, wear-it-on-his-sleeve Canadian nationalist, and he didn't like losing to Péladeau. He and Chagnon, for better or worse, believed that one giant communications company delivering content and services in both official languages would benefit Canada long-term. Remember, the friendly deal between Rogers and Vidéotron occurred less than five years after the 1995 referendum that came within 54,288 votes of Quebec seceding from Canada. It had been a razor-thin win, with the No side against Quebec separation taking 50.6 percent to the Yes side's 49.4 percent.

But back to the Blue Jays. It was my friendship with Paul Beeston, who at the time was president of Major League Baseball, that helped Rogers attain preferred purchaser status with commissioner Bud Selig. In 1976 Paul had become the Blue Jays' first employee, before the expansion franchise had even played a game. Our friendship went back almost that far through our mutual friend Paul "Leaky" Little, who worked for my political mentor Darcy McKeough before moving on to management roles at Labatt. Beeston was absolutely essential to our purchase.

Ted recognized the financial and brand implications of the deal, even though, as I said, he knew nothing about the game. (One time he yelled at a Jays player to run faster to first base after receiving a base-on-balls free pass. Another time, in the Jays' press box, he introduced himself as "the village idiot" to *Toronto Star* reporter Dave Perkins and complained about the low Canadian dollar, calling it the "peso.") But Ted knew the business of sports—and that baseball could fill our cable pipes and radio airwaves with content for six months of the year. Indeed, the asset has since exploded in value. In December 2017, *Forbes* magazine estimated that the Blue Jays were worth US$1.3 billion. Remember, we paid all in roughly US$200 million.

As Ted noted at the September 2000 news conference announcing the purchase,

> We've seen a trend in North America of entertainment and commu-nications companies being more and more involved in sports, and I think that's a good trend because I think those companies can help sports and sports can help those companies. We've seen that with Time Warner, with News Corp and Disney, and it's probably time that there be a Canadian company in that league. I don't know about you, but I'm tired of always reading about everything happening south of the border. The city and the country love sports and we love sports, and that's why we're here.

Here's a little-known fact that underlines Ted's ability to understand the business of sports. The very popular *Jays in 30* TV program was his idea—an idea that would be copied by other TV rights holders of professional sports teams across North America. Ted had initially suggested that Sportsnet rerun Blue Jays baseball games to sell more ads. When our TV folks told him that no one would spend three hours watching a taped base-ball game, Ted said, "Edit it down to 30 minutes and people will watch." And he was correct. The numbers show that Jays fans will watch *Jays in 30*—especially after a win—even if they've already watched the game live.

And one must remember that when Rogers bought the Jays the financial community thought it was a dumb idea. So we'd rarely talk about the team during analysts' calls. We even rolled the team into Tony Viner's division of Rogers Media so as not to break out the Jays' financial numbers on their own. (In his memoir, Ted acknowledged that the Jays had cost Rogers $300 million up to that point, including the purchase price.)

From 2000 to the time of Ted's death in December 2008, at every RCI board meeting some director would bitch about the Jays and ask when we would divest. To his credit, Ted always defended the move, although when the issue arose at the board, he'd often say "Phil, that question is for you."

Out of the gate, we hired Paul Godfrey as president of the Blue Jays. As chairman of Metro Toronto in the mid-1970s, Godfrey had actively tried to get an MLB franchise for Toronto. We believed his stature would help. And initially, Tony Viner, Albert Gnat (who died of cancer far too young in 2004), and I really liked the Godfrey hire. Now, I've got no axe to grind against Godfrey, but there are certain things that are worth mentioning.

Early in his tenure, Godfrey talked Ted into a few really dumb things. The dumbest was purchasing an Arena Football League team and moving it to Toronto. Godfrey convinced Ted that, since several NFL owners also had Arena football teams, it would be the best way to eventually get an NFL franchise ourselves. I was opposed to the idea, as was Tony Viner and John H. Tory, who was cable president and very close to Ted. But Godfrey persuaded Ted to put up more than $6 million for the team and then put his son, Rob Godfrey, in charge of it. After two seasons with sparse crowds in the 20,000-seat Air Canada Centre, the Toronto Phantoms were no more. I'll say this about Ted: he might be talked into ideas when executives are new and shiny, but he wouldn't put up with underperformance for long.

In Godfrey's case, it was his skills as a political operative that allowed him to fly under the radar and survive longer than we'd thought he would. Few are better political operatives than Paul. At virtually every one of the Jays' 81 home games each season, Paul Godfrey would entertain in luxury box 337, located between home plate and third base. Sometimes it was business with politicians and partners who could help the Jays and Rogers, but many times it was a "friends and family" thing.

After a few years Ted had had enough, and told Tony and me to let him go. Godfrey pleaded with us to give him another couple of years. We told him it wasn't going to happen, but that I'd talk to Ted about one more year, and only one more year. Ted grudgingly did give him that, and as it was coming to a close, Godfrey came back to Tony and me, pleading again. When things became clear to him, Godfrey stood down and thanked us. Then he asked one more favour: could I line up a meeting with Ted so that he could personally thank him?

By this point Ted was fed up, tired, and only months away from death. He didn't want to meet with Godfrey and told me so. I said, "Ted, it's only 15 minutes." Ted agreed to meet him, but made it clear that he didn't have a good feeling about it. To be honest, I had trepidations, too. Anyway, Godfrey arrived at the executive floor in our building at 333 Bloor Street East, and as soon as he walked through Ted's office door he started trashing both Tony Viner and me, asking Ted to keep him. How do I know this? Simple: as soon as Ted ended the meeting he came over to my office in a fury. He started swearing at me, calling me a fucking idiot for letting Godfrey into his office and detailing what Godfrey had said. He was livid, and, of course, I was the villain.

Oh, well. That was Ted.

On September 29, 2008—just two months before Ted's death—Rogers Media issued a press release: "Blue Jays President and CEO, Paul Godfrey, has decided not to renew his Blue Jays contract and will leave his position at the end of 2008." Both Ted and I were quoted about the outgoing president, but Tony's comment was the best. You have to know that Tony Viner has a great sense of humour, and I bet he, not the PR department, actually wrote his quote because Tony had seen the bills for Godfrey's luxury box 337. "Paul has provided inspirational leadership to the team," Tony said. "He has eaten, slept and breathed the Blue Jays for eight years."

When I returned to work in the summer of 1999, I could feel that something was amiss between Ted and me. For one thing, my daily physiotherapy appointments meant that I wasn't as visible around the executive offices. Ted always liked you to "be there," and so he became more involved in regulatory affairs, now often directly approaching those who reported to me, like Ken Engelhart, vice-president of telecom regulatory, and Michael Allen, vice-president of cable regulatory. He also tried to rework my contract with less favourable terms. Ted would send me memos outlining his suggestions, but after I didn't reply several times, the issue went away.

The biggest change in our relationship was that I could no longer verbally spar with Ted. For years we'd hash things out this way. He appreciated my direct approach and honest style of telling him exactly what I thought. We wouldn't always agree, and Ted held the hammer: his name was on the building, not mine, so it was his ultimate decision. But sometimes he could be moved on a position.

I'll let a few others comment on our relationship here. John A. Tory, Toronto mayor John Tory's father, sat on the Rogers board for more than 40 years. He and Ted were very close. Indeed, the John and Liz Tory Eye Centre at Sunnybrook Health Sciences Centre in Toronto was created in 2008 by a $7.5 million donation from Ted and Loretta Rogers to honour their friends. "My dad used to say, 'Ted always wanted to bet the farm and thank God Phil was there,'" says John H. Tory. "Phil was the one guy who was there the whole time. His counsel was so important to Ted."

Alan Horn, longtime chairman of Rogers Communications, says much the same. "Ted and Phil's relationship transcended everything else. Before the stroke, it was almost equal. Phil kept Ted a little bit grounded." In 1999, at a dinner to celebrate my thirtieth anniversary at Rogers and my having worked so closely with Edward Samuel Rogers (nicknamed ESR), Alan put a special twist on the story by playing on Mark Antony's famous speech in Shakespeare's *Julius Caesar*. "Friends, Rogers, countrymen, lend me your ears," Alan said to the assembled guests. "Lind's here thirty years ... he came to berate ESR, not to praise him."

I liked to think of myself as Ted's true partner—a non-equity partner, but partner nonetheless. Bob Buchan says, "Ted used to use the words as a compliment, but he meant it when he'd refer to Phil as 'my partner.' The relationship became one of near equals as time went on. Ted was always the boss, but Phil was right more often than he was wrong, and Ted took his counsel."

But after my stroke, things were different. Partly because of my weakened state, but also because of the explosive growth of wireless, Ted began to look elsewhere for counsel, too.

As I mentioned earlier, the clinical term for the post-stroke inability to come up with the right words is aphasia. Even if you can imagine the right words, they can be elusive. Where aphasia can be terrifying is in verbal debates, either in expressing the right words or in understanding what others are saying. Ted had many virtues, but patience wasn't one of them, so he probably felt that it wasn't worth the bother.

But Ted was also a bully. That's one of the reasons for all his successes in business. He'd bully people into doing what he wanted done, whether they were employees, bankers, suppliers, or partners. When he sensed vulnerability, Ted would hone in on the perceived weakness and work it to his advantage. That was now happening to me, and it forced me to change tactics when dealing with him. So I developed a strategy of sending him memos, in which I'd express concerns and suggest other alternatives when I saw fit. It was here that I received tremendous help from my assistant, Michelle Cha, who took dictation and was good at coming up with the words I was looking for when I couldn't find them. And when I'd write those memos, instead of being straight up I'd inject nice things about Ted to get him fluid with the idea, whatever it happened to be, and to hold his attention. This memo approach gave me time to formulate my ideas better and to find the right words. We'd been brothers in arms for years and had fought many battles side by side. I always knew who was in charge, but that never stopped me from jousting with Ted. The stroke did that.

And in some ways, Ted resented me. It simmered, and from time to time it would bubble up—not often, but sometimes. Even before my stroke. We were once at a company Christmas party and in the presence of John H. Tory when Ted said to me, "There are two camps in this company, mine and yours. Let me tell you, my camp is going to win." Shit, no kidding, I thought. "It's your name on the building, not mine," I replied.

Ted was a lot of things. He had thousands of traits. He was fearless, but he was afraid of certain things. He was outspoken but sometimes shy. He was a bully yet tremendously compassionate. Although he was impatient, he had the ability to bide his time, if need be. He was magnetic, but he could often be totally unreasonable. He would yell at people and call them names, yet for the most part people were attracted to him, and would mostly forgive his outbursts no matter how hurtful they were at the time. I remember countless meetings where he'd be rude and "out of control," but at the end of them he'd say, "Well, that was a productive meeting." We would all be amazed at this. It should be noted that the company had a high turnover of executives during those years.

To the outside world, the Rogers executive team was a unified force. But amongst his executives, Ted sowed seeds of discord and encouraged backbiting, much like Franklin Roosevelt did with his cabinet. Due to our closeness, Colin Watson and I refused to play his game of divide and conquer. Others fell prey to Ted's guile.

He was brilliant, and a great debater. He would probe and probe your argument until he found a weakness, and then he'd exploit it relentlessly. He would never, ever give up. All one had to do was tell Ted that what he was suggesting was impossible—then he would push harder. And many times he was right. After all, people are pretty conservative. He was wrong many times, too, but unafraid to change course when he was on the wrong path. And usually when it became obvious that his idea was unattainable, he'd say "Well, let's try something else." And quite often Ted would have an idea that would surface years after we thought he had given it up. His perseverance was truly astounding.

Ted was also permanently dissatisfied, always thinking things could be done better, success achieved more quickly. I wish for his sake that he could have celebrated victories, but he just couldn't sit back and savour. Instead, he was on to the next battle. Even at victory parties, he was always thinking—and usually talking—about what was next.

His ideas were numerous, often coming out in written edicts. He might have 100 ideas in a week, and most were ridiculous, but one or two would be brilliant. One time when he was wearing his executive team down with so many crazy ideas, I had to confront him. "Ted," I said, "we've got a horrible problem. There's some maniac out there firing off memos and signing your name to them."

Our relationship has been compared to that of an old married couple. But it was more complicated than that, especially after my stroke. We got along great, but we bickered. We squabbled. Neither of us was ever afraid to tell the other what was on his mind. (Later, I'll tell the story about the time he wanted to change the name of the company from Rogers to Cantel. It was one battle that he came to appreciate having let me win.) Most of all, there was a great deal of mutual respect between the two of us.

Just five weeks before he died, I wrote him this letter:

Dear Ted,

Last weekend marked the 39th year that we have been together at Rogers. I remember October 20, 1969 as if it were
yesterday. Daphne Evans was in your office when I arrived
reporting to work. She dispatched me down the hall to
meet Barry Ross, whom I took an instant liking to, and thus
my journey with you began.

But, as you noted in your book, we started even before
that date. Our grandparents had worked together and we
knew each other from political dealings. You were the elo-
quent, high energy, ever faithful crusader ... and I was the
more pragmatic organizer who could count votes! Together
throughout the years we've made a very good team. We've
certainly had our disagreements (mainly on politics, even
to this day!) but on the substantial issues, we have always
been as one ... with you leading the charge and me fighting
the battles by your side.

I was thinking about this recently when I was preparing to do a video appearance on our behalf honouring the
CRTC's 40th anniversary. I had to mentally scroll through
the Chairmen and acting Chairmen during these years and
think about how many times we've been in front of them! It
is well over 100 times and some of those appearances were
absolutely critical to us. In fact, on several occasions they
were "make or break" affairs. But we always managed to
pull through when it really counted. With so many years
behind us, it's impossible to overlook how important the
CRTC has been to us—and they continue to be important
to this day!

I really enjoyed your book. As you've shown many
times on deals—or issues we'd frankly sometimes wished
you'd forgotten—you have an incredible recall. As I read
the book, it was fun remembering the countless number of

people we've met, the opportunities we've had, the mistakes we've made, and the victories we've won. All in all it has been an incredible ride—and it's not over yet—not by a long shot.

The business books like to say—no one is irreplaceable. While technically correct—no one could have given our company the shining purpose and sheer drive that you give it. Our successors (as we fade away) will come forward and provide strong leadership. But there can only be one Ted Rogers—who took an idea and through hard work and incredible motivation converted it into a raging force of 30,000 warriors.

As someone who has been with you almost from the beginning, I want to say what a joy and pleasure it has been to serve as your lieutenant. It hasn't always been easy for either of us but in the main it has been entirely fabulous! At age 65, with the benefit of perfect hindsight—I'm able to clearly see the key to whatever level of success I've achieved is being with you—so closely aligned over all these years. You are my great mentor—and my wonderful friend!

But as I said earlier, it isn't over yet. There are still several mountains to climb and countless problems to overcome. So we continue, but I just wanted to reminisce a bit and to say thanks from the bottom of my heart for what you have done for me over the years.

With love and respect,
Phil
October 24, 2008

Ted and I started working together around the time man first landed on the moon. And working with Ted was not dissimilar to a moon shot. He always aimed for the stars; full speed ahead.

I remember once, after a particularly long day, Ted and I were having dinner together and the subject of best friends came up.

"Without doubt, your best friend is Toby Hull," I said.

Ted looked at me plaintively and said, "I thought you were my best friend?"

I was astounded. He and I were close, but Toby really was his best friend, even if he thought that way about me. But it got me thinking about his friendships. I don't think Ted had many close friends, really close friends. He simply didn't have time to develop or nurture them. He was almost 100 percent work.

But on the other hand, he had thousands of friends. He had such charisma and he was always reaching out his hand to everyone he met and saying "How are you?" To this day, everyone who met him remembers him and considers him a friend. From a company standpoint, this was terrific. We had thousands of motivated employees, all working hard for him. It is an honour I hold close to be one of Ted's closest friends.

And while our relationship changed after my stroke, it was strong enough to bend, but not break.

20

Regional Sports and a National Dream

I became a diehard Cleveland Browns fan in the late 1950s, listening to games on WGAR-AM 1220 radio while I was at Ridley College and later watching them every Sunday on CBC-TV (in the pre-satellite/cable era, Ontario was in the Browns' territory). My friend Gordie Chaplin introduced me to the Browns, and 60 years later, I'm not sure if I should be grateful or peeved.

The team captivated me. In 1957, a 21-year-old rookie named Jim Brown was running over and through defenders on his way to one of the greatest careers in NFL history. And in 1964, before there was a Super Bowl, Brown led the Browns to a title championship. I've been a long-suffering fan and season-ticket holder ever since.

When owner Art Modell moved the team to Baltimore in 1996, I grudgingly went with him. After all, we were quite close, and had been friends since 1993, when the Browns were in Toronto playing an exhibition game and I threw Modell a VIP luncheon at the Rogers Centre (then called SkyDome). After that, I'd go down at least once a year to see games with him in Baltimore. (Later, having been vilified as Public Enemy Number 1 for moving the team and even receiving death threats, Modell never returned to Cleveland.) So on January 28, 2001, there I was in Tampa with Modell, cheering on the Baltimore Ravens to a crushing 34–7 Super Bowl victory over the New York Giants. But in my heart, the Ravens weren't the Browns.

Meanwhile, in 1999, the NFL had reactivated a Cleveland Browns franchise with the familiar orange and brown uniforms. But the new Cleveland Browns have struggled, achieving only two winning seasons and only one brief playoff appearance. Still, they're my team. And sadly, I've passed this Browns affliction to my son, Jed, but misery loves company, especially when the team goes 0–16, as it did in 2017.

Modell was a good man and an NFL innovator. He helped increase the game's popularity through his work as chairman of the NFL's Television Committee from 1962 to 1993, spearheading things like Monday Night Football and other pioneering ideas. As for moving the Browns, he'd had three choices: move the team, sell the team, or go bankrupt and forfeit the franchise. "Let me put this in perspective," Art Modell told the *New York Daily News* a few years before his death in 2012. "I didn't give up 35 years of my life, where I was part of everything that went on in Cleveland, because I happen to like crab cakes. I moved for a legitimate reason. It was tough."

I mention the Browns story because it underlines the passion stoked through sports. I love sports—the excitement, the fan loyalty, and the way it can bind people together, as it does from coast

In October 1999, Ted threw a party for my thirtieth anniversary with Rogers. The invite included this fun road map of some of our achievements together over those first three decades. Just three months back at work after my stroke, neither of us knew if the road map would continue. It did.

PHIL AND TED'S EXCELLENT 30 YEAR ADVENTURE

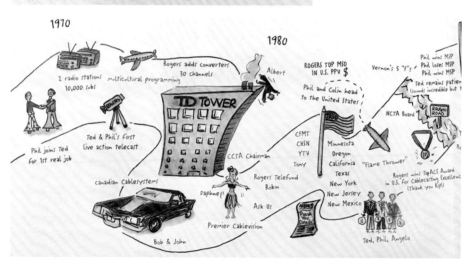

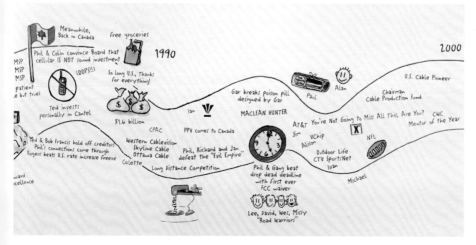

Top: With Adrian Montgomery, who contributed greatly to Rogers securing the Toronto Buffalo Bills Series.

Middle: Blue Jays spring training in Dunedin. With the Jays' inimitable president Paul Beeston and Nadir Mohamed.

Bottom: Nadir and me with Francesco Aquilini, owner of the Vancouver Canucks, announcing the naming of Rogers Arena in Vancouver. A major coup for Rogers.

Top: (L–R) Jake Kerr, owner of the Vancouver Canadians (Northwest League affiliate of the Toronto Blue Jays); Paul Beeston; me; and Jays GM Alex Anthopoulos.

Middle: In 1997, NFL Enterprises senior vice-president Tola Murphy-Baran and I announced the groundbreaking NFL–Rogers deal to bring the exclusive U.S. DirecTV satellite package to cable in Canada. Helping promote the launch is NFL Pro Football Hall of Famer Ronnie Lott.

Bottom: (L–R) Former Rogers Media president Tony Viner, me, and Ted with the NFL's Vince Lombardi Super Bowl Trophy.

Enjoying lunch with JR Shaw and Ron Joyce, Tim Hortons co-founder, at Eagle Pointe Lodge in British Columbia. Like Ted, JR is a cable giant who built his small family business into an empire.

Ellen Roland and I out for an evening with our friend John Tory, Toronto mayor and former president of Rogers Cable. Following my stroke, every Saturday morning for weeks John would come to my room at Toronto Rehab and read the newspapers to me.

ROGERS
50th
Anniversary
Celebration

Above: (R–L) Robin Mirsky, executive director of Rogers Group of Funds, with board member Alison Clayton.

Left: At Rogers's fiftieth anniversary party with five women who've made extraordinary contributions in their fields to Rogers. (L–R) Jan Innes, Pam Dinsmore, Susan Wheeler, Colette Watson, and Alison Clayton.

All three parties in the House of Commons gave a standing ovation to CPAC on its twentieth anniversary. (L–R) Yves Mayrand, Colette Watson, me, Ken Stein, Serge Sasseville, and Bob Buchan.

Top: My favourite U.S. ambassador to Canada, David Jacobson, and his wife, Julie.

Middle: Toronto Star reporter Bob Brehl and Ted Turner at a CCTA convention in the 1990s (25 years later, Bob and I would collaborate on this book).

Bottom: Two of my closest Vancouver friends, David Barnhill (left) and Peter Hyndman. Barney, my roommate at UBC, came to Toronto in 1998 to live with me for several months and help guide me through my stroke recovery.

Left: One of scores of fishing trips with my son, Jed. He's a better fisherman than I am.

Bottom: Sharing a special moment with my daughter, Sarah, at my sixtieth birthday party at the Power Plant in Toronto.

THE CABLECENTER

Top: A Cable Guy through and through, I loved this moment in Boston before a roomful of my peers. 2012 US Cable Hall of Fame.

Left: My Order of Canada ceremony in 2002 with Missy Goerner—a U.S. Road Warrior, friend, and colleague for nearly four decades.

Bottom: I'm frequently told I lack patience, whereas Michelle Cha, my executive assistant for nearly 20 years, has the patience of Job with me ... most of the time.

to coast during Blue Jays post-season runs or gold-medal hockey games. But sports can also create villains, rightly or wrongly, like Art Modell or visiting superstars like LeBron James or Yankee sluggers. Sports is wonderful theatre.

For the longest time, I wanted Rogers Communications to be part of the show—and not just by delivering sports content across our cable networks, but by producing and owning our own sports content. That opportunity came in the mid-1990s when a good friend named Peter Barton suggested that a regional sports network could work against the mighty TSN in Canada. Peter had had the vision to go up against the enormous Disney-owned ESPN and create such networks in the States. And now he'd help us create Sportsnet here.

Peter had been a key player in growing Tele-Communications Inc. (TCI) into a mammoth U.S. cable operator. John Malone— undeniably the smartest and craftiest cable operator I ever met, and that's no slight to Ted, the Shaws, or the Roberts—put Peter in charge of Liberty Media, Malone's cable programming company. Peter and I had a lot in common. He used to say we belonged to the "squadron of second bananas" along with Terry McGuirk, former CEO of Turner Broadcasting, because we had an ability to work closely with hard-charging men and handle the details to implement their visions.

Peter Barton, who in September 2002 died way too young of stomach cancer at the age of 51, is a significant slice of the Sportsnet story, as is another man who happens to be a villain in the eyes of many Canadian hockey fans: NHL commissioner Gary Bettman. I'll get to Bettman's role in the Sportsnet story shortly, but first I will say this about him: Gary Bettman is a man of his word who has always treated Rogers fairly.

Returning to the mid-1990s, I told Peter Barton about the one fundamental difference between Canadian and American broadcast regulations that could really hamper the Sportsnet idea. Unlike their U.S. counterparts, Canadian cable operators couldn't control programming entities beyond local cable Channel 10. (As I've said, Rogers was the owner of the multicultural television network only because no one else was interested in saving it from bankruptcy.) Other money-making specialty cable channels were verboten to cable operators. I talked earlier about how the broadcasters, in general, held great sway at the CRTC. Their lobby group, the Canadian Association of Broadcasters (CAB), were effective campaigners in keeping cable out of programming.

And when we were formulating the Sportsnet idea, broadcasters had a powerful ally in maintaining the status quo: CRTC commissioner Andrée Wylie, who would go on to become vice-chairman of broadcasting. Ken Engelhart says that during her 10 years with the Commission we never once won a major broadcast decision— except when we ultimately gained control of Sportsnet, which even she couldn't block as powerful events unfolded.

We also needed to tackle the CRTC's "genre protection" policy, which in those days effectively gave a monopoly to the first licensed service in any category. The Sports Network (TSN) held that monopoly.

Initially, Peter and I started thinking about Sportsnet as a network to be part of, but not control. We came up with a 20 percent stake each for Rogers (all we were allowed at the time) and Peter's Liberty Media, and a plan to find other Canadian partners. I got CTV president John Cassaday on board (40 percent) and then Molson Breweries (20 percent). We now had a solid partnership.

In the early stages, Ted Rogers was lukewarm, at best, to the Sportsnet idea. But he came around, especially after we bought the Toronto Blue Jays.

So we presented our arguments to the CRTC, but lost our first licence application in 1994. And although Cassaday resigned from CTV in June 1997 to work for the Shaws, our partnership remained solid with the new CTV president, Ivan Fecan. We regrouped, made another application, and in 1998 won our licence, with a launch date planned for that October. But victory presented us with several challenges: How do we get on air? Who's going to carry us beyond Rogers Cable? And what kinds of sports properties are available for us to buy the rights and broadcast? We could have been a stillborn service.

That's where NHL commissioner Gary Bettman comes into the story. Out of the blue, Gary called and asked me if we'd be interested in buying the national rights for NHL games in Canada.

You bet we were interested. I immediately went to Ted and said, "I can't believe this, but Gary Bettman just called and offered us the NHL rights if we're willing to pony up." Ted knew a business opportunity when he saw it: "Go for it," he said. "We'll have an instant network." We were able to negotiate a national NHL package that gave us the strong programming cornerstone we needed in order to be relevant. In fact, without Gary Bettman's initial approach, I'm not sure Sportsnet would have worked; certainly it wouldn't be as successful as it has become today.

Gary was good to Rogers in other ways. Shortly after we purchased the Blue Jays in September 2000, Gary called me to say he'd love to see Rogers owning an NHL club, too. With both Montreal and Ottawa having ownership troubles in those days, he said that Rogers would look good "in the club" of NHL owners.

I reported this to Ted in a memo dated September, 8, 2000—more than a decade before Rogers and Bell teamed up to buy 75 percent of Maple Leaf Sports & Entertainment and thereby finally "join the club."

Over my career at Rogers I've been involved in a whole series of campaigns, and the basic thrust of every one of them has been to grow the company. I realized early on that, although Ted had countless objectives, this was his main one. I too always liked the idea of growing the company, and the Sportsnet story is one of those examples.

After that first NHL deal, a whole bunch of interesting dominoes fell that ultimately gave Rogers 100 percent of Sportsnet, which is now in about 12 million Canadian homes and holds a far bigger viewership than TSN. Those dominoes included Bell's $2.3 billion purchase of CTV Inc., which also owned TSN, in February 2000. This had two major ramifications for Rogers generally and Sportsnet specifically.

The first came later that year, when the CRTC approved the CTV takeover but told Bell it would have to divest one of its sports networks. The choice was obvious: TSN was a powerhouse, Sportsnet was a fledgling network. We'd already been granted approval to buy Molson's stake, so with 40 percent ownership, we were the obvious buyer of CTV's shares. Second, and even more importantly, with Bell now owning specialty channels and the CTV network while also owning a satellite TV company and having plans for wireline TV delivery to the home, the CRTC could no longer block cable operators from controlling specialty channels. After all, Bell was a BDU (Broadcast Distribution Undertaking), just like cable.

The headline for *The Globe and Mail*'s lead editorial on September 6, 2000, said it all: "Playing ball on a level field: Cable

giant Rogers deserves same rules as telephone competitor BCE."
And that forced the CRTC to allow us to pick up CTV's stake—and
control—of Sportsnet.

This was the dawn of an important new era for Canadian
television. Two decades after U.S. cable could move into programming, Canadian cable could finally own and operate specialty
channels and TV networks. Today, Rogers owns the OMNI and
City TV networks as well as specialty channels WWE, FX, FXX,
OLN, Sportsnet, Sportsnet360, Sportsnet World, and Sportsnet
One. In September 2018, I was honoured to be an inaugural
inductee into the Sportsnet Hall of Fame.

———————————

It's worth noting the August 2010 launch of our new Sportsnet
One channel because of the strain it put on my friendship with
Paul Beeston. A year earlier, in 2009, Tony Viner and I had con-
vinced Paul to take on a second term as president of the Toronto
Blue Jays. He accepted on an interim basis, but it was our fervent
hope that he'd stay longer, which fortunately he did.

When Sportsnet One launched we needed some relevant content to attract customers, and so we decided to air a few dozen
Blue Jays games on the new channel for a couple of years. (Most
games remained on the regular Sportsnet, but some were shifted
over.) This really pissed off Blue Jays fans, who couldn't watch
those games without getting a digital set-top box and paying for
the new premium Sportsnet One service. They'd call Paul Beeston
and the Blue Jays and scream bloody murder that this was no way
to treat their loyal fans.

Well, Paul was getting more and more angry at me and the
rest of us at Rogers for making him look like the bad guy. He'd call

and holler at me to put all the Jays games back on the regular Sportsnet. "But Paul," I'd say, "there's a really important British darts tournament on tonight that Sportsnet needs to carry, and next week there's a highly anticipated tractor pull, so that's why the Jays have to go on Sportsnet One."

He knew it was all bullshit, of course, and I think he even kind of understood that we needed to do it in order to push the digital set-top boxes. Today we laugh about it, but back in 2010 and 2011, Paul didn't find it funny. It's all a moot point now, given that Jays fans either have Sportsnet One or stream the game to their phones and tablets. When the odd game is shown on Sportsnet One today, few if any complain.

Ted's terrific successor as Rogers CEO, Nadir Mohamed, tells another story about Paul Beeston and the Sportsnet One launch. Before the final game of the 2010 season—and a month after the launch—the club was honouring retiring manager Cito Gaston, who'd led the Jays to two World Series. It was a big deal; former star players and other dignitaries would be on the field with Cito, giving him gifts and tributes. "I thought I should be there representing ownership," Nadir says. "Three times Paul called me asking if I was sure I wanted to attend. Each time I said yes." After Nadir confirmed his attendance for the third time, there was a pause. "You know you're going to get booed because of Sportsnet One," Paul remarked. Nadir knew that Paul didn't want anything spoiling the tribute for his friend Cito.

But Nadir did attend, receiving only a smattering of boos, and the emotional event went off without a hitch.

Returning to the early days of the original Sportsnet, a few years after that first NHL contract expired, we let TSN get the national NHL rights back and concentrated on regional rights.

Then, in late 2013, we really shook things up again with a 12-year, $5.2 billion agreement giving Rogers the national rights on all platforms to NHL games through the 2025–26 campaign— including all playoff games and the Stanley Cup Final.

Ted had died five years before this, so a lot of credit goes to Rogers CEO Nadir Mohamed (who would soon leave the company), along with Rogers Media president Keith Pelley and Sportsnet president Scott Moore. Of course, there's a back story to this NHL agreement as well.

Pelley and Moore had negotiated with the NHL with a proviso: if you like this deal, take it, but if you want to negotiate with TSN or anyone else, then the deal is withdrawn. By the time Bell president and CEO George Cope heard what was going on, it was too late. Cope phoned Gary Bettman and offered him more than our $5.2 billion. But Bettman, with his long history with Rogers, was true to his word, telling Cope that the NHL already had a deal with us.

There was another dimension to Bettman's decision as well: senior executives at Bell had made the mistake, for whatever reason, of marginalizing Rick Brace, who in 1984 had played a key role in starting TSN but in 2013 was shuffled over as Bell Media's head of specialty channels and CTV production. Now, Rick is well known and liked at the NHL. Bettman and deputy commissioner Bill Daly no doubt had a level of trust and comfort with Rick that they didn't have with his successor at TSN. To close the loop, when Pelley left in 2015 to run the European PGA Tour, we scooped up Rick Brace to replace him as president of Rogers Media.

As for Bettman, in 2018 he celebrated his twenty-fifth anniversary as NHL commissioner. I believe he too often gets a bum rap from Canadian hockey fans, who blame him for the three lockouts during his tenure and for disrespecting Canadian franchises by favouring American franchises in the U.S. Sunbelt. But to me, Gary Bettman has been good for the game and good as his word.

There are many other sports stories involving Rogers, but I'll limit it to just one more here: the story behind the NFL Sunday Ticket.

Today, with new technologies and on-demand viewing across numerous platforms, the NFL Sunday Ticket may not seem like a big deal, but back in its day it was a very, very big deal. And I'm proud that Rogers was the cable operator to land it and bring it to Canada. This may be a slight exaggeration, but Sunday Ticket was like crack for the diehard NFL fan. It forever changed how some fans watched the game.

On June 1, 1994, the NFL announced a deal with DirecTV satellite service to provide fans with the NFL Sunday Ticket— meaning that those with direct-to-home DirecTV dishes could now watch whichever NFL games they wanted. It was a boon for bettors and diehard fans alike who wanted to follow their favourite team's every minute of action. Bar and restaurant owners loved it, too, because they were attracting more patrons and increasing beer-and-wings sales.

The shackles that had bound fans to watching "local games"— even if their favourite team was playing on the other side of the country—were suddenly released. Meanwhile, U.S. cable had no means to fight back, since the deal south of the border was exclusive to DirecTV. (Of course, the exponential demand for high-speed Internet would soon more than make up for any U.S. cable losses to DirecTV.)

And there was spillover into Canada. With the CFL waning and the NFL waxing in much of the country, the NFL had become an increasingly attractive form of programming—meaning that the deal had major implications for Canadian cable.

Technically, DirecTV was available only to U.S. customers, but a "grey market" was growing fast in Canada for customers who wanted the satellite service; its receivers were so small that they could be placed on a home's roof or hooked to an outside wall or apartment balcony. These pizza-sized dishes were a threat to Canadian cable and to the Canadian broadcasting system in general. And Sunday Ticket was a catalyst for increasing grey-market sales.

What to do? If you can't beat 'em, join 'em. I was bound and determined to get NFL Sunday Ticket for Rogers so that we could offer it to our customers, too. This is a story untold until now.

It seemed an impossible task, but Missy Goerner and I started meeting with the NFL to try to find a way. To us it was simple: the options in Canada were satellite or cable. Back then, in the mid-1990s, the licensed Canadian satellite companies were new and puny, hardly attractive to the NFL. And we offered cable.

We worked with the NFL for months trying to explain how they could realize significant revenue from Canada—how they could have their cake and eat it too. Our foray on this score yielded some positive results, but after a while we recognized significant opposition within the league. We couldn't convince Neil Austrian, the NFL's president and COO, nor Phil Hochberg, an NFL lawyer in Washington, D.C., who until that time had worked on many U.S. files for us at Rogers. I considered him a close associate, and indeed a friend. Austrian and Hochberg felt that the major problem with selling the rights in Canada to Rogers was that DirecTV wouldn't like it—they'd view it as some sort of back-door entry for U.S. cable to get Sunday Ticket.

So we were at a bit of a standstill when John H. Tory—CFL commissioner at the time and a Rogers loyalist through and through—suggested we talk to Pat Bowlen, the Denver Broncos owner who'd recently succeeded my friend Art Modell as chairman of the NFL's TV committee. Born in Wisconsin, Bowlen knew Canada after making his fortune in Alberta oil, and his wife, Annabel, had been born and raised in Edmonton. As fate would have it, the 1997 Grey Cup was about to be held in Edmonton, and both Pat and Annabel Bowlen would be attending.

I headed to Edmonton on a mission. During Grey Cup week, John Tory had me seated beside Pat Bowlen at a dinner—and so I was able to explain to him how Rogers getting NFL Sunday Ticket would make sense for both of us. He told me to leave it with him, and that he'd get other owners on board.

Now, over the preceding two and a half years there'd been a number of false starts on this file, so I wasn't holding my breath. But Bowlen was as good as his word: a few weeks later, NFL commissioner Paul Tagliabue, another fine guy, decided that Rogers could have the rights for NFL Sunday Ticket in Canada.

I regarded it as a huge victory, and told the entire story to the Rogers board. Directors expressed some enthusiasm, but none more than Ted Rogers—again, never a sports fan, but an expert on the business of sport.

Other Canadian cable companies instantly expressed interest, and Missy did a tremendous job of bringing them on board and making the launch a success.

There are a couple of sad postscripts to this story. The first is personal: Pat Bowlen has been stricken with that horrible disease Alzheimer's, which afflicted my mother and took her from us. I wouldn't wish it on my worst enemy, and certainly not on a gracious man like Bowlen, who was too ill to celebrate his beloved Broncos' latest Super Bowl win in February 2016.

The second relates to the business: Sunday Ticket—and the other sports packages Missy lined up with other major sports leagues—had been a tremendous win for Rogers, but that victory was squandered by our marketing people, who refused to recognize its importance.

Now, when you get something that your competitor doesn't have, you hammer that point home again and again. We'd done it in 2008 when we were the first in Canada to offer the iPhone, but we dropped the ball on NFL Sunday Ticket.

Meanwhile, Bell—hysterical about not being able to offer Sunday Ticket to their TV customers—fought it on the basis that we had an exclusive and they didn't. Legal battles ensued for months and months and we won them all, but the marketing department lagged. After several years, Bell did get the rights, and now everyone has these types of sports packages. In my mind, our tremendous success wilted into a mere moderate success.

There is a silver lining, though. Ever the optimist, Ted came up with the idea to bundle all the sports packages together in a Super Sports Pak (SSP), which Missy figured out a way to get all the leagues to agree upon. Today we offer great value, with 3000 to 4000 games per year for $35 a month. Paul Beeston calls it the greatest value in sports.

This behind-the-scenes look at TV sports packages underlines a broader point about Rogers: that it's always trying to get more programming, more choices, and more value for Canadians. And although I regard the creation of SSP as a tremendous achievement, I still feel bad that our marketing people didn't see Sunday Ticket's potential and recognize it as an important differentiator with satellite that it was at the time.

21

The Buffalo Bills in Toronto Series

On February 6, 2008, 24 television camera crews, numerous radio stations, and dozens of print reporters, web writers, and photojournalists from the Greater Toronto Area, western New York, and further afield swelled into the largest-ever sports news conference in Canadian history. Rogers was about to announce the $78 million deal we'd negotiated that would bring the Buffalo Bills to Toronto for one regular-season game per year for five years and a pre-season game every other year.

And by the time the media congregated at Toronto's Rogers Centre, it wasn't even news.

Six days earlier, we'd sent out an official press release: "The Buffalo Bills will play a series of eight games over a five-year period at the Rogers Centre in Toronto beginning in 2008, Bills owner Ralph Wilson announced today in conjunction with Ted and Edward Rogers and Larry Tanenbaum." I was quoted in the release, too: "This is like a dream come true. Canadians love NFL football and this series will let Canadians see the games live in Toronto."

Wilson had presented the plan to the NFL owners for approval three months before, and that story had leaked to the media, too. So it was hardly a scoop, and yet so many media representatives had still shown up to cover the news conference: it was a can't-miss event. Such is the public appetite for the NFL in Canada.

At no time—dating all the way back to the 1950s, when NFL teams made their first appearances north of the border for exhibition games—was anyone as close as we were to getting an NFL team permanently in Canada. And although we played down speculation about this being step one in a master plan to bring the NFL here, that was most certainly my goal, and the goal of Ted Rogers and Maple Leaf Sports & Entertainment chairman Larry Tanenbaum, too. We were tantalizingly close.

Which made our disappointment all the greater when it ultimately didn't happen. When I reflect back on a wonderful career and life, few things disappoint me more than failing to bring an NFL team to Canada. It still really bothers me.

Nonetheless, at the time, getting those Bills games in Toronto represented a significant achievement. It began when, together with a young colleague at Rogers named Adrian Montgomery, we mapped out a plan. Adrian had been a lawyer in our content group when I seconded him for this project. He's personable, energetic, and smart. In fact, he shared many traits with the members of my original U.S. franchising team decades earlier. Like them, he didn't know the players when the game began, but in no time he was carrying the ball down the field with me and helping us get into the end zone with a deal to get Bills games played in Toronto.

As I've said, Ted Rogers was no sports fan, but he was knowledgeable when it came to the business of sport. And he was

100 percent behind the plan to get the Bills here, and to bide our time until the day they'd be for sale.

No doubt, had he lived longer and seen the plan flop, Ted would have called it another "Lind Lemon" or "Phil's Folly," as he loved to do when something didn't immediately take off. And I'll certainly take responsibility for mistakes made at our end. But we also faced obstacles we had no control over. Namely, the Bills were a bad team, and seemingly getting worse each year of the deal. Plus, the NFL often scheduled us lacklustre opponents that produced lousy games, and often toward the end of the season, when Buffalo was completely out of contention.

First, some background. For more than 30 years, others had tried to get an NFL team in Canada. There was Montreal mayor Jean Drapeau and councillor Gerry Snyder leading a charge for that city throughout the late 1960s and 1970s. Toronto, too, saw many attempts from various groups, including one headed by Paul Godfrey—and throughout the 1990s, when several exhibition NFL games were played in the city, then NFL commissioner Paul Tagliabue would routinely muse about what a terrific market Toronto would be for his league.

Then in September 2006, shortly after Tagliabue retired and was succeeded by Roger Goodell, Ted Rogers and Larry Tanenbaum (who happened to be Ted's across-the-street neighbour) announced a partnership to try to bring the NFL to Toronto. "We hope to pursue [a franchise] vigorously as soon as the NFL gives us the word" on expansion, Larry said at that news conference. Everything was pointing toward that inevitability.

The Bills in Toronto Series was a test for us and the Toronto market. It was also a lifeline to help the Bills, or as the Bills spun it, "our franchise's regionalization plan."

Although the NFL shares the massive national TV money, local revenues aren't shared. And Buffalo was a shrinking market, with high unemployment and one of the lowest average family incomes in any NFL market, which was reflected in how much the team could charge for tickets. We were paying almost $10 million per game—double what the team was getting from the gate in Buffalo.

Bills owner Ralph Wilson, who was 89 when we signed the deal, was on record as having declared that after his death his estate would sell the franchise to the highest bidder.

So why all the media at the 2008 news conference? On the one hand, Buffalo and Rochester media were concerned that the team would be heading up the Queen Elizabeth Way and leaving western New York. On the other, Toronto media were thrilled that NFL games were coming to town. There was also speculation that, if we did end up with an NFL team in Toronto down the road, it would spell the end of the Canadian Football League, which by this point wasn't much of anything east of Manitoba.

Before the news conference, I advised Ted to tone things down and make no reference to any permanent NFL franchise in Toronto. What we'd just achieved was exciting enough: our research had indicated that sports fans were hungry for the NFL in Toronto, and that going to these games would be a hot ticket. This really pumped Ted's tires. So as we headed down to the Rogers Centre, he was in an "I've just conquered the world" mood, and there was no stopping him.

Ted was especially revelling in the fact that people had to buy all their tickets up front for games five years down the road against unknown opponents. This was a decision he alone made. I thought it was absolutely nuts asking people to fork over a few thousand dollars in advance, and I'd argued and argued against it.

But Ted couldn't be swayed. He just did not understand how the average fan would react to such a proposal.

We'd done our research and had found that professional sports fans in southern Ontario preferred the NFL over the CFL brand of football. And in doing the math, we knew that paying almost $10 million per game meant that the average ticket price had to be $175 just to break even. And so at the news conference, I made a point of telling reporters that not all ticket prices would be exorbitant.

This is how Stephen Brunt of *The Globe and Mail* reported an exchange between Ted and me on the ticket price issue:

> "There will be some tickets priced under $100 (Canadian) for the game," Rogers lieutenant Lind said.
> "Two of them," Rogers interjected.

The news conference went from bad to worse when Ted started gloating about how taxpayers had paid for Toronto's domed stadium but that he'd ended up buying it for a song. "It cost other people $600 million to build it ... and we salute them today. We paid $25 million for it," Ted said.

As Brunt suggested, "All that was missing was a knee-slapper about reverse billing." Thankfully, Brunt didn't use the phrase "negative option" billing, a term that drove Rogers customers crazy. Our corporate culture had become much more customer-focused and less arrogant toward subscribers since the negative option disaster 14 years before, but at this epic news conference, Ted was putting at risk the softer corporate image we'd all worked so hard to cultivate.

And after the news conference, plenty of voices—from CFL commissioner Mark Cohon to Senator Larry Campbell of British

Columbia—were ringing the protectionism bell. Campbell even brought a bill to the Senate floor calling for a ban on the NFL in Canada. And B.C. Lions' David Braley went so far as to suggest that western Canadians would boycott Rogers wireless phones if we brought the NFL to Toronto. As sports journalist Sean Fitz-Gerald wrote, "To many, that possibility looms like a guillotine over the Canadian Football League. They see the NFL as a vacuum, sucking up corporate money, television viewers and fans."

It was all a bunch of noise, but admittedly, I got caught up in it. As a result, I came off sounding a little too confident when I told the *National Post* in June 2008:

> In Southern Ontario, this is NFL territory. The CFL's great, wonderful, terrific, but this territory is NFL territory, at least if you're 50 and under. If you're older, fine, you can go for the Argos or Hamilton or whatever....
>
> The reason Toronto hasn't gotten a team is because Toronto hasn't come even close to getting a team until this latest move. It's great to say hello to the [NFL's] owners and everything like that, but there wasn't a deal on the table. There hasn't been a deal. And there isn't a deal now—but some people have argued there's a possibility of a deal now.

The *Post*'s 3000-word article, entitled "A cultural icon at stake," presented both sides of the debate over the NFL coming to Canada. The sheer investment of that much space underlines just how hot the issue was.

The first regular-season Buffalo Bills game in Toronto was on December 7, 2008—just five days after Ted Rogers's death—when they played their arch rival, the Miami Dolphins.

December 7 is Pearl Harbor Day in the U.S., so maybe this foreshadowed the torpedoing of our plan. Tickets didn't sell as well as we'd thought, and there were as many fans in Miami teal as there were in Buffalo blue. Some Miami fans even booed the Bills when they took the field.

As the Bills in Toronto Series would prove, southern Ontario may prefer the NFL to the CFL, but fans cheered for different NFL teams. Or, as Bills president Russ Brandon wisely said after that very first game, "This is a very good NFL market, but not a Bills market yet."

Indeed, Toronto simply wouldn't embrace the Bills. Although we slashed ticket prices, attendance remained sluggish. It never became the hot-ticket event we'd expected. To make matters worse, a few Buffalo players began complaining about giving up their home field advantage by coming to Toronto, especially in December, when they played indoors at Ralph Wilson Stadium in Orchard Park, New York, instead of in the snow and cold. And when the Bills had a 1–6 record in their regular-season games played in Toronto, more and more fans booed.

In January 2013 we extended the series. "Ticket prices will remain consistent with last season's game, with more than 60% of tickets less than $100," our joint news release declared.

Then, when Ralph Wilson died in March 2014, Ted's son Edward and Larry Tanenbaum teamed with Jon Bon Jovi to submit a bid to purchase the team. Reports surfaced later that Donald Trump had also been interested in bidding, and that he'd been behind a grassroots campaign, called the 12th Man Thunder, that tapped into anxiety about the team's possibly moving to Toronto. "He wanted to be the hometown favorite because he would keep the Bills in Buffalo," Michael Caputo, a Buffalo public relations consultant who would go on to work on Trump's presidential campaign, told the Associated Press in November 2017. "It was always his intention to come in here on a white horse and save the team."

But none of it ended up mattering. Buffalo Sabres owners Terry and Kim Pegula topped everyone with a bid of US$1.4 billion and kept the Bills in Buffalo.

On December 3, 2014, the Toronto Series was officially cancelled. With so much fanfare leading up to the series, it all faded away relatively quietly. For me, the agonizing disappointment still lingers. But as a lifelong Cleveland Browns fan, disappointment is nothing new.

As an addendum to this story, I've kept in touch with Ralph Wilson's remarkable widow, Mary Wilson. Still a devoted Bills fan, Mary has a box at New Era Field, formerly Ralph Wilson Stadium, and each season she and I get together for a game. Mary and Ralph were both devoted tennis players, and in the 1980s and early 1990s they'd spend summers in Europe winning age-group mixed doubles titles before returning to their Michigan home and travelling to watch their beloved Bills.

Physical activity was important to Ralph, and is still really important to Mary. Using most of the proceeds from the sale of the Bills, Mary and the Ralph C. Wilson, Jr. Foundation are in the process of giving away $1.2 billion to improve the quality of life for so many people in both southeastern Michigan and western New York. The foundation gives to many organizations aimed at getting people more physically active, especially in the battle against childhood obesity. What a terrific legacy for Ralph.

22

The Brand and Other Battles

The so-called "negative option," introduced in late 1994, was likely the lowest point for Rogers Communications, and would profoundly change our company. It's a good time to go into more detail on that, because it ultimately led to two major disputes between Ted Rogers and me.

The negative option worked this way: we tied the launch of new Canadian specialty channels to popular existing services, and if customers didn't want the new service, they could lose an existing service. Plus, the onus was on the customer to call us to cancel; otherwise, the new charges would appear on their bills.

Customers grew livid when they found out that they could lose popular channels like CNN and A&E if they didn't pay for Canadian channels they didn't want. The media had a heyday with us. There was story after story, day after day, about Rogers stuffing unwanted programming down people's throats. The *Toronto Star* was particularly relentless in attacking us in its business and entertainment sections daily and on the front page multiple times per week.

Where it got really nasty, though, was Vancouver and the lower mainland. During the early to mid-1990s, we'd grown tremendously there—first with the 1990 purchase of Western Cablevision Ltd., and then by swapping our minority ownership in kids' channel YTV for other small systems in the lower mainland. And after paying $84 million to Shaw Communications, we got back cable subscribers in North and West Vancouver. This really gave us heft in the area, adding to the base we'd acquired from the 1980 Premier cable takeover. But while the West Coast is known for its laid-back lifestyle, it was anything but when it came to the negative option.

A few people were pelting rocks at our red Rogers Cable trucks. Even our video stores were under pressure, and started posting signs in their windows saying that they weren't connected with Rogers Cable. Luckily, none of our employees were seriously hurt, but many were very nervous, and I couldn't blame them. "The anger was intense," Jan Innes recalls. "I'd been doing public relations in politics and the corporate world for 15 years, and I had never seen anything like it."

After a couple of months of this PR calamity, Ted finally relented and sent Colin Watson to Vancouver to give his famous mea culpa news conference. And if there was anything humorous at all during this period, it was Colin at that news conference. He was uncomfortable, to say the least. We used to tease him that he looked like Richard Nixon at the president's famous "I'm not a crook" press briefing.

No question, it was a marketing disaster, and the buck stopped with Ted Rogers. But two important things should be clarified.

First, the CRTC remained quiet—as did shrewd cable operators like Shaw—but the Commission played a significant behind-the-scenes role in the story. The CRTC's general view was that the new services needed a fixed amount of money each year to fulfill their business plans, which had been approved by the Commission. This meant that if the new services struggled and achieved only low penetration into Canadian homes, we'd face regulatory pressure to pay the programmers a higher wholesale fee per subscriber. In other words, it was a sort of nudge-nudge, wink-wink from the Commission to link these new Canadian services to popular existing channels and boost penetration levels. So they were kind of onside with this plan. Still, in trying to promote Canadian programming and ensure the long-term success of new Canadian specialty channels, we forgot about the customer. It was a huge mistake.

Second, the repercussions on the company were profound, and continue to this day.

The first big battle between Ted and me that the negative option sparked came when he insisted on changing the name of the company. This occurred almost immediately after we apologized and told customers that we wouldn't link the new Canadian services to existing services, nor would we bill them unless they asked for the new channels.

In early 1995 we were doing pretty intense market research to measure how broad and how deep the damage was to the Rogers brand. And each market research firm report we saw seemed to be worse than the one before. Our image was particularly bad in western Canada. The Rogers brand was one of innovation along with strong technical and programming services. Now, all that meant nothing. We'd have these meetings where researchers would come in with charts and screens, layering bad news on top of bad news. Ted would seethe, and sometimes he'd even storm out before the presentation was complete.

One day, he told me that the Rogers brand was so damaged that he was going to change the name of the company to Cantel, the brand of our wireless phones at the time. The Rogers name, he said, would be dropped and cease to be linked to the Cantel brand. Every platform would be renamed Cantel—phones, cable, business networks, video stores, and media.

I was aghast. It was such a bad idea. We had a lot of brand equity tied to the Rogers name, and most importantly, that name meant everything to Ted. After all, this was the guy whose father had died young, causing the family to lose the Rogers radio company, and from the age of five Ted had dreamed of getting it back. It made no sense to toss the name away after everything he'd achieved over the previous 35 years. No sense at all. Rogers had been such a proud name.

I just could not let him make such an immense mistake, but I also knew Ted well enough to know that you couldn't change his mind with mere opinion. You needed hard data and logical argument.

So Jan Innes and I kept compiling research, measuring and weighing the brand equity against the damage done. We had focus group after focus group telling us what they thought. And we kept stalling Ted, telling him to give it another month or two and we'd see what the market research said then. We also had our ad agency, Garneau Wurstlin Philp, come up with new ideas to boost the brand, including the now-familiar Rogers tag, that *ba-ba-boom* sound at the end of radio and TV commercials.

We'd have meetings with Ted where we'd present him with all sorts of brand-enhancing ideas, complete with audiovisual demonstrations. But Ted was determined, and I started to worry that he'd make the name-change announcement at the next quarterly call with financial analysts.

Luckily, he didn't go public. We dragged out the issue long enough that Ted finally decided not to do it. It was a major battle, but it was a finesse battle. Although I don't remember a lot of yelling and haranguing between us, it was certainly a fight that many days I thought I could lose.

The rock-throwing incidents in Vancouver pissed Ted off and stuck in his craw for a long, long time. To have a city rise up against us like that was something he couldn't comprehend, nor could he forgive the people there. Even if there had been good reason for it. And not only that, Ted was never totally comfortable in western Canada, kind of like how he'd felt in the United States. He just didn't have strong ties to either place in the way I did.

The second big battle with Ted began in 2000, about five years after the negative option, when an opportunity arose to trade cable assets with Shaw. Ted jumped at the offer. He was getting very concerned about Shaw's buying up of cable systems around our core holdings in the Greater Toronto Area. And, still smarting over the negative option shenanigans in Vancouver, he was more than willing to pull out of B.C. The problem, though, was that he'd be trading top-end cable systems across the lower mainland for some mid-tier systems in Ontario and subpar systems in New Brunswick.

So I was absolutely opposed to the trade, and argued as forcefully as possible that Vancouver was a key urban centre with high growth potential, especially with money flowing in from Hong Kong (which had moved under mainland China's control in 1997, after the 99-year British lease expired). Lots of money was moving into Vancouver's lower mainland from elsewhere, too. But at that point I was only two years removed from my stroke, and I just couldn't get Ted to recognize the downsides in vacating B.C. I could definitely see the logic of consolidating around the GTA, as Ted argued, but a footprint in western Canada outweighed that—especially with wireless phone growth exploding.

I mentioned earlier that over all my years working with Ted, we had only four big disagreements. And this losing battle to convince him to keep Vancouver, the second of two that stemmed from the negative option, was the only one of the four that happened after my stroke. Ted was brilliant most of the time, but in my opinion, Jim Shaw got the better of him on that deal.

Ten years after the swap, in 2009, new Rogers CEO Nadir Mohamed lamented the weakened Rogers brand in British Columbia. And Nadir, who'd worked for Telus in Vancouver years before, was aware of my love for B.C. and my long list of friends and contacts in the West Coast. So he asked wireless president Rob Bruce and wireless marketing officer John Boynton to talk to me about somehow acquiring a signature piece in the province to help grow our brand awareness there.

Off I went to Vancouver. There I met with Francesco Aquilini, eldest son in the family that owns the Canucks NHL hockey team and, more importantly for Rogers, its arena. We hit it off immediately, and I quickly got to know his brothers, Paolo and Roberto, and their father, Luigi, who has a true rags-to-riches story.

Luigi had come to Canada in the 1950s—penniless, without a word of English, and with only a Grade 5 education. Starting out in construction, he worked 16-hour days, and probably still works longer hours than most people half his age. Today Luigi's family enterprises employ 10,000 Canadians from coast to coast in real estate, financial services, entertainment, and more. And the Aquilinis are one of the most generous philanthropic families on the West Coast, giving tens of millions to hospitals, schools, and Indigenous charities.

When I first met the family, the Canucks arena was called GM Place and was under contract until 2015, but back in 2009, GM was in financial trouble. Francesco—who remains a good friend still—was happy to reduce GM's sponsorship to in-arena advertising, and the automaker agreed. Francesco then sold us the naming rights for a 10-year period.

And so, ever since the 2010–11 hockey season, the Canucks have played in the Rogers Arena, which has helped immensely with brand awareness in the area.

Nonetheless, I'm convinced that pulling Rogers Cable out of B.C. in 2000 is the reason Rogers—with the highest wireless market share nationally at around 33 percent—trails Telus on the West Coast.

The third major disagreement I had with Ted was selling the U.S. cable assets, which we've already explored. The fourth and final one occurred in 1992, when we were invested in Unitel Communications, and was over the selection of an American long-distance partner.

To me, the obvious choice was to partner with AT&T and their platinum brand. But Ted had other ideas. He and I had just been to Kansas to visit Sprint's Overland Park headquarters and meet top executives. They wooed and flattered Ted, but I had my bullshit detector up, and I didn't like what I smelled.

On the flight home, Ted was going on about how Sprint was entrepreneurial, just like us, and so would make a great partner. I pointed out that it had been only two months since we'd won the long-distance competition battle at the CRTC, and we weren't even up and running for the public yet. We needed legitimacy in the eyes of Canadians, and AT&T would give that to us instantly. Our Unitel partner, Canadian Pacific, also favoured AT&T.

"Besides," I said, "Bell hooking up with MCI must have really pissed AT&T off, and they'll be keen to inflict damage on both MCI and Bell." (In the summer of 1992, Bell and its partners in the Stentor Alliance of local monopoly phone companies surprised everyone by partnering with MCI Communications Corp. Unitel had been in talks with MCI until they called it off and partnered with Bell, which had had decades of business ties with AT&T.)

But Ted was still enamoured, and the Sprint–Unitel "preliminary talks" progressed into September. We were candid in telling Sprint that we were talking to other carriers too, and said we'd get back to them by the end of November.

Around early October, at a Rogers board meeting, Ted threw me for a loop by moving a motion that we partner with Sprint. I couldn't believe it, and looked over at the chairman, Gar Emerson, expecting him to say something. After all, through Gar's investment firm Rothschild Canada Inc., he'd done work for Canadian Pacific. (As Lawrence Surtees writes in *Wire Wars*, "Emerson had been involved in most of the major mergers and acquisitions of the

1980s and had acted for Canadian Pacific in its purchase of voting control of Laidlaw Transportation Ltd.," adding that CP chairman Bill Stinson had retained Rothschild "to act as CP's investment banker in its tripartite talks with Rogers and AT&T.")

When Gar stayed silent on Ted's motion, I spoke up. And for the next 10 minutes I argued against Ted's Sprint idea. The board ended up voting the motion down. Then, in mid-October, Unitel and AT&T entered serious and lengthy negotiations.

In January 1993, we reached an agreement with AT&T. Our partnership with them wasn't perfect, but AT&T's deep financial pockets made it a heck of a lot better than if we'd followed Ted and lined up with Sprint.

Of those four disputes between Ted and me, I won the AT&T partnership and the Cantel brand change, and lost U.S. cable and Vancouver cable, the two in which I knew Ted's mind was made up. With the former two, I was able to change Ted's mind— and he never held it against me for doing so, including in front of the board of directors of his company. I think that speaks highly of his leadership qualities.

Actually, there was a fifth dispute. Both Colin Watson and I— and the entire board, including Ted's wife, Loretta—initially voted against going into Cantel, since we'd been hard pressed by the banks to stop spending. Ted accepted that vote, and invested his own personal money in Cantel at the beginning. Kudos to his foresight there.

The Shaw–Rogers corporate relationship is complex, partly because of the personalities involved and partly because for the last 25 years we've been first and second, respectively, in the rankings of Canada's leading cable companies. We weren't direct competitors (except with Shaw's direct-to-home satellite service), and in many ways we were allies and partners. Still, there was always friction when we did deals. Even if we were both working for the benefit of the cable industry, each side put their company's interests first, and rightly so.

JR Shaw, originally from southwestern Ontario, moved out West in 1961 and got into the cable business with Edmonton's Capital Cable in the late 1960s, around the same time as Ted Rogers started his cable company in Toronto. After a series of financial and regulatory setbacks, in July 1970 Capital Cable finally received a licence to serve half of the Edmonton market by cable, and JR hooked up his first customers the following year.

I made a point of getting to know JR in the mid-1970s, and I count the entire Shaw family as close friends. Right from the start, JR impressed me greatly. You could just tell he was going to be big, unlike most of the ma-and-pa cable operators of the early days.

Like us at Rogers, JR was convinced of the importance of programming. Today, Shaw and its subsidiary, Corus Entertainment, own 39 radio stations, 44 specialty television channels, and 15 conventional television stations, including the Global Television Network.

Over the years, as JR's children entered the company, he made them start at the bottom, installing cable or handling customer complaints. His eldest son, Jim, rose to replace JR as CEO in 1998, a position he held until 2010. Over the course of his reign the company revenue rose from $646 million in 1998 to $3.7 billion in 2010. Jim was a living example of the maxim "The first generation builds it, the second generation grows it, and the third generation blows it." I'm sure the last part won't apply in this case.

Sadly, in January 2018, Jim died at age 60 after a brief illness. "Jim's countless contributions to our company are integral to Shaw's long-term strength and growth as a Canadian industry leader," said his brother Brad, now the CEO, at the time of his passing. "As an operator, a deal maker, and a strategist, Jim continued building the foundation started by our father, JR, to create a Canadian business leader and household brand across western Canada." JR's daughters, Heather and Julie, also work for the family firm. And JR, now 84, remains Shaw's executive chairman. I can't imagine the pain he and Carol, his wife of more than 60 years, went through in losing their eldest son.

Jim's story is both exhilarating and distressing. In the early 1980s he dropped out of the University of Calgary, sold Christmas trees one season, and then went straight into his father's cable business in 1982. He was a real character, with a blustery style that intimidated many people, and yet he'd undoubtedly mastered the art of negotiation. In fact, some in the Rogers organization, including me, thought Jim could prevail even over master negotiators like Ted—which he did in 2000 with the Vancouver cable swap. In the mid-1990s, when I convinced JR to sell us the three Vancouver-area cable systems, Jim was not pleased and told me so. But in only five years he more than made up for it by reacquiring those cable subscribers, and a whole lot more.

Jim had a way of dealing with people that made them think they'd done very well when in reality they hadn't. Such was Jim's style: all guns blazing in business, and a softer side, too. For people he liked, he could not do enough. To him loyalty was everything, so if you were in Jim's good books you could do no wrong. The reverse was true as well. But I will remember him as having a big heart and as a truly good person. He was a great guy.

Since his death, I've thought about our relationship. I'm nine years his dad's junior and 14 years Jim's senior. In a way, he was kind of like a rambunctious kid brother I could never control, nor would I want to try. And I've had some of my most memorable fishing experiences when Jim and JR hosted me at Eagle Pointe Lodge, north of Prince Rupert, B.C.—a spectacular, breathtaking resort that the Shaw family owns. I miss him a lot.

On a personal level, I've counted the Shaws as friends for a very long time; on the business level, it's a little more complicated.

We've worked together on things like CPAC, CCTA, CableLabs, a failed digital streaming service called Shomi, programming funds to help independent Canadian film and television producers, and many other ventures. And in 1994, JR was integral to helping us land Maclean Hunter by swapping assets with Ted instead of entering the fray as a white knight for MH executives.

Still, over the years, we've also had some corporate friction—over things like Shaw Direct, the direct-to-home satellite service with almost one million subscribers, some of whom were Rogers customers, and deals that have been far more favourable to Shaw than to Rogers. Sometimes I was a conduit between Jim and Ted, just as I'd been between JR and Ted. Ted had a great affection for the Shaws and it was mutual, but JR and Jim were two of the very few people who could rattle him, especially during negotiations.

Having said that, we've had lots of corporate fun with them, too. In the late 1990s, Jim and Ted bet a steak dinner on which company would reach one million high-speed Internet users first. After Shaw won, Ted sent a 900-pound steer to Jim's downtown Calgary home, dropping manure all over the front lawn. It was a classic Ted move. Not to be outdone, some months later Jim had a 2000-pound iron sculpture of a bull, by famed sculptor Joe Fafard, delivered and placed in the middle of Ted's office while our board meeting was taking place. When Ted returned to his office, he saw a note attached: "You see Shaw for the beef and Rogers for the bull." Ted loved both those pranks. He had the iron bull moved from his office, but for a decade or more he kept it prominently on display on the executive floor of Rogers's corporate offices.

23

Art and the Beauty of British Columbia

As a young UBC student in the 1960s, I fell in love with art and the city of Vancouver. One day I wandered into the campus gallery and encountered a challenging work: called *Bagged Place*, by Iain Baxter and his then wife, Ingrid, it was made up of a series of rooms in which all the household items were encased in clear plastic bags. It was the most unusual thing I'd ever seen. And it marked the beginning of a personal journey into both contemporary art and my fascination with Vancouver and the entire province of British Columbia. That afternoon, I stood in the gallery pondering *Bagged Place* for a very long time. Even though I knew nothing about contemporary art at the time, I saw in Iain's work a talent that was unexplainable. His work made me think in new and different ways.

Iain would inspire and influence many Vancouver contemporary and photoconceptual artists. Indeed, the city is alive with a number of internationally renowned artists, among them Jeff Wall, Rodney Graham, Stan Douglas, Ian Wallace, and Geoffrey Farmer. Jeff Wall and Stan Douglas have both won the prestigious Hasselblad Award, an international photography prize handed out each year in Sweden. It's a very big deal in the international arts community.

I believe in contemporary art and the role it plays in society. I believe that through art audiences can engage with the experience of citizenship and gain knowledge and ideas that build and enlighten. Art gives us a way to think in new ways about the world in which we live.

Marshall McLuhan believed that artists are the best predictors of the future, and that contemporary art helps us think about ways to anticipate that future. I know it gives me great joy and happiness.

Contemporary artists are themselves interesting and multidimensional personalities. Their work can be interpreted in a number of different ways, and I find that conversations with them are often captivating. "My father is fascinated with artists, not just their art," says Jed Lind, a multimedia artist in Los Angeles with an MFA from CalArts (California Institute of the Arts) in Santa Clara. "He's intrigued by what makes them tick, their struggles, their successes. He's most fascinated by those at the top of their game."

Over the years, many have helped with my personal journey into the world of contemporary art, perhaps none more than Jeannie Parkin. Jeannie is a dynamo. Now into her nineties (though no one but she knows her exact age), she's vibrant, energetic, incredibly knowledgeable, and as hip as ever. And Jeannie, one of the first to recognize the genius of Andy Warhol, has advised me more than once on what to buy, and perhaps more importantly, what not to buy.

My collection includes works by Greg Curnoe, who in 1992, at the age of 55, died tragically when a distracted pickup driver plowed into him while he was cycling. Greg, who was from London, Ontario, was an interesting guy whom I was introduced to in the early 1970s by my dad's old pal Jake Moore of Labatt. He was also one of the artists who had a tremendous influence on me when I first became interested in Canadian art. Greg's work seemed to express so much more than what could be put into words. His sentiments just seemed to soar in the air. I was so impressed.

And I never let his political views get in the way of my fondness for his work. Greg was an ardent Canadian nationalist, or, more precisely, he was fervently anti-American. Greg thought that almost everything American was to be feared. I'm definitely not that way at all; I continue to be fascinated by America (yet disgusted by some of the current goings-on).

But I do think that the spirit of expressing oneself as being a Canadian is just as relevant today as it was when Greg was doing his thing. It's vital for Canada that this expression takes place. Greg's death meant that Canada lost not only a terrific artist but also one whose living talents could have inspired and taught others for 20 or 30 years more. (A discussion with Greg today about Trump's America would surely be entertaining, too.)

Speaking of America and my art collection, a few years ago I got a call from the wife of David Jacobson, the former U.S. ambassador to Canada. David and I first met in 2009 at a Bills game in Toronto. We share many interests, but especially sports and politics, including our admiration for his former boss, Barack Obama. I became close friends with David and his wife, Julie, and sometimes when I had to stay in Ottawa overnight I'd stay at their official residence. Anyway, Julie called to tell me that friends of theirs were coming to Toronto to visit art galleries, and were looking for an interesting private collection to see as well. These people were on the board of the Georgia O'Keeffe Museum in Sante Fe, New Mexico, where Julie and David have a home. O'Keeffe was, of course, one of the most significant artists of the twentieth century.

Julie asked for a Saturday evening art tour of my place, and that was fine with me. It was all arranged. The only possible wrinkle was that I'd be returning from Europe that day, but I expected to be home by two p.m. When the day came, though, my flight to Toronto was cancelled. As soon as I got the news of the cancellation I called David. "I kind of freaked out because we had 50 people coming to Phil's place," David Jacobson says. "But in typical Phil fashion he figured it out. His assistant, Michelle Cha, would be there and would look after the caterer, and Michelle and I hosted in his place. Phil solves problems."

My involvement in the contemporary art world goes beyond collecting. In Toronto, I'm on the Art Gallery of Ontario's board of trustees and serve as chairman of its Modern Contemporary Acquisition Committee. The AGO is important to me—as the most significant platform for art in this country, it's a national treasure. Its new director Stephen Jost is terrific, as is Kitty Scott, AGO's Contemporary Curator. As well, since its inception in 1987, I've been involved with the Power Plant Contemporary Art Gallery at Toronto's Harbourfront, including serving as board chairman.

I also have great admiration for the Albright-Knox Art Gallery in Buffalo and the team under current director Janne Siren, and serve as a director of the Canadian foundation that undertakes projects and promotes awareness of the museum's collection here.

In western Canada, I'm on the board of trustees at the Vancouver Art Gallery; I'm very fond of Kathleen Bartels, VAG's director. I'm also friends with Reid Shier, director of the fabulous Polygon Gallery in North Vancouver, which opened in November 2017. Major funding for this architecturally stunning waterfront gallery included contributions from the Audain Foundation and Polygon Homes, both established by the local developer and philanthropist Michael Audain, whose support led to the name change from Presentation House Gallery to the Polygon. Together, the Polygon and VAG (which is planning to open a beautiful new building within the next few years) are why the lower mainland is establishing itself as one of the epicentres of contemporary art in North America. "It's a city on the edge, nearer California and away from New York and London," says Kathleen Bartels. "I came from Los Angeles, and Phil has been a mentor to me, someone from whom I often seek advice."

Kathleen organizes exclusive, once-a-year international art tours for gallery donors. Ellen Roland and I have gone together on several of these trips; usually in a group of 10 or 20, we travel to Berlin or London, Chicago or Los Angeles, Tokyo or Hong Kong. In each place the group spends three or four days touring the homes of private local collectors, getting behind-the-scenes tours of local museums, and lunching with prominent players in the local art scene. In the art world you have to earn people's trust in faraway places, and Kathleen certainly does.

During our London tour we visited the studio of sculptor Antony Gormley, whose trademark for the last 20 years has been the male figure. When we visited his studio, I told Gormley that one of his pieces (titled *Antony Gormley*, and made of three large blocks of concrete) sits in my living room. He smiled and said that it had been one of his first major self-portrait sculptures, and that he was so pleased to now know its owner. We were to meet again; as Ellen recounts, "Two years ago, when Antony visited Phil's Toronto apartment, he walked up to the sculpture and put his nose to the head, as they were the same height. Antony was quiet and reflective."

I love attending popular art fairs, like Frieze in London and New York, and Art Basel in Miami Beach. I find these big shows to be a driving force in supporting the role that galleries play in nurturing the careers of their artists. You just never know what you'll find. My friend Richard Stursberg has accompanied me a couple times to Art Basel. "Going to Art Basel with Phil is an experience all on its own," Richard says. "He knows all the dealers and they all know him. He gets lots of attention, and you hear the most thoughtful and marvellous discussions about contemporary art just by tagging along with Phil."

Over the years I've invested a lot in art, not only through my collecting but also by fundraising. Three initiatives deserve mention, as they're aimed specifically at young and aspiring men and women.

The first is the Lind Family Art Fund, which I set up at Upper Canada College after Jed graduated from there in 1997. The beauty of UCC is that it didn't peg him in one place. A guy like Jed could win the art prize and still be a captain of the rugby team. That happened. I appreciated it, and wanted to celebrate it.

Becoming an artist is a 10- to 20-year process, and at UCC kids with interest and talent are at the age where they're entering or just about to enter this lengthy process. And so this project supports student trips to important exhibits in major art centres, including London and New York City; it also helps beef up UCC's art book collection, helps with art room renovations, and helps fund visiting artists.

The second is the Phil Lind Scholarship Fund at CalArts. "Without this scholarship I don't know if I would be able to go to CalArts," the 2017 recipient wrote me. "My family and I are not well off, and my sister and my mom are both getting their master's degrees the same time I am going to school ... I can't thank you enough."

The third is the Philip B. Lind Emerging Artist Prize in British Columbia, which Rogers set up as a retirement gift to me. It was established in 2016 to support young artists working in photography, film, and video. The province's postsecondary visual arts instructors nominate students, and the shortlisted students have their work exhibited as part of the Lind Prize exhibition.

I believe passionately in nurturing new generations of artists. Everyone in society benefits from a strong, vibrant arts community.

Beyond the contemporary art scene, there are so many other reasons I love Vancouver and British Columbia. I knew it right away when I arrived at UBC in the 1960s. The mountains, the natural beauty, and, of course, the fly fishing all combined to make me fall hopelessly in love with the place.

I've gone on countless trips to various places in the province, including Tofino with the Stanfords, Qualicum Beach with the late Harvey Southam and his sisters Martha Lou and Stephanie, up the coast with the late Bob Healey, Prince George with my brother Ron, Prince Rupert with the Shaws, the Bulkley River system with Lindsay Everts and Wade Davis, Haida Gwaii with Steve Macdonald, the Gulf Islands with Kevin Leslie, and the Cowichan River with Peter Hyndman.

B.C. is the most fascinating place in the world to me.

And, over the years, the area has been so important in both my business and personal life, with the two often overlapping. People in business—like Jimmy Pattison, the Aquilinis, Bob Lee and his daughter Carol, and Bob Rennie—have become special friends.

I consider Jimmy Pattison both a good friend and mentor, as did Ted Rogers. I know Ted regretted not asking Jimmy to join the Rogers board because he thought Jimmy was too busy running his multi-billion-dollar enterprises. When Bell scooped him up on their board, Jimmy was so loyal he kept his Rogers phone and received much ribbing for it! I learned so much sitting on the Brookfield board with Jimmy.

Bob Lee, for example, has impressed me in so many ways. He's a real estate developer, and, like Luigi Aquilini, embodies a rags-to-riches story. Bob was born in Vancouver and grew up in Chinatown, where his dad worked days in a greenhouse and evenings in a restaurant to make ends meet. Although we were raised in very different economic classes, Bob and I are similar in that we both struggled in school until we found our passion: the real estate business for him, the communications industry for me. After he graduated from UBC, Bob really capitalized over the years on the many wealthy people leaving Hong Kong for Vancouver. And he's given back to the city time and again, especially to our alma mater. As a founder of UBC Properties Trust, Bob played a pivotal role in the development of housing on the Point Grey campus, which has generated windfall revenues for the university. More importantly, he came up with the idea to lease instead of sell its endowed lands, meaning that the university will earn more money in the decades ahead.

Bob Rennie is Vancouver's "condo king" and owner of his own contemporary art museum in the city. He's also the best and smartest collector of contemporary art in Canada. The thing about Bob is that he's outspoken, opinionated, and often controversial. He can get in hot water with many in the Vancouver arts community, of which I am a member. In one instance of this, he was a vocal opponent of VAG's $350 million expansion to a new downtown site. "Arts and culture has a hard time attracting the big dollars," Bob told *Artnet News* in October 2017. "My suggestion was that the city should sell that piece of land at today's value—a couple hundred million dollars—give the money to the Vancouver Art Gallery, and let them stay on their old site and not have to drain the shallow philanthropic pool here, our government and taxpayers' money. I think we've passed the 'starchitecture' age and it should be about the contents, not the box." I don't always agree with Bob Rennie, but I certainly give him credit for supporting the arts.

I've also had strong relationships with many B.C. premiers over the years, in particular Gordon Campbell, Christy Clark, and Mike Harcourt, who was a chum of mine at UBC back in the 60s. It's not difficult to point to the direct, tangible benefits these friendships have had for Rogers Communications, and having access to premiers on various issues sure helped over the years.

I've mentioned many other lifelong friends and political pals from B.C. elsewhere, but there's one I'd like to single out here. Her name is Cindy Grauer, and I've known her since the 1970s. In fact, Cindy knows virtually everyone in Vancouver, and certainly all the people in politics. She's my political guide in the province.

Two of my longest friendships in B.C. are with Jake Kerr and David Barnhill, both of whom I met on my first day at UBC. Jake is a tremendous guy who's travelled similar paths as my own, socially and in business. He truly belongs to the west coast— Vancouver and San Francisco alike. Together with Jake I attend the Bohemian Grove, the exclusive, 140-year-old retreat that's held each July in Monte Rio, California, and is filled with prominent politicians and business leaders. David was my first roommate; he was tremendously helpful after my stroke, and we travel the world together. And the Canucks' Francesco Aquilini is also a great friend. A true entrepreneur like his dad, Luigi, Francesco lives life to the fullest in B.C.

With all my ties to—and love for—British Columbia, the natural question is, Why don't I just live there? The answer is that my roots are in Ontario. Most of my family and friends are here, and, of course, there's the farm and the mill.

Even though I'm not a permanent resident, I always look forward to my trips to B.C. I'd estimate that, in total, I spend a month or two every year in Vancouver, and always in the same room on the eighteenth floor of the Westin Bayshore. Overlooking Stanley Park, the ships in Coal Harbour, and beyond to the Burrard Inlet, its view is breathtaking, something I always anticipate seeing again and again. My affection for that great province cannot be overstated.

24

Post-Stroke Campaigns and CRTC Chairs

T hree of my favourite campaigns occurred after my stroke, and to be honest, they were a physical struggle at times. A real struggle. But that just made the victories all the sweeter.

One involved increasing programming choices for Italian Canadians and everyone else whose mother tongue wasn't English or French; another involved blocking broadcasters from charging cable to carry their signals; and the third was keeping a giant U.S. wireless company from unfairly entering Canada at the behest of former prime minister Stephen Harper. By comparison, earlier campaigns—Canadian Cablesystems, U.S. franchising, Unitel, and Maclean Hunter—were larger, but these three were important in their own right. Ted Rogers was somewhat disinterested in the first campaign, and he died just as the second one was heating up. So I wasn't only quarterback on these files, but also acted as coach, general manager, and owner.

A more personal reason to tell these stories is simply because they *did* occur after my stroke. The point is not to say "Look at me, look at me," but rather to help those who've suffered a stroke to look at themselves and their situation. There is life after a debilitating stroke. Lots of life. I relearned how to read, write with my other hand, walk, talk, and more. I battled aphasia, and I underwent endless hours of physiotherapy and speech therapy. There were many dark days. But these campaigns are proof that, at the end of the dark tunnel a stroke can bring, there can be life, lots of productive life.

RAI (Radiotelevisione Italiana) is Italy's equivalent to the CBC, a government-owned broadcaster that's filled with news, public affairs, and other terrific programming. In 2003 RAI (pronounced "rye") wanted to come to Canada, and Rogers wanted to offer our customers this new digital channel. After all, more than 500,000 Italian Canadians live in the Greater Toronto Area, the core of Rogers Cable.

The problem was that the existing Italian-Canadian channel, Telelatino (TLN), was Canadian owned, and it wanted to ensure that its primary language, Italian, had an exclusive in Canada. To me, the issue was very simple. In southern Ontario, if you're English Canadian you have hundreds of networks to choose from on our cable system. If you're French Canadian you have several dozen channels. But if you're Italian Canadian, before RAI you had just one. That was the problem right there.

A near-spontaneous grassroots campaign arose. A petition demanding more choice for Italian Canadians gathered 100,000 signatures and was sent to government and the CRTC. Busloads of Italian Canadians from Toronto and Montreal arrived at CRTC headquarters in Gatineau, Quebec, calling for RAI's inclusion in Canada. And these placard-waving protesters—estimated at 1000 to 2000 people—were mostly seniors, which made the network newscasts' visuals even more powerful.

During the two-year campaign I worked closely with Pam Dinsmore and Jan Innes. We would talk to RAI executives in Italy every few days (these were the early days of videoconferencing). We'd map out strategies, and fine-tune the promises we could make to the CRTC to convince commissioners that more third-language programming was needed, and that it wouldn't negatively impact TLN.

But TLN wasn't rolling over. They got some big names on their side, like novelist Nino Ricci and even Robert Fowler, the Canadian ambassador to Italy at the time. (Later, after the whole issue was settled, I very undiplomatically blew up at Fowler at a lunch meeting in Italy in the Ambassador's residence, accusing him of stepping beyond his rightful duties as ambassador by ignoring the wishes of thousands of Italian Canadians.)

We had our supporters, too, including Italy's ambassador to Canada. The giant Columbus Centre—the pre-eminent arts-and-culture destination for Toronto's Italian-Canadian community—organized people to contact politicians and the CRTC. And Toronto's *Corriere Canadese*, the largest daily Italian newspaper in the world outside of Italy, published countless articles and editorials pointing out the unfairness: other international channels like BBC Canada were available, and RAI should be, too. The RAI network itself was, and still is, skilfully managed in Canada by Cristiano De Florentiis, a charismatic Italian who has tremendous social skills.

We got deep into the Italian community, but the campaign was even bigger than Italian programming. Foreign-language programming in general was in high demand, and if it wasn't readily available on TV, consumers (many of them "cable cord cutters") would find it via the Internet. This was a fight to increase programming choices for all Canadians. And it was a bitter battle, very political, reaching right into the Prime Minister's Office.

On May 13, 2005, although the CRTC didn't like it, it finally approved the RAI signal. (But they did have one stipulation that let them claim it wasn't a total victory for RAI: any cable or satellite company wanting to carry it also had to offer TLN.) *Vittoria!*

Few things get me seething like the Canadian television networks' attempted fee-for-carriage cash grab, the so-called "TV tax." After everything cable did to increase their TV licences' value over the years, in 2006 the broadcasters ignited a six-year battle to get us to pay them for carrying their signals. It went all the way to the Supreme Court of Canada, and they came very close to winning.

Just writing this raises my hackles. Ken Engelhart and Jan Innes would joke that fee-for-carriage was my "Wullerton." I had no idea what they meant until I watched an episode of *Corner Gas*, set in the fictional town of Dog River, Saskatchewan. The characters all despised the nearby town of Wullerton for its arrogance. Every time the word "Wullerton" was mentioned, the Dog River people would spit in disgust. "Fee-for-carriage made Phil see red," Ken says. Or as Jan puts it, "You had to be careful even *mentioning* the words fee-for-carriage around Phil." (As it happens, in 2011 UBC awarded its first Phil Lind Multicultural Artist in Residence to Lorne Cardinal, one of the stars of *Corner Gas*. As RCMP Sergeant Davis Quinton, Cardinal was perhaps the most voracious Wullerton spitter in Dog River.)

The fee-for-carriage approach originated in the U.S., but in 2006 Lenny Asper, then CEO of CanWest Global—a company awash in debt of its own making—brought the idea to Canada. And with a new Conservative government threatening budget cuts, the CBC also liked the idea, as did CTV. Then in 2010, when Shaw bought Global, that network stepped back and let CTV— also awash in debt—carry the torch. The CBC was still harping on fee-for-carriage but in a different category, given that it was a publicly funded broadcaster.

All this debt talk sounds funny from someone who works for a company famous for being soaked in it, but at least we figured out our own solutions. And our solutions did not involve others.

In their frantic efforts to claim "We're Number 1" bragging rights and win the ratings game, both Global and CTV had indulged in out-of-control bidding contests for the rights to popular U.S. prime-time programs. They also spent large amounts buying up other media properties. Predictably, both found themselves struggling to meet the profitability levels their investors expected. Then, on top of all that, the 2008 recession began and advertising started to dry up.

So what to do? Naturally, CTV started crying poor all the way to the CRTC, hoping that a tax imposed on their satellite and cable TV subscribers would bail them out. (As I said, Global did the same until 2010.) CTV threatened that without it they might have to shut down local TV stations across the country. Taxing customers, CTV claimed, was the only way to ensure they'd have sufficient cash on hand to meet their commitments. Heaven forbid they take on less debt, rein in their spending, or explore new revenue opportunities. It was so much easier to ask someone else to do it for you.

Depending on where they lived, many Canadians would find themselves facing bill increases of up to $10 per month—$120 a year more—and for what?

Consumers, along with cable and satellite companies, were already making significant and ongoing contributions to CTV, Global, and other television broadcasters' bottom lines. By CRTC order, monthly bills contained a hidden 5 percent consumer tax, money that goes to the Canadian Television Fund and is used to subsidize the cost of making Canadian programs. That amounted to more than $150 million per year.

And, at their own expense, cable and satellite distributors had helped make local broadcasters wealthy by substituting Canadian versions of popular U.S. shows for the original versions transmitted into Canada by U.S. networks like NBC and CBS. Canadian viewers don't get the originals; they see a CTV or Global version complete with Canadian ads—ads that generate the easiest money anyone in the television business has ever made.

Yet, in the case they brought to the CRTC, CTV and Global blithely insisted that they were saviours of Canadian broadcasting. Never mind that they were reneging on their promise to provide their signals free and to produce Canadian programming in exchange for the privilege of receiving an exclusive broadcast licence.

We won the first and second CRTC hearings, but lost the third. In 2010, CRTC chairman Konrad von Finckenstein astonishingly flip-flopped and granted the over-the-air broadcasters the right to charge a fee for their signals. We took the CRTC decision to the Federal Court of Appeal, and then we ended up at the Supreme Court of Canada.

And that's when things got really interesting.

First off, the landscape changed dramatically when Bell bought CTV and Shaw bought Global before the case even got to the Supreme Court. Both Bell (which owns a direct-to-home satellite company) and Shaw (with both cable and satellite) had been vocal anti-tax supporters. I wondered what the networks' position would be now.

To no one's great surprise, Bell suddenly became wildly in favour of the tax. But Shaw, although a little less vocal publicly, stayed with us; they even helped fund our legal challenge. This move by Brad Shaw certainly ensured that Shaw was in the cable camp. It was now Rogers, Shaw, and Cogeco that would be the main cable companies fighting the TV tax. (Vidéotron owned a Quebec network, and so was on the other side too.)

At this point CBC entered the fray as CTV's ally, somewhat negating their loss of Global as a supporter.

So off we went to the Supreme Court. Now, at Rogers we'd pioneered the art of practising for appearances before the CRTC. Before every hearing we'd work long and hard on our rehearsals, anticipating any questions that might be asked and formulating decisive answers. The same would be the case now. We hired two former Supreme Court justices—Michel Bastarache from Quebec and Jack Major from Alberta—who listened to our legal team's arguments, critiqued their performances, and asked penetrating legal questions. Our two main lawyers were Jay Kerr-Wilson, an expert on copyright law who worked with Bob

Buchan, and Neil Finkelstein, one of Canada's best-known lit-
igators, who recently passed away at age 66. We did have
one snag, though: Finkelstein wasn't interested in coming
to the rehearsal. Over his career he'd taken 28 appeals
to Canada's Supreme Court, and didn't feel that practice was
necessary. I had Bob call him and persuade him otherwise.
As Bob recalls, "Finkelstein came, and after the rehearsal
he told me he enjoyed it and found it very helpful."

The case hinged on copyright: specifically, could Canadian
broadcasters legally stop cable and satellite from freely taking
their signals when they didn't hold the copyright to most of their
programming (whether popular U.S. shows or independently
produced Canadian shows)? "I'll never forget the rehearsal that
day," says Jan Innes. "We totally changed how we positioned
our case based on the input from the former judges."

Ken Engelhart recalls that our argument boiled down to this:
"We know the CRTC has the power under the Broadcasting Act,
but because it's copyright, they can't do it. And the other guys
were saying 'Copyright, schmopyright. It's broadcasting and
we've got the power of the Act.'"

The Supreme Court ruled that the CRTC had overstepped its
authority in granting CTV and other companies the right to charge
for their signals because the broadcast regulator does not have the
authority to rule on copyright issues. We won the case, but it had
been touch and go. "As Phil always says, 'When regulators over-
reach, they get slapped down,' and that's what happened here,"
Ken remarks.

The Supreme Court decision was issued on December 13,
2012. Pam Dinsmore and I were celebrating in the office of Rogers
CEO Nadir Mohamed when I introduced a little doubt, cautioning

that the devil is often in the details, and that the decision might contain some legal argument that could lead to the court re-examining the case. "We can't get ahead of ourselves," I said. "We've still got to read the decision."

To which Nadir responded, "Phil, we don't have to read it, *they do!*"

In 2013, halfway through its mandate, Stephen Harper's government was looking tired and bereft of captivating political ideas for the next election. It was then that the Conservative PM wrapped himself in his "Captain Consumer" cape and launched an assault upon Canada's big three wireless phone companies: Rogers, Bell, and Telus. He and his government were going to lower monthly wireless bills for consumers by cracking the cartel. Harper painted us as Russian-style oligopolists who feared increased competition, which was unfair and untrue: genuine and vigorous competition exists between the three.

Nonetheless, in May 2013, Industry Canada officials were dispatched to New York to hold talks with U.S. giant Verizon Wireless, offering enticements like discounted spectrum to help persuade the Americans to set up shop in Canada as the fourth wireless carrier.

We never feared competition. Verizon—or any other huge multinational—could come to Canada. But the rules had to be fair. And Harper was inviting Goliath in and taking the slingshot away from David.

When word of this leaked to Nadir Mohamed, it put Rogers on an immediate war footing. (I'm sure Bell and Telus were, too.) Our own government was helping a foreign company, and one

with annual revenues of $75 billion—more than the market capi-
talization of Rogers, Bell, and Telus put together.

Think about that: Verizon was pulling in more dollars each
year than our combined worth on the public stock market. And
our federal government was courting them in the misguided
view that it would benefit Canadians. At what cost? How many
Canadian jobs would be lost and moved to Verizon's U.S. offices?
(Not to mention that if Verizon entered Canada they'd cherry-pick
the densely populated urban markets and invest nothing in rural
areas, instead riding on the infrastructures Canadians had built.)
Just the talk of it clipped $5 billion off our market caps in one day.

This was not going to happen without a fight, especially given
our history at Rogers. "As campaigns go," says Ken Engelhart,
"on a scale of 1 to 10, this was an 11. Verizon and its sheer enor-
mity made it a gut-churning file."

It's important to step back for a moment. In 1983, Ted Rogers
asked his board of directors for $500,000 to invest in a new technol-
ogy called wireless telephony. Every board member, me included,
voted against the idea as too risky. Even his wife, Loretta, voted
against Ted's idea. Although he controlled the company, Ted
accepted the board's decision; as I mentioned earlier, he instead
put his own money into the first wireless competitor in Canada,
then known as Cantel. Then, some years later when his vision was
borne out, Ted sold his Cantel shares to Rogers Communications
Inc. Today, thanks to Ted's initial risk, Rogers's shareholders,
employees, and Canadian customers from coast to coast all enjoy
the benefits of wireless.

By the time of Harper's attack, Rogers had invested $30 billion
in wireless infrastructure on top of the $500,000 Ted had plunked
down; Bell and Telus had invested similar billions. We receive tax

credits for this, but our companies are still writing the cheques and providing more than 100,000 jobs for Canadians.

But Harper and his government decided to put it all in jeopardy, from Canadian jobs to investment and retirement income, by offering Verizon Wireless spectrum—for which Rogers, Bell, and Telus weren't even allowed to bid—and by allowing Verizon to buy smaller Canadian wireless operators we were prohibited from buying. He was changing the rules, and badly.

We moved to DEFCON 3, not quite all-out war but ready for immediate action. Heidi Bonnell, our fabulously connected government-relations operative in Ottawa, led the charge as we met with Conservative MPs to tell them why this policy was dangerous. And Heidi had a strong relationship with Industry Minister James Moore; she talked to him often, and would fill us in on his thinking. But we found out firsthand that he was as zealous as his boss.

It was quite bizarre. When discussing broadcasting and other matters, Moore went off on a libertarian tangent. But when talk turned to wireless he was the complete opposite, a "central planner," saying that it was incumbent on his government to create a fourth national carrier, by hook or by crook. He simply wouldn't listen to us. And it was clear that you had to buy into every last thing Harper believed in or you'd be out of cabinet. It quickly became apparent that no one in his government was going to stand up to the prime minister on the Verizon file.

Then the PMO got really nasty when it ran advertisements attacking us (ads that, of course, taxpayers paid for). It was ridiculous. We let the government punch us again and again, until finally we said "That's enough. No more."

We moved to DEFCON 2. In the summer of 2013, the CEOs at Rogers, Bell, and Telus appointed internal teams to coordinate a publicity campaign, called Fair for Canada, through which we'd inform as many Canadians as possible about the dangers of Harper's policy. I was head of the Rogers team; Joe Natale (Rogers's current CEO) led the Telus team; and Wade Oosterman led Bell's. Jan Innes, as the fourth member of this tri-party team, coordinated media relations and advertising. Each of the three companies had people reporting to us, and we'd meet weekly, either in person or via conference call, to discuss tactics and overall strategy. We worked extremely well as a team.

The media was the lowest-hanging fruit. Executives and high-profile experts like former communications minister Francis Fox penned opinion pieces supporting us and calling on the government to make the rules fair. We also held news conferences in cities and towns across Canada. Heidi had us out meeting MPs on their own turf in ridings all over the country. Our unions explained the risk to jobs. Investor-relations people talked to telecom analysts about the potential impact. We lobbied the CRTC asking for their support. And we hired an advertising and marketing firm to blast out our messages.

We visited every and any newspaper editorial board who would have us. Our old foes at the *Toronto Star* staunchly supported us when publisher John Cruickshank put his name to an August 21, 2013, editorial entitled "Stephen Harper betrays Canada's interests in telecom fight." Cruickshank went for Harper's jugular: "What do you call a man who betrays the interests of his country for a foreign power? The Americans call him a Benedict Arnold. In Canada, we call him Prime Minister," he began. And it got even more hard-hitting as it went along. We just couldn't believe it. It was wonderful.

Our sights were firmly set upon Ottawa, but we knew that our Fair for Canada campaign would also be heard loud and clear at Verizon headquarters in New York.

Verizon CEO Lowell McAdam must have sensed that an entry into Canada would be no cakewalk. About a week after the *Star* editorial appeared, he told *Bloomberg News* that his company would not be expanding into Canada to buy one or both of Wind Mobile and Mobilicity, two smaller carriers we'd been forbidden from purchasing. McAdam added that public discussion of Verizon's interest in Canada was "way overblown."

In the end, Shaw Communications Inc. bought struggling startup carrier Wind Mobile Corp. in 2015. And in that year's federal election, for the first time in my life, I did not vote Tory.

Over the 50-year history of the CRTC, I've appeared before all 10 chairmen (and two interim chairmen) who preceded the current office holder, Ian Scott, who took over in September 2017. From 1970 to 2014 I had the pleasure of representing Rogers more than 100 times before the Commission. And over that time I've formed some opinions about each chairman, which I'd like to share here. Rightly or wrongly, these are my views—based on watching their performances in setting policy and on reading their decisions.

André Bureau (1983–1989) was the best. He had an analytical approach to issues, and with his legal background he was terrific at striking a fair balance between the interests of industry players and of consumers. He also had a terrific vice-chairman of broadcasting, Fern Bélisle, at his side. The first CRTC chairman, Pierre Juneau (1968–1975), would be a close second to Bureau.

Harry Boyle (1975–1977) and Pierre Camu (1977–1979) were both solid as well. Boyle had actual on-air experience in both the private and public broadcasting sectors, and had a real sense of the problems and opportunities of programmers like me who would appear before him. Camu was a smart businessman who'd come out of the transportation industry. He understood the economic and cultural importance of networks, whether they were rivers, railways, roads, or telecommunications and cable networks.

At the other end of the spectrum were Françoise Bertrand (1996–2001) and Charles Dalfen (2002–2006). I got the sense that Bertrand didn't fully grasp the industry and its myriad issues. Her leadership was also mired in sniping and backroom politics, which found their way into the press. Dalfen, ironically, had been one of the best vice-chairman in CRTC history, but once he got the top job several decades later he got bogged down in the details and in putting his personal stamp on everything. This choked the Commission when it came to carrying out policy and making decisions.

I would place Keith Spicer (1990–1996), Konrad von Finckenstein (2007–2012), and Jean-Pierre Blais (2012–2017) in the "grandstander" category. Each one seemed more concerned with newspaper headlines and positive coverage on the nightly news than with getting the policy right.

John Meisel (1980–1983), an erudite and gracious man who's now well into his nineties, was a Queen's University professor when Joe Clark appointed him to head the CRTC. The really interesting thing about him was that he didn't own a television set, and proudly said as much while he was chairman of television's regulator. I just couldn't believe that, and I still shake my head thinking about it.

25

Close Calls, Gender Equality, and Loyalty

My stroke very nearly killed me, but I've had several other close calls, perhaps more than most.

In the 1980s, Jim McCoubrey and I took our families on a safari and sightseeing trip to South Africa and Zimbabwe. At the time, Jim was chairman of Young & Rubicam, one of Canada's biggest agencies and part of the multinational advertising conglomerate headquartered in New York. He knew plenty of people in both African countries, and had lined up a great adventure for us.

One day, Jim and I decided to go rafting with an internationally recognized whitewater rafting company called Sobek on Zimbabwe's Zambezi River. Thankfully, it was just us and not our families.

This was a relatively new venture for Sobek. According to the company's website, "Sobek made the first descent of the

Zambezi in October 1981 and is legendary on this stretch of the river. The Zambezi River is home to some of the most exhilarating rapids in the world and the combination of its beautiful scenery, fascinating wildlife and unique African culture makes this trip world famous."

Our group had three rafts, two piloted by experienced Californian guys and ours by a local. They decided to launch the rafts right near Victoria Falls, a point at which the Zambezi is a seething, madly uncontrollable river. It looked very dangerous, but we were assured that the guides would be extremely careful and that we'd be safe.

After launching, I noticed these massive whirlpools that opened up for no apparent reason—and Jim and I were in the raft that got caught in one of them. Down we went, descending 10 to 20 feet below the water's surface. It was unbelievable. There was much consternation, of course, and the people who were organizing the rafting were trying to recover everyone who went overboard and get our raft right side up, which they did.

Fortunately, Jim came up and was quickly rescued. But I was caught in a downward draft and could not for the life of me get close to the surface. I struggled for what seemed an eternity. The lifejacket felt useless. I was even seeing bright colours in some kind of out-of-body experience. I was sure I was going to drown.

Just then I started rising. The downdraft was loosening its grip, the lifejacket's buoyancy was working, I was getting ever closer to the surface—and then I popped up, gasping for air. I could see a raft quite a ways away, and the organizers trying furiously to get closer to me. At one point they threw a rope, but I was too exhausted to grab it or swim closer. The raging water was relentless.

Then, all of a sudden, they screamed at me to turn around. A massive rock structure loomed just ahead. I hit it, and once more I got sucked down. The people in the raft were frantic. But somehow I came up again, and finally they were able to pull me into the boat. I threw up everywhere. And for the remainder of the trip I stayed on the boat, tightly grasping the ropes the entire time until we reached the debarkation area an hour or so later. Then, to get out of the canyon, we had to climb a kilometre up a steep incline. Never have I felt more beaten and exhausted. I sure was thankful to be alive.

I've heard that drowning is a peaceful way to die, but I don't believe it. Just thinking about that violent struggle to survive gives me a less than peaceful feeling.

About 15 years before the Africa incident, I was involved in a harrowing airplane episode. After founding the Ontario chapter of the Sierra Club environmental group, we were called upon to get involved in the James Bay Project. Hydro-Québec's massive hydroelectric development initially involved three major rivers in the northeastern part of the province: Nottaway, Broadback, and Rupert. The main opposition to the project were the Cree peoples, whose lands would be impacted by the dams. And so the Sierra Club took a scouting trip up there to meet Chief Billy Diamond and his Cree brethren.

On the way back we chartered a plane that would take us from Moosonee 300 kilometres south to Cochrane, Ontario. In addition to the pilot there were three other pilots in passenger seats, including my father. We took off late in the afternoon in a de Havilland DHC-2 Beaver aircraft, known as the "workhorse of the north." But owing to a bad calculation by the charter company, before we could reach Cochrane we found ourselves in pitch darkness.

The problem was that Beaver floatplanes don't have radar; they fly under visual flight rules (VFR)—meaning we couldn't tell exactly where we were.

We flew around for 40 minutes—our fuel getting lower and lower—looking desperately for a car so that we could follow its headlights, hopeful that it would be heading to Cochrane. Without that visual guidance we'd have to crash land in the dark, and almost certainly perish because we couldn't be sure we wouldn't set down in water. All the pilots aboard were extremely tense, which made other passengers like me even more nervous, knowing now that we were in real trouble.

Fortunately, we spotted a car's headlights, found the lake where we intended to stay, and landed safely. By then most of the cottages were lit up; people had heard about our distress over the radio. And as we walked up from the dock, we were told that a task force had been set up to look for our wreckage at first light. Thankfully, that task force wouldn't be needed.

Believe it or not, I was involved in three other airplane mishaps that could have been disastrous.

In 1982, Colin Watson and I boarded a small plane in the town of San Angelo, Texas, northwest of San Antonio. The plane—a twin-engine turboprop Mitsubishi MU-2, made in San Angelo—was owned by UA/Columbia, our U.S. cable partner. Right after takeoff, as we were ascending, I noticed oil and fuel spewing all over the wing. I quickly alerted the pilot, who shut off the left engine and somehow manoeuvred the plane back for an emergency landing. It turned out that the fuel cap either hadn't been put on correctly or had malfunctioned. Four years later, in 1986, they stopped making the MU-2: it had been deemed too dangerous an aircraft.

Another time, Larry Black and I were flying into the B.C. interior, northeast of Prince Rupert, for fly fishing on the gorgeous Sustut River, which is renowned for its steelhead. Everything was going smoothly as we descended for our river landing as planned, but the Sustut was moving rapidly. The pilot came in for the landing too quickly, the plane bounced in the water, and it didn't stop. We ended up onshore, right in the middle of the bush. Rescuers had to cut down trees with chainsaws just to reach us and get us out of the plane. It had been a smash landing, and quite frightening.

The third alarming plane excursion happened in Erie, Pennsylvania, when we hit a deer running across the runway while we were taking off. Miraculously, the pilot kept control of the plane, and was able to power down to stop, right at the end of the runway.

One of the most tragic plane crash stories happened in Alaska, and it didn't involve me but rather a very good friend of mine, Bill Phillips, along with his son Willy and several others.

But first a little background. I'd met Bill through his wife, Janet, who worked at the National Cable Television Association when I was on its board. Bill was chief of staff for longtime Alaska senator Ted Stevens. We became good friends, and shared a passion for not only fly fishing but also football: Bill had played at the University of Evansville in the 1970s, and Willy's three older brothers played at Stanford, Virginia, and Indiana.

When Rogers sold the U.S. cable systems in 1989, I convinced Ted to let me purchase a small American system so as to preserve our grandfathered rights. We debated long and hard but eventually decided on Alaska, for a couple of reasons. One, Stevens was a force in the U.S. Senate. Known as a "homer," he managed to get hundreds of millions of dollars a year funnelled from D.C. to Alaska, he was mean, nasty, and incredibly focused on taking care of his constituents and Alaska businesses. Two, Bill Phillips was back in Alaska and investing in a number of ventures there. He recommended that we buy the small cable system in Palmer/Wasilla, a suburb of Anchorage (where then-unknown Sarah Palin was a local politician, about 15 years away from running for U.S. vice-president).

Anyway, years after we bought that little cable system, on August 9, 2010, Bill, Willy, Ted Stevens, and six others flew to a fishing lodge on Lake Aleknagik, about 500 kilometres southwest of Anchorage and about as remote a place as you'll find on earth. The plane, a de Havilland DHC-3 Otter, and the lodge were both owned by an Alaskan telecommunications firm, GCI. (A few years before this Bill had taken my son Jed and me to the same lodge, and we'd flown there aboard a GCI plane, too. Probably the same plane. We had a wonderful fishing experience—and saw grizzly bears, moose, and other wildlife in the middle of nowhere. It was a marvellous trip.)

But tragedy struck for Bill and the others that evening when their plane slammed into a mountain slope. The weather was precarious, and rescuers couldn't get anyone off the mountain until morning.

Bill died immediately on impact. Ted Stevens also died. Seated beside Bill was Willy, whose ankle was shattered but who miraculously survived. Three other men survived, and in total, five died. It still sends shivers down my spine thinking of Willy and what he went through that night. He was only 13 years old at the time.

There's something I'd like to address about women in business. I've been pointed to as someone who was ahead of his time in promoting women and encouraging gender equality in the workplace. I've been honoured by such organizations as Canadian Women in Communications for what is described as male leadership and mentorship. Many people have said gracious things, including Toronto mayor John Tory, who remarks that I "always promoted women to senior executive levels and relied on their counsel. He has often pushed for more women on the boards of directors he serves on and, on more than one occasion, Phil would only accept a board appointment if the organization promised to appoint women to serve along with him."

Those are all nice accolades, but the truth is a little more selfish. I've consistently relied on the sage advice and hard work of women as far back as I can remember because the ones on my various teams were all extremely good, often great. Women like Jan Innes, Missy Goerner, Alison Clayton, Pam Dinsmore, Robin Mirsky, Colette Watson, Heidi Bonnell, Kaz Flinn, Heather Armstrong, and Liane Langevin constantly exceeded expectations.

To be honest, for me it's not a question of gender equality in business. I just want the best talent. It's exactly why I don't care that Ken Engelhart, Michael Allen, Vernon Achber, Adrian Montgomery, Wes Heppler, David Jones, and Lee Sheehy are men.

So instead of tossing accolades in my direction, we should be asking simple questions: What took business leaders so long to realize that talented women are all around us? And speaking as someone who loves fly fishing, why would male business leaders fish in only half the talent pool?

Now that we've dispensed with that, let's move on to the characteristics I looked for in my team members and the type of work environment I liked to foster.

Obviously, I looked for intelligence and a strong work ethic. But soft skills—like emotional intelligence, good humour, and a sense of fun—were important; after all, we'd be working long and hard together. I also looked for confidence, not arrogance— the confidence to stand by their ideas, and to stand up to me and Ted if necessary (although as best I could, I always tried to shield my people from Ted in a tirade). "Phil was clearly the boss, but everybody could speak up," Ken Engelhart says. "There was never a sense of 'This way and only this way.' Phil created a marketplace of ideas. Now, if your idea was goofy and not well thought out, he'd attack it."

"My first meeting with Phil's team was an eye-opener," says Pam Dinsmore, who joined our team in the mid-1990s after a career in government and the CRTC. "Thoughts and ideas were being tossed around. People were yelling at times, and every second word was fuck. 'Fuck this' and 'fuck that.' Coming from the Commission, I'd never experienced anything remotely like it."

"Chaos," adds Jan Innes, "is a good word to describe our work environment." Jan loves to tease me about how my office was a beehive of activity, with people coming and going and me answering the phone during a meeting, making her— or whoever was in my office at the time—wait around while I had my phone conversation. It wasn't out of rudeness. It's just that there were so many things going on all the time.

Colette Watson says I was a pioneer when it came to the concept of telework, or remote work. "Phil invented the concept of allowing women to work from home 25 years ago—although most other people call it mat leave."

Jan tells the story of me arriving in her hospital room shortly after her first child, Evan, was born in 1991: "It was eight a.m. and before visiting hours. Phil had flowers—and papers for me to go over." But Jan's favourite story involved her third child, Stuart, who was born in 1995. When he was two months old, Jan brought him with her to a late-afternoon team meeting at Rogers. Stuart slept in his car seat the whole time. At the end of the meeting, I suggested we all go out for dinner. I love to have informal dinners for team bonding rather than those hokey team-building seminars and HR exercises. "I told Phil I had to get Stuart home and so I couldn't join the dinner," Jan says. "And Phil says: 'Send him home in a cab. He's already in a car seat.' Everybody in the room cracked up—except Phil. Actually, he probably wasn't serious. But that's Phil. It was all about work and fun."

I'm very big on loyalty, and it works both ways. Ken tells the story about how, early in his career at Rogers, he sent out a regulatory memo without fully vetting it with me. Ted didn't particularly like what the memo said and confronted me with it. "It would have been easy for Phil to tell Ted that he hadn't seen it and that I'd been a bit overzealous," Ken says. "But he didn't. He said, 'Ted, that's our position in the regulatory department.' That was the first time, but not the last, Phil had my back.".

Missy talks about my fictitious "white book" and "black book" containing the names of people I like and those on the other side. "Once you're in one book, it's pretty difficult to move to the other," she says. "But if you do something Phil perceives to be disloyal, you'll move from the white book to the black book in an instant."

Richard Stursberg, who'd been Unitel's senior vice-president of regulatory, went on to work for Shaw, and even Telus, but he never moved to the black book because he was upfront and honest about it. Even my co-author, Robert Brehl, wrote some stinging things about Rogers when he was at the *Toronto Star* and later *The Globe and Mail.* Some of his articles launched me into more than a few F-bomb tirades, especially during the "negative option" months, but he always gave us our say, and I understood that he was doing his job.

But over the years there were others, who shall remain nameless, who have really ticked me off. And each case boils down to disloyalty, to pulling some Machiavellian stunt against Rogers. When I meet these people, I'm cordial. Some have no idea they're in what Missy calls the "black book." I may forgive, but I won't forget.

Now it's time to mention some quirks of my character. I know we all have quirks, but that doesn't make it any easier admitting them on the record like this. I'm not relishing this part, but several friends have insisted that my story would not be complete without pointing these things out. Some are small, like using only a purple pen, and others are a little bigger, but they're still just quirks.

I'm on airplanes more than most, but people generally don't like to be seated nearby, especially in the seat directly in front of me. I have a tendency to strew papers everywhere within a 10-foot radius. "Don't even try to recline your seat if Phil is behind you," Paul Temple says. "He'll start pounding the seat until you put it back in the upright position."

I also have a pet peeve about arriving too early at the airport just to sit around and waste time. Robin Mirsky tells the story about me cutting it a little too tight for a flight to Halifax, where I was due to give a speech. "We arrived at the gate after it had just been shut," Robin says. "Phil started arguing with the Air Canada rep—and rather vociferously, demanding to get on the flight—but we were denied, and soon the RCMP showed up to investigate the commotion. We didn't make the flight and Phil didn't deliver his speech. At least he wasn't tossed in jail."

I also don't like to waste time when I'm driving alone for any distance, so I phone people. "He'll call and go through the business of the day," says Heidi Bonnell. "It doesn't matter if you're in the middle of preparing dinner or overseeing homework, the phone rings and it's Phil. Just imagine how much time he has to kill when he's driving two and a half hours to the farm!"

And I love my calendar: 75 sheets or so of 8.5 x 11–inch paper stapled or clipped together, with everything unfolding in my life for a year or more out. Meetings, trips, movies, breakfasts, lunches, dinners, art shows—all that stuff is in my calendar. Compiling and updating it is a large part of my invaluable assistant Michelle's job. "He can sit on a plane and amuse himself reading the calendar for two hours," Jan says.

Ted and I had exactly the same calendars. Actually, it was Ted who got me and Colin started on these, since he always wanted to know where we were and what we were doing on any given day. Ted's calendar was legendary, too. He later insisted that all C-level executives do them, with a duplicate copy going to his office. So during the franchise wars, Colin and I would come up with code words to throw Ted off the scent. (Ted liked us to have fun, just not *too* much fun on his dime and time.) For example, while in Oregon, if I wanted to spend some time fly fishing on the Rogue River, my calendar entry might read "Inspect rogue cable headend."

Colin and I would even "help" others with their calendar entries. After Bob Francis's death and before Graham Savage got the job, we had a short-term CFO who we thought was a little too full of himself. Ted had this way of showering new executives with praise for a short period of time while they were his flavour of the month, and his comments had made this particular guy's head swell. He was actually saying he might just be Ted's successor and shit like that. One day, he asked Colin and me how much information was needed for his calendar.

We suggested that, since Ted expects his senior people to work really hard and then relax and enjoy themselves, he should put as many things in his calendar as possible so that Ted would know he was working and *playing* hard. Before we knew it, the guy was entering golf games in Palm Springs, skiing in Colorado, and sailing near British Columbia. When he saw these entries Ted must have blown a gasket, because the guy wasn't around much longer. "They had a lot of fun and sometimes acted like frat-house boys," says Alan Horn, who would one day be a fine Rogers CFO and a terrific chairman.

My last admission has to do with food. For example, I love hot dogs, but only if they're burnt to a crisp. As well, I hate to eat alone, and rarely do.

"He also eats off other people's plates," Ken Engelhart says. "Now, there are lots of cultures where taking food off another person's plate is acceptable. But it's quite unusual in the culture of Phil's Anglo-Saxon Protestant upbringing." Adds Jan:

"And he loves dessert but never orders it. He just eats other people's dessert. He says the calories don't count that way."

I may have broken many management-book rules about team building, but it worked for us on the Rogers regulatory team, and we had far more successes than failures.

26

Reflections

Whe n you're referred to as a "Cable Guy," you wear it as a badge of pride. Today, Rogers is a telecommunications company with more than two-thirds of everything—revenue, earnings, stock value, you name it—coming from our wireless operation. But once a Cable Guy, always a Cable Guy. That's me. I remain vice-chairman of Rogers Communications Inc.

I'm one of the lucky ones who can honestly say that I've loved my work and my career. I was honoured to work with Ted Rogers for nearly 40 years—and we accomplished some great things.

I'm passionately interested in the arts, in nature and the outdoors, in Canada's West Coast and the Klondike, and finally, in people and politics.

Over the years I've been extraordinarily blessed. It's obvious that I've had one or two bumps along the road, one in particular in 1998. And during that time—and the years since—I've had not only the support of my family and countless friends, but also extraordinary help from a small group of friends, whom I've already mentioned. I will always be in their debt.

I feel extremely fortunate in every way. For my fabulous immediate family, I'm proud of my two wonderful children, Sarah and Jed, and Jed's daughter James. For my extended family— it's difficult to imagine a better set of brothers and sister, their spouses, and my collection of nieces and nephews. The family farm brings us together; the familial love keeps us together. And for my longtime relationship with Ellen.

In 2002, after being nominated by former CRTC commissioner Sally Warren and former Rogers colleague Kevin Shea, I was awarded the Order of Canada for my career and my input into Canadian culture and broadcasting. These included things like initiating funds for programming that have exceeded $600 million to date in needed cash for independent Canadian producers and my 30-year support for the Banff Film Festival. That same year, my alma mater, the University of British Columbia, bestowed upon me a Doctor of Laws honorary degree, and some years later, an Alumni Award of Distinction. Those are two honours I hold very dear.

After my hundredth-and-something appearance before the CRTC, CARTT publisher Greg O'Brien wrote, "His fingerprints are all over broadcasting policy in Canada." CARTT.ca is the industry bible for those working in cable, radio, television, and telecom in Canada.

In 2012 I was deeply honoured to be elected into the Cable Hall of Fame in the U.S. It meant all the more because I was only the third Canadian selected for the hall; the other two were Ted Rogers and JR Shaw, both held in such high regard in both countries.

Looking back on a tremendously exciting career, one of the things I enjoyed most was travelling with Colin Watson and Vernon Achber. We had so many great times, with stories that remain vivid even as I move into my fourth quartile.

In the 1980s, when we owned U.S. cable systems, we'd sometimes travel with Ted on the company jet, affectionately referred to as "The Flame Thrower" (or as "Quiz Air" by whoever drew the short straw to sit beside Ted for the long flights). In our typically whirlwind fashion, over a span of two or three days our corporate group would visit cable systems in California, Oregon, Minnesota, and Texas to review budgets, assess building progress, and tally how many paying subscribers we were hooking up (which was so critical to keeping us ahead of our creditors).

"It's hard to adequately describe the terror some of our team experienced during the Toronto quarterly review visits," Missy Goerner says. A good illustration I can recall was Ted grilling a new San Antonio finance director during his very first presentation. This poor guy was named Richard, but Ted kept calling him "Dick," even after Richard had pointed out his preference. Throughout Richard's presentation Ted would interject often, and sometimes about the advance book, a large three-ring binder filled with operational data that the local teams would always provide us with.

"Dick, is it in the book?"

"Yes, Ted, it's in the book," Richard would reply.

"If it's in the book, Dick, I've read it and I don't need you to repeat it."

Rattled, Richard would begin to explain something else. Then Ted would interrupt him again.

"Dick, is it in the book?"

"No, Ted. It's not in the book."

"Then Dick, if it's not in the book, I haven't been able to read it so I don't want to hear about it."

These were our "seagull visits"—we'd fly in, swoop down, shit all over the local folks, and then fly away.

But it wasn't just the local teams who got razzed during these trips. There was a Toronto guy who never quite meshed with the rest of the senior team. In those heady days we were very clannish, and anyone who took themselves too seriously would pay a price. And on one of our seagull tours, this Toronto guy had what appeared to be an amazing string of unlucky circumstances befall him, a laundry list of bad luck. For example, upon arriving in a city past midnight and after everyone else had checked in, he'd find his hotel reservation mysteriously cancelled. In another city, he'd be awakened at five a.m. by the unexpected delivery of breakfast to his room. And in the days before cell phones and setting your own alarm, no matter how many times he'd check and confirm, his seven a.m. wake-up call would be mistakenly moved to eight-thirty. Ted was furious that he was never on time while we all waited downstairs for him. As a topper, one night this fellow naively placed his shoes outside his door for polishing. The hotel staff only located them in the ice machine hours after we'd flown on to another city. That morning he'd been on time for once, and hadn't kept Ted waiting for our trip to the airport. But he'd been in his stocking feet.

Ted pretended to believe that these misfortunes were just coincidental. But all had been covertly carried out by the mischievous known offender in our group, Kevin Shea.

And what can I say about Ted Rogers that hasn't already been said? Ted was everything they say about him—brilliant, creative, tireless, a visionary, a crusader.

But he was not proficient with technology—ironic, considering he built his company on the latest and greatest high-tech things of the day: FM radio, cable TV, wireless phones, high-speed Internet, and more. Ted could never get the hang of a computer.

He tried unsuccessfully to take lessons, but he didn't use one, not even for email. He could barely figure out his wireless phone, let alone how to mute the ring.

At one Christmas party for dozens of senior Rogers people at Toronto's posh, private York Club, Ted got up to say a few words. I was standing at the back of the room beside John Tory, who was president of Rogers Media at the time.

"Watch this," John whispered to me. Then he dialed Ted's private number. So just as Ted started talking to the assembled audience his phone started ringing, which everyone could hear through the microphone in his hand. He fumbled around, searching for the correct pocket, and finally found his phone. Just as he pulled it out, John hung up and the ringing ceased. Ted put it back in his pocket, resumed his speech, and a few seconds later John dialed again. Ted fumbled around again. He was getting more and more annoyed. Meanwhile, John and I were dying in muted laughter at the back of the room.

Finally, an exasperated Ted gave up. He said, "Merry Christmas. Enjoy the evening," put the microphone down, and the music and party continued. (Today, the York Club has a strict "no cell phones" policy—maybe because of that incident!) Ted knew he was being pranked by one of us; he just didn't know who. As I've said throughout the book, Ted was a prankster himself, and while sometimes he would rage and call us all juvenile delinquents, he never attempted to shut us down or rein us in.

John's phone prank with Ted was classic Tory. His business achievements are well chronicled, not the least of which is his current role as mayor of Toronto. And he's been a fantastic mayor, restoring Toronto's good name around the world after the Ford years. Working 18-hour days, John continues to make Toronto the best place to live and the best place to do business.

There was another prank pulled on Ted by another of his senior guys—and I got into hot water that time because I just could not contain my laughter.

Ted had invited about 20 of us to his beautiful cottage on Muskoka's Tobin Island for a two-day planning session. This was the late 1990s—high-speed Internet was exploding and digital TV was just beginning. High-definition TV was in its infancy, with only a couple of broadcasters experimenting with it and very few people even owning high-def TVs. So the biggest issue at the session was how to allocate the limited spectrum on our cable wires going into homes. Our thick planning-session binders—and virtually everyone in the room—recommended giving more space to Internet use, thereby blowing the doors off Bell Canada's slower Internet service. The faster the Internet, the more new customers Rogers could grab.

We recommended allocating space for only four HD channels. One person in the room argued against this, saying that HD was the future of television—and, of course, that person was the visionary Ted Rogers.

He was railing that morning, cursing and calling us names. It was very unpleasant, and we were all looking at our watches, waiting for the noon lunch break. When it finally arrived, an unnamed executive pulled from his briefcase a magazine ad for penis enlargement procedures. Ever the planner, this prankster already had three holes punched in it, and after everyone had left the room he placed it in Ted's binder. "Maybe this will break the ice when Ted comes back," he said to me.

When we returned, Ted's binder was open with the ad staring him in the face. But Ted didn't seem to notice it, and launched back into his tirade about needing more allocation for HD channels. This went on for several minutes. I was quietly cracking up as I watched Ted waving his arms in the air, calling us all dummies, and apparently still not noticing the ad in his binder. Finally I couldn't contain myself any longer and broke out laughing uncontrollably, kind of like Mary Tyler Moore in that famous scene at Chuckles the Clown's funeral. Ted's reaction was different from that of the consoling minister in *The Mary Tyler Moore Show*.

"Philip," he said, "get out of here and go somewhere and compose yourself."

Two lessons from that story. One, Ted wouldn't give us the satisfaction of even acknowledging that he'd seen the ad. Two, Ted was correct—as was so often the case. HDTV took off, and in those early days before emerging digital-compression technologies arrived, we needed the space so that we could offer both HD channels and the highest-speed Internet on the market.

There are so many stories like these that still make me laugh out loud. Just recalling them makes me think of something a little more serious, though. Ted was not an easy man to report to, and many men (not women, because Ted unfortunately didn't promote too many women to the highest levels) just couldn't hack it and either left Rogers or were fired.

Colin and Graham Savage were probably the most high-profile departures (both on their own accord), but there were many others over the years. And when we smelled trouble for one of Ted's senior executives, others would be eyeing the furniture and plants in his office to grab immediately after the execution.

So why did I survive so long?

The role I filled for Ted was different from everyone else's. I was adviser, confidant, sometime gatekeeper, definitely sounding board, and probably a lot of other things. My friend Peter Barton, who held a similar role with Liberty Media's John Malone, once said that while other executives acquiesced to Ted and John, he and I had to be our respective boss's "Abominable No Man."

Ted worked from morning until midnight, so I was on call 18 hours a day. My only escape was on the weekends at my farm, where, for the entire time we worked together, I convinced Ted that I didn't have a telephone (I did) and couldn't be reached. He'd often call on Sunday evenings when I came back to town, just as we were sitting down to dinner, and ask, "Have I got you at a bad time?"

In addition to my own responsibilities, I always had to know what Ted was doing. I synched his calendar with mine. Up until my stroke, everything that Ted was working on would ultimately impact my job, and I could be called upon at any moment to offer advice and counsel or to take action.

Looking back, although we often argued stringently, I've wondered why Ted was harder on his other senior guys than me, and why he gave me far more autonomy than he did Colin, Graham, and others. One reason, I believe, is that my areas—programming, regulatory, and understanding the public's mood toward our company—weren't Ted's strong suits, which included such areas as finance and cable operations.

Ted prided himself on his breadth and depth of knowledge concerning tax implications, recurring revenues, EBITDA (Earnings Before Interest, Tax, Depreciation, and Amortization), high-yield junk bond financing, bank loan covenants, and a heck of a lot more. And even though he'd speak nostalgically of his early days in radio programming, he also thought of himself as a cable operator, not a programmer.

He just didn't push back as hard on the things I specialized in, like the CRTC, the U.S. franchising, programming, and what the public was feeling. I got to know individual commissioners, politicians, public-policy players on both sides of the border, consumers through focus groups, and more. Ted had neither the time nor the patience for that sort of thing. So in my areas of expertise, Ted would basically acquiesce—that may be too strong a word to apply to Ted Rogers—or at least he'd agree more than he'd battle me on my files and my decisions. Colin, Graham, and others weren't as fortunate, and Ted would relentlessly push them harder than he pushed me.

And finally, Ted gave me more leeway because he knew that I distinguished him — the man — from the company. When he was alive, virtually everyone saw Ted Rogers and Rogers Communications as the same thing: interchangeable. Not me. Maybe because we went back so many years — in politics, business, even our ancestors and their ties — Ted understood that I viewed him as the captain of the ship, not the ship. He was an integral part of the company, the most integral part, but he was not the company.

So, when I deemed something was taking us off course, I could boldly tell Ted this. It was not personal; just me advising the captain how best to protect the ship. I was like a first mate spotting an iceberg and vigorously telling the captain to change course. Sometimes, he'd heed my advice and get completely out of harm's way (not changing the company name to Cantel or not partnering with Sprint). Other times, the first mate's warnings didn't work and we'd graze the iceberg (negative option, selling Vancouver cable assets). The ship never went down, in part, because Ted Rogers allowed me to stand up to the man when it came to the company's best interests.

Ted was a giant, the Mount Everest of Rogers CEOs, but I would be remiss not to mention the three men who have succeeded him. Before I do, though, a few words about two integral qualities that I believe are essential for any CEO in any business. One can be a successful CEO without these two things, but one can't be a great leader without them. The first is humility; even a modicum of humility takes a CEO into a whole new world. It also dovetails into the second: the ability to listen. Too many CEOs stop listening, except to those who tell them only what they want to hear. It is so harmful to themselves and their company when they stop listening. Now back to Ted's successors.

Nadir Mohamed is a brilliant guy, and I was close to him after he took on the very difficult role of filling Ted's shoes. I count both Nadir and his wife, Shabin, as good friends. Even though I was no expert on wireless, Nadir would often call on me for advice and counsel, including ways to strengthen our brand in western Canada so as to increase phone subscribers. It's on public record that Nadir found it untenable having two of Ted's children report to him in operations while he reported to them at the board level. After five years as CEO, Nadir and the controlling family mutually agreed to sever ties.

The next CEO, Guy Laurence from the U.K., was brash and full of confidence. A good way to describe him would be a bull in a china shop. His background was wireless, and he didn't know or care to learn about cable. He refused to listen to anyone. Nor did he understand the culture and history of Rogers; for example, he cut back on engineering, something Ted would never have allowed. Rogers was built on innovation and quality. After a number of bad decisions, the board voted to sever ties with Laurence less than three years after he'd been appointed CEO.

The current CEO is Joe Natale, who came to us from our competitor Telus. So far, I'd describe his tenure as terrific; he's exactly the person we need. I got to know Joe well during the Fair for Canada campaign when he was still at Telus. He has all the right instincts, and he inspires people. Ted was a master at cordially talking to all levels of employees on elevators, in the cafeteria, or at company meetings (it was only with his leadership team that he'd blow his top)—and Joe is exhibiting this Ted-like town-hall flair. He's amiable and very approachable. Everything points to a great tenure as Rogers CEO.

Alan Horn, who's been Rogers's acting CEO twice, heads Rogers Telecommunications Ltd., the family holding company, and for more than a decade he was an exceptional chairman of Rogers Communications Inc. Alan and I had distinctly different styles when it came to dealing with Ted. Mine was more direct, especially before my stroke, and Alan's was more nuanced and serpentine. But while our styles differed, the results were generally the same: convincing Ted to slow down or to look at something a different way.

Alan still chuckles and says I paid him one of his favourite compliments ever. Many years ago, at a private Rogers company meeting, the late John A. Tory was talking about how a complicated tax plan to move the radio stations into RCI had Alan Horn's fingerprints all over it. "Ah, Horn," Alan quotes me as saying, "Rasputin's Rasputin."

I don't actually remember that comment about Alan and the Mad Monk who befriended the family of Russia's last tsar. But I do know that the well-read and witty Scotsman Alan Horn has served the Rogers family diligently and brilliantly for 30-plus years. During Ted's last few years, no one, including me, was closer to Ted on business matters than Alan.

One cannot reflect upon the history of Rogers Communications without citing two people integral to the development of the company: John W. Graham and John A. Tory.

John Graham was Rogers's first chairman and Ted's stepfather. But Ted always called him his "second father." They were that close. John was a steadying hand who could tug on the string when Ted's kite got too high and into buffeting winds. He was also the person who believed in preparation and hours of rehearsal before CRTC hearings. I learned much from him in that regard.

John A. Tory was a sharp, skilled lawyer who succeeded at whatever he did in business. He's best known as the man who guided and built the Thomson family empire for many years, taking it from a string of Canadian newspapers to an international conglomerate. He was also, in my opinion, the best director to ever serve on the Rogers Communications board.

The two Johns have other things in common: they lived their lives with great integrity and were two of the nicest gentlemen I've ever come across in the business world. Their word truly was their bond.

It's also worth mentioning that Ted's widow, Loretta, has been a staunch supporter of the company from the very beginning. Loretta has served on the board for more than 50 years, and invested her family money in the company during its rough patches.

And their son, Edward, is looking good as chairman of Rogers Communications Inc. I can't imagine it would be easy being the son of a business titan like Ted, but Edward has acquired tremendous industry experience over the years, and at the board level and elsewhere, it shows.

The Rogers staff physician, Dr. Bernie Gosevitz, has been a good friend; in the face of the extreme physical challenges Ted and I both faced, he gave us each sage advice and special care that kept us going.

There's more to me than Rogers, and I'd like to close the loop on a couple of things. First, the Klondike, which is so rich in history and colourful stories. I urge anyone who hasn't visited Canada's North—especially the Yukon, but other territories, too—to do so for its sheer beauty and to find out firsthand what the North means to our country.

My huge private collection of Klondike paraphernalia will be donated to a museum in western Canada, likely Vancouver. I'd love to see it all go to the Yukon, but so far its government hasn't seen fit to invest in infrastructure that would be able to house and preserve the books, documents, photographs, and other memorabilia, some of which is quite fragile. In 1998, along with my dad, brothers, and sister, the Lind Family donated money to the Dawson City Museum to help build storage facilities. But it isn't nearly enough to house a collection like mine. I have to find a solution in the next few years so that it won't be a problem for Bob Reeves to work out. Bob is a terrific financial planner, and I value his friendship and advice. He's also vice-president of investments at Rogers Telecommunications Ltd. He's low key, self-effacing, smart, and invaluable to me.

Incidentally, there is a terrific documentary, *The Klondike Gold Rush*, produced in 2014 by my pal, Don Boswell, president and CEO of WNED, the public broadcasting station in Buffalo. It ran all across the U.S. and Canada on the PBS system.

I am just so fascinated by the Klondike. Stephen Armstrong tells a story from the early 1990s, during our cross-country campaign to bring competition to long-distance phone service. Stephen was consulting with us at the time, as well as doing some work for the Yukon government.

We were in Whitehorse for meetings, and afterward I saw him sitting in the hotel coffee shop with an Indigenous man and his wife. When Stephen introduced me, it turned out that this fellow, George Henry, was from Northern Native Broadcasting. We started talking about programming and things like that, and at one point he mentioned that he was from a place called Carcross, near Bennett Lake—which had been an important place in my grandfather's journey to the Klondike. John Lind had hired Chilkat guides to get him and his supplies through the treacherous Chilkoot Pass to the headwaters of the mighty Yukon River at Bennett Lake. Here they felled trees and made boats—more like rafts—to get them up the river.

I thought this was an interesting coincidence, and given that the population of Carcross is only 300 people today, I wondered aloud whether my grandfather might have hired any of George Henry's ancestors way back in 1894 when he first went to the Yukon.

A terrific discussion followed. "Phil talked about the Yukon, the Klondike, and the various Native bands who played a role in the Klondike's history," Stephen says. "George Henry was completely blown away by this big-shot communications southerner telling him stuff about his territory and the Native people who live there."

Another thing that fascinates me is the United States, and specifically our relations with it. Canada is both profoundly different and profoundly similar to our southern neighbour. No other country in the world enjoys such closeness to and affection for the U.S. Americans consider Canadians not as foreigners but more as distant cousins—and no other country can make this claim. Sure, we've got our differences, but we also have many similarities. "Phil understands U.S. politics as well as anybody in Canada," says former American ambassador to Canada David Jacobson. "He may be the best ambassador to the U.S. that Canada never had." That's kind of him, but I'm not sure what to think of Trump's America these days. I'm so disheartened by some of the things going on down there.

I suppose that makes my Phil Lind Initiative—an annual dialogue series and course hosted by UBC's School of Public Policy and Global Affairs—all the more important. Big-name Americans come to offer perspectives that UBC students wouldn't get otherwise. Some come to deliver a single lecture and others to teach for an entire semester; these visitors have included such luminaries as Nobel Laureate Joseph Stiglitz and former U.S. labor secretary Robert Reich. Now, students at Yale, Princeton, Harvard, and other Ivy League schools have access to these types of brains all the time—speakers travel an academic route around the Northeast, and there's a smaller route around California—but nothing like this had existed in the Pacific Northwest. So I felt that students up here should have the opportunity to learn from the best minds as well. Dr. Taylor Owen and Victoria Austin are the critical components in making this initiative a success, and I've set it up with enough funding to continue its great work for years to come.

What we're trying to do with the Phil Lind Initiative is teach future Canadian business leaders more about the U.S. than we think we know. Here in Canada, there's a tremendous yearning for learning about the United States—and yet today, as I've already mentioned, there aren't a hell of a lot of Canadian companies succeeding in the U.S. in the way Rogers did decades ago. Although plenty of individual Canadians have found success there, especially artists and performers, very few Canadian corporations have done the same (these exceptions include the BMO Financial Group, of which David Jacobson is currently vice-chair, and TD Financial Group). Indeed, it's much tougher to make it in the U.S. than it is here—so if we're to succeed economically and culturally in that country, it's critical that Canadians know more about it. And that's why the Lind Initiative offers such a fount of information on "American things," whether economic, political, or sociological. And one of its central purposes is to help Canadians use this information to better deal with Americans.

We have much to learn and understand about our neighbours, including their methods in, and approaches to, business. But it's too easy *not* to learn. Once people get to be big shots in industry, whatever industry that may be, for some reason most of these people just stop listening. I don't know why that is, but they do. They think they know it all because they've come to the top. That's not the case, so you should always listen and try to understand why people think the way they do.

That was part of Ted's genius: no matter how big he got, he never stopped listening and learning. We used to fight and argue all the time, but he listened. I would listen too, and we'd compromise.

It was mainly Ted's ideas, mainly Ted's relentless energy that drove our success. But he listened and supported, sometimes unconditionally, my plans for how to achieve his vision.

Think about it: fifty years ago, there was a lowly little cable company with one franchise in Toronto and one in Brampton, Ontario—and all of a sudden, we're the largest telecommunications company in Canada. It's an amazing story.

Why?

Because we had ambition and drive. And because Ted had the guts to risk everything over and over to make it a great company. And because each time a new opportunity arose that made sense, he had a lieutenant who would say, "Buckle up, team. Here we go again!"

Index

Note: MH—Maclean Hunter
PBL—Philip Lind
TR—Ted Rogers

A

Aberdeen Farms Ltd., 194
Achber, Vernon, 109–10, 114,
    129–30, 136, 139, 140, 146–47,
    151, 156, 158, 234, 319, 328.
    See also Road Warriors
Aitken, Max (Lord Beaverbrook),
    37
Ali, Muhammad, 108
Allen, Michael, 7, 110, 130, 164,
    170, 242, 319
Alliance Atlantis Communications
    Inc., 206
Ambler, Charles, 82–83
Anderson, Charlie, 25–26
Anstey, Gary, 171
Aquilini, Francesco, 278, 279, 296
Aquilini, Luigi, 278–79, 294, 296
Aquilini, Paolo, 278
Aquilini, Roberto, 278
Alexander, Lincoln, 63
Armstrong, Heather, 319
Armstrong, Stephen, 94, 101–2, 217,
    340–41
Ask Us (TV show), 90
Asper, Lenny, 301
Atkins, Norman, 62, 63
AT&T, 123, 177, 280–81
Audain, Michael, 291
Audet, Louis, 208
Austin, Victoria, 341
Austrian, Neil, 261

B

Baker, Howard, 116
Barnhill, David "Barney," 53, 197,
    225, 232, 296
Barrett, Dave, 104
Bartels, Kathleen, 291

Barton, Peter, 153, 253, 254, 334
Bassett, John, 72, 167
Bastarache, Michel, 303
Baxter, Iain, 287–88
Beeston, Paul, 238, 257–58, 264
Belcher, Jonathan, 29
Belchertown, 29–31
Bélisle, Fern, 181, 310
Bellamy, Francis, 149
Bell Canada, 87, 259, 305, 306, 307,
    308
    contribution rates to, 177
    and CTV purchase, 256, 303
    and fee-for-carriage, 303
    long-distance monopoly of,
        164–65, 169, 170–71, 172, 173,
        174, 175
    and MCI partnership, 280
    PBL attitude to, 166
    Rogers's desire to compete with,
        236
    and sports packages, 263
Bennett, Bill, 103
Bennett, Jalynn Rogers, 220, 221,
    222
Bennett, William, 193
Bertrand, Françoise, 102, 310
Bettman, Gary, 253, 255, 259, 260
The Big Blue Machine (Boyer), 61
Black, Larry, 115, 135–36, 317
Blais, Jean-Pierre, 310
Bliss, Ray, 63, 71
Blue Circle America Inc., 220
Bon Jovi, Jon, 271
Bonnell, Heidi, 164, 307, 308, 319,
    323
Bos (ad agency), 172
Boswell, Don, 340
Bowlen, Pat, 262, 263
Boyer, Patrick, 61
Boyle, Harry, 310
Boynton, John, 278
Brace, Rick, 259

Braley, David, 270
Brandon, Russ, 271
Brascan Ltd., 91, 93
Brehl, Robert, 322
Bridgman, Ann, 33
Bridgman, Elijah Coleman, 31
Bridgman, Philip Ashley, 29, 31–32, 83
Bridgman, Susan, 29, 32, 33–34. *See also* Lind, Susie
Brokaw, Tom, 202
Bronfman, Edward, 91
Bronfman, Peter, 91, 92
Brookfield Asset Management Inc., 93
Brown, Jim, 251
Brown, Peter, 104–5
Bruce, Rob, 278
Brunt, Stephen, 269
Buchan, Bob, 5, 91, 123, 164
    and cable ownership, 85
    CBC withdraws from CPAC, 210
    CNCP negotiations and, 167
    on CPAC and PBL, 207
    and CRTC hearings letters, 173
    and fee-for-carriage, 303–4
    on Juneau and PBL, 209
    and MH acquisition, 185, 189
    on PBL and TR relationship, 243
    on PBL's feelings about Bell, 166
    and PBL stroke, 227–28
    reaction to Premier purchase, 97–98
    on Rogers's desire to enter TV, 217
Buffalo Bills, 265, 266, 267–72
Bureau, André, 309–10
Byrne, Greg, 171

C
Cable Public Affairs Channel, 164, 207–12
cable TV industry
    "benefits package," 94
    Canada as leader, 86
    Canadian compared to U.S., 115–16
    Canadian content in, 76
    challenges facing, 87
    changes in, 110, 111, 217–18
    changing landscape of, 85
    clustering concept, 87, 98
    commercial deletion in, 77–78
    CPAC in, 208–12
    CRTC effect on, 74–75
    debate over regulation of, 100
    and fee-for-carriage, 300–04
    innovations of, 74, 75–76
    introduction of HDTV, 332–33
    and local ownership, 98
    Ontario's desire to regulate, 100–02
    programming allowed in, 257
    rate hikes, 145
    rates in U.S., 144–45
    during recession, 139
    restrictions on, 254
    Rogers and Shaw relationship, 281–82, 284
    and satellite services, 260–61
    simultaneous substitution and, 75–76, 77
    in United States, 107–8
    violence in shows, 213–14
Cable Value Network Inc. (CVN), 206
Cablevision, 145
Caisse du dépôt et placement du Québec, 237
Camp, Dalton, 62
Campbell, Don, 181
Campbell, Gordon, 295
Campbell, Larry, 269–70
Camu, Pierre, 89, 310
Canada Cement, 37
Canadian Association of Broadcasters, 254
Canadian Broadcasting Corporation, 210, 301
Canadian Cablesystems Limited (CCL), 85, 86, 87, 89–96, 97, 99–100, 107, 108, 111, 113
Canadian Cable Television Association (CCTA), 76
Canadian Home Shopping Network (CHSN), 206

Canadian National, 165
Canadian Pacific, 165, 166, 170, 175, 176–77, 280, 281
Canadian Pacific Investments Ltd., 103
Canadian Radio-television and Telecommunications Commission
    application for Sportsnet, 255
    approval of local programming, 90
    breakup of phone monopoly, 164
    broadcasters' sway with, 74, 80, 205–6, 218, 254
    and cable TV industry, 116
    and CCL deal, 94–95, 97, 98, 99
    CFMT transfer approval, 217–18
    chairmen of, 309–11
    and commercial deletion, 77
    and companies' business plan, 169
    and fee-for-carriage, 302–4
    and Italian programming issue, 299–300
    multilingual programming decision, 216, 217–18
    negative option controversy, 274–75
    policies, 74–75, 85, 89, 205–7, 217–18, 254
    and Premier deal, 104, 106
    rate increases requests, 166
    restrictions on Rogers, 106
    Rogers and jurisdiction issue, 100
    Rogers' desire to break Bell monopoly, 167
    Rogers' long-distance competition application, 170–75
    and Rogers-MH deal, 185, 188–90, 211
    and Rogers' public affairs channel request, 209
    ruling on Bell and and CTV, 256–57
    support for local cable companies, 98
    and TV violence warnings, 212–14
    and Unitel venture, 163–65
Cantel, 246, 276, 281, 306, 335
CanWest Global, 301, 302, 303
Capital Cable, 282
Capital Cities Communications Inc., 77
Caputo, Michael, 271–72
Cara Operations Ltd., 196
Carbone, Al, 229, 231
Carbone, John, 231
Cardinal, Lorne, 301
Carmack, George, 21–22, 23
Carmack, Kate, 21
Carpenter, Dennis, 144
Carroll, Carleen, 171
Carter, Jimmy, 140
Cassaday, John, 254, 255
CBC, 210, 301
CCL. *See* Canadian Cablesystems Limited (CCL)
CCTA, 76
Cerio, Skip, 110, 147–48
CFMT, 215, 216–18
CFTO, 73, 74
CFTR-AM, 73
Cha, Michelle, 244, 290, 323
Chagnon, André, 237, 238
Chaplin, Gordie, 42, 46–47, 55, 251
CHFI-FM, 73
Chrétien, Jean, 43
Cisneros, Henry, 132
City TV, 83, 215–16, 257
Clark, Christy, 295
Clark, Joe, 62, 100, 310
Clasen, Bob, 110, 147
Clayton, Alison, 5, 213, 224, 225–26, 227, 229–30, 232, 319
Cleveland Browns, 251–52, 272
Clinton, Bill, 132, 232
CN (Canadian National), 165
CNCP, 164–65, 167, 168. *See also* Unitel Communications Inc.
CNN, 110
Cockwell, Jack, 92
Cogeco, 208
Cole, Ed, 55–56

Collings, Tim, 213
Comcast, 160–61, 188, 190
Cook, Chuck, 210
Cope, George, 259
Corner Gas (TV show), 300, 301
Corporate Catalyst (Griffiths), 89
Corus Entertainment, 282
Courtois, Bernard, 166
CP (Canadian Pacific), 165, 166,
    170, 175, 176–77, 280, 281
CPAC, 94, 164
Craig, Bill, 110, 124
Crist, Johnny, 19, 20, 24, 27
CRTC. *See* Canadian
    Radio-television and
    Telecommunications
    Commission
Cruickshank, John, 308–9
CTV, 72, 254, 255, 256, 301–2, 304
Cubberley, Amy, 39
Curley, Paul, 68, 171
Curnoe, Greg, 289

D

Dalfen, Charles, 95, 310
Daly, Bill, 259
Davis, Bill, 67, 68, 100–101, 104
Dawson City Museum, 27, 339
De Florentiis, Cristiano, 300
Desbarats, Peter, 209
Devlin, Jack, 196
Diamond, Chief Billy, 315
Dickinson Pacific Cablesystems,
    145
Diefenbaker, John, 58, 59, 60, 63
Dinsmore, Pam, 5, 164, 299, 304,
    319, 320
DirecTV, 260–61, 262
Dodge, David, 50
Dolan, Chuck, 145
Domtar, 103
Douglas, Stan, 288
Dow Jones/Knight Ridder, 127
Drapeau, Jean, 267
Drossos, Angelo, 130–32
Dubin, Charles, 72
The Duke of Kent (McKeough), 66,
    67

Dunbar, Lawrence, 174
Dunlop, Susan, 43
Durham Cement Company, 38

E

Eaton, John Craig, 198–99
Eaton, Sherry, 198, 199
Eaton, Thor, 42
Eaton, Timothy, 40
Edper Investments Ltd., 91–92
Emerson, Gar, 180, 181, 182,
    280–81
Engelhart, Ken, 5, 7, 164, 178, 230,
    242, 319
    and CRTC, 169, 173, 304
    on fee-for-carriage and PBL, 300
    on PBL, 153, 196, 320, 321, 324
    on PBL and TR, 170
    on TR at hearings, 190
    on Verizon, 306
    on Wylie, 254
Evans Products, 138
Eyton, Trevor, 91, 92

F

Fafard, Joe, 285
Farmer, Geoffrey, 288
Fascell, Dante, 78, 115
FCC (Federal Communications
    Commission), 108, 116, 117,
    183, 184, 185, 186, 187
Fecan, Ivan, 255
fee-for-carriage, 300–304
Fensom, D.S., 49
Fierheller, George, 99
Finkelstein, Neil, 304
fishing
    family love of, 1–2, 32
    PBL excursions, 107, 135, 142,
        202, 284, 317, 318
    PBL interest in, 105
FitzGerald, Sean, 270
Flatt, Bruce, 93
Flinn, Kaz, 319
Fowler, Robert, 299
Fox, Francis, 181, 308
Fox, Lou, 156, 157, 158, 159
Francis, Bob, 84, 136–37, 324

Frank (magazine), 227
Fraser, Don, 122
Fraser, John, 53, 61
Frazier, Joe, 108
Fulford, Robert, 209
Fulton, Davie, 53, 61, 62, 68

G
Gamey, Ron, 176–77
Gardiner, George, 196
Garneau, Wurstlin, Philp, 276
Gaston, Cito, 258
Gates, Michael, 27
Global Television Network, 282
Gnat, Albert, 95, 96, 217, 236, 240
Godfrey, Jack, 43
Godfrey, John, 43
Godfrey, Mary, 43
Godfrey, Paul, 240–41, 267
Godfrey, Rob, 240
Goerner, Missy, 146, 184–86, 319
    and TR and Angelo Drossos, 130,
        131
    and approach to NFL, 261
    and L. Fox, 158, 159
    meets PBL and TR, 128
    and PBL's stroke, 4-5, 7, 224,
        225–26, 227, 229, 232, 233
    on PBL's white and black books,
        321–22
    on quarterly reviews, 329
    and Schwab, 140–41
    and sports packages, 263
    as U.S. Road Warrior, 109, 128,
        155, 156, 190–91
Goldschmidt, Neil, 141–42
Goldwater, Barry, 71
Goodell, Roger, 267
Gooderham, John, 38
Goodman, Eddie, 45, 63, 64, 72
Gorbachev, Mikhail, 172
Gormley, John, 171
Gormley, Antony, 292
Gosevitz, Dr. Bernie, 7–8, 339
Gotlieb, Allan, 113
Graham, Ann, 72–73
Graham, John W., 338
Graham, Rodney, 288

Grauer, Cindy, 171, 296
Green, Howard, 60, 61
Green, Zollie, 121–22, 123
Grey and Bruce Cement Company,
    37
Griffiths, Tony, 89, 91, 95, 96, 107

H
Hamilton, Dr. John Russell, 48, 49,
    58
Hamilton-Piercy, Nick, 95, 110, 144
Harcourt, Mike, 295
Hardin, Herschel, 104
Harper, Arthur, 19
Harper, Stephen, 297, 305, 306,
    307, 308
Harvey, George, 167–68, 176–77
Healey, Bob, 53
HBO, 108, 110
Heart and Stroke Foundation
    of Canada, 228
Heming, Gertrude, 38. *See also*
    Lind, Gertrude Heming
Henderson, Robert, 21–22
Henry, George, 340–41
Heppler, Wes, 109, 146, 156, 184,
    185, 186, 187, 188, 319. *See
    also* Road Warriors
Herman, Skip, 202
High Wire Act (Van Hasselt), 89
Hill, James J., 17
*The History of Western
    Massachusetts* (Holland), 30
Hochberg, Phil, 262
Hoey, Eamon, 173
Holland, Josiah Gilbert, 30
Home Box Office. *See* HBO
Home Shopping Network (HSN),
    206
Horn, Alan, 243, 324, 337–38
Houston Industries Inc., 110, 155,
    157, 159
Houston Light & Power, 155
Hoy, Alix, 201, 220
Hull, Toby, 249
Hunt, Dawn, 164
Hyndman, Peter, 53, 103, 105–6,
    138

I

Iannuzzi, Dan, 215, 216, 217
Innes, Jan, 164, 171, 172, 200, 319
  and brand damage, 276–77
  and fee-for-carriage, 300–301,
    304
  hiring of, 168
  LBJ Ranch visit, 233
  and negative option billing, 274
  on PBL, 196, 324–25
  and PBL stroke, 5, 7, 8, 224, 225,
    231
  and RAI, 299
  on Regulatory work
    environment, 320
  stories about PBL, 321, 323
  and wireless competition issue,
    308
Innis, Harold, 89
I Was There (Tyrrell), 14–15

J

Jacobson, David, 289–90, 341, 342
Jacobson, Julie, 289, 290
Jamieson, Nancy, 233
Jarmain, Ed, 77, 87
Jarmain, Ted, 77, 91, 95
Jays in 30 (TV program), 239
Jerrold converter box, 79, 215
John G. Lind Storage Facility, 27
Johnson, Janis, 64, 171
Johnson, Lyndon, 71
Jones, David, 109, 119, 121, 125,
    146, 185, 319. *See also* Road
    Warriors
Jones, Russ, 46
Jost, Stephen, 290
Juneau, Pierre, 85–86, 185, 209, 310

K

Keaton, Michael, 202
Keaton, Sean, 202
Kelly, Chris, 168
Kennedy, Robert, 64–65
Kerr, Jake, 53, 197, 296
Kerr-Wilson, Jay, 303
Kierans, Tom, 68
Killory, Diane, 184, 185, 187

King, Martin Luther Jr., 65
Kinsella, Patrick, 171
Klondike Gold Rush, 11, 12–13,
    18–19, 21–25
The Klondike Gold Rush
    (documentary), 340
Konig, Jacques, 176
Kossar, Leon, 215

L

Langevin, Liane, 110, 147, 148, 319
Langford, Stuart, 164
Larsson, A.G., 38
Laurence, Guy, 336–37
Lawrence, Allan, 67
Lawrence, Bert, 67
Leary, D.J., 124–25
Lee, Bob, 294–95
Lee, Carol, 294
Leranbaum, Michael, 203
Lewis, Drew, 139
Lewis, Hugh, 84
Liberty Cable, 138
Liberty Media, 253, 254
Lind, Ada, 27
Lind, Anne, 3, 43, 194, 197,
    198–201, 222, 230
Lind, Geoff, 41, 44, 193, 194, 196,
    221
Lind, Gertrude Heming, 196–97
Lind, James, 328
Lind, Jed, 1, 5, 43, 52, 152, 194,
    202–3, 222, 230, 252, 288, 292,
    318, 328
Lind, Jenifer (Jenny) Burbidge, 41,
    193, 195, 196, 221, 232
Lind, John Grieve (Johnny), 219,
    220, 340
  birth, 17
  business undertakings, 11–12
  buys Rocky Saugeen property,
    193
  character and personality, 11, 12,
    16, 38
  contributions to St. Marys, 39–40
  death and funeral of, 11, 12
  early years, 17–18
  education, 16

enters cement business, 37–38
entrepreneurial undertakings, 23–25
generosity of, 11, 12
as inspiration for PBL, 13
life in the north, 13, 16, 18–27
love of fishing, 1
parallels with PBL, 16
reading interests, 16, 26
saves "Christmas Eve" baby, 13–14
Lind, John Skiffington (Uncle Jenny), 35–36, 37, 44, 193, 197
Lind, Philip Bridgman. *See also* fishing
accepts job with Rogers, 73
airplane mishaps, 315–17
as art patron, 201, 287–93
attraction to career in media, 72
becomes chair of Rogers' U.S. cable, 109
birth, 33
and calendars, 323–24
character and personality, 45–46, 55, 102–3, 135, 201, 322–25
as Cleveland Browns fan, 272
contacts T. Rogers about job, 72, 73
country property, 193–94
on CRTC chairmen, 309–11
defends simultaneous substitution policy, 78
early years, 41–42
eating habits, 324–25
education, 42, 43, 44, 50, 51, 52–54, 198
end of marriage, 3, 203, 222
fascination with Klondike, 339–40
first girlfriend, 43
health and stroke, 3–9, 59, 222–32, 228–34, 298
hijinks at Ridley College, 45–49
honours received, 328
influences on, 16–17
interest in politics, 44–45, 57–58
love of B.C., 287, 293–96
love of sports, 251–53

marries Anne, 198
meets TR, 60
nickname, 49
opinion of the U.S., 341–42
political activity and interests, 53, 62–64, 66–69, 71–72
relationship with mother, 42–43
relationship with TR, 73–74, 133, 160–61, 242–49, 334–36, 337
and Rogers's move to U.S., 110–18
sale of St. Marys Cement, 219–21
team members, desirable traits of, 320–22
white and black books of, 321–22
whitewater rafting experience, 313–15
and women in business, 319
Lind, Ron, 41, 42, 44, 193, 195, 221
Lind, Sarah, 1, 5, 44, 152, 194, 199, 200, 202, 203, 221, 222, 230, 327
Lind, Susie, 12, 42–43, 194–95, 196, 222
Lind, Walter (Jed), 1, 12, 28, 33–35, 36, 37, 193, 194, 195–96
Lind, Wilhelmina, 27
Lind Family Art Fund, 292
Lind Gallery, 27
Little, Paul, 68, 238
Lombardi, Johnny, 215
long-distance phone competition, 164–65, 168, 169, 170–71, 172, 173, 174, 175

M
Macadam, Bill, 53
Macdonald, Jim, 218
MacDonald, Donald, 104
MacDonald, Finlay, 72
MacKay, J. Stuart, 72
Maclean Hunter Ltd. (MH), 179, 180, 181, 182, 183–90, 284
MacMillan Bloedel, 103
Major, Jack, 303
Major League Baseball, 238, 240
Malcolm, T.R. Anthony, 51

Malone, John, 111, 153, 253, 334
Maple Leaf Sports & Entertainment, 256, 266
Marr, Al, 90
Martin, Joe, 66, 67, 68
Mason, Skookum Jim, 21, 22
Matheson, Jack, 47, 48, 49, 50
Mazankowski, Don, 63
McAdam, Lowell, 309
McArthur, Cammy, 58
McBrien, Bill, 34, 35
McCaw, Craig, 151, 153
McCoubrey, Jim, 51, 55, 90, 313, 314
McCoy, Chuck, 103
McDonald, Steve, 107
McGill University, 52–53, 59
McGuirk, Terry, 253
MCI Communications Corp., 280
McInnes, Stewart, 171, 174
McKenna, Frank, 172
McKeough, Darcy, 65–69, 101, 152, 238
McKeough, Joy, 66
McLaughlin, Jim, 197
McLeod, Gordon, 49
McLuhan, Marshall, 79, 99, 288
McMillan, Tom, 68
McNaughton, Charlie, 67
MCTV (Multicultural Television), 215–16
Meighen, Michael, 53
Meisel, John, 310–11
Miles, Gary, 103
Miller, David, 186, 187
Mills, Victor, 51
Mirsky, Robin, 5, 7, 164, 214, 215, 224, 225, 231, 319, 323
Mitchell, Skiffington, 19, 20, 21, 23, 24, 27
Mitchell, Steve, 47–48
Modell, Art, 251-52, 253, 262
Moffat, Randy, 72
Mohamed, Nadir, 258, 259, 278, 304, 305, 336
Molson Breweries, 254, 256
Montgomery, Adrian, 266, 319
Monty, Jean, 172

Moore, Jake, 91, 95, 196, 289
Moore, James, 307
Moore, Scott, 259
Moorecroft, Arthur "Kip," 81, 83
Moores, Frank, 64
Morris, Gwen, 49
Moss, Steven, 110
Moulton-Patterson, Linda, 110, 146–47
Mount Sinai Hospital, 4
MTV (Multilingual Television), 216
Mulroney, Brian, 53, 62, 209
Murray, Lowell, 62

N
Nader, Ralph, 174–75
Naify, Marshall, 127, 128–29
Naify, Mike, 128
Naify, Robert, 127, 128–29
Natale, Joe, 308, 337
National Cable Television Association (NCTA), 111, 116, 117
National Hockey League (NHL), 255–56, 259
National Trust, 220, 221
negative option billing, 72, 214, 219, 269, 273–75, 277, 278
NFL, 265–71
NFL Sunday Ticket, 260, 261, 262, 263
Nixon, Martha, 52, 198
Nixon, Richard, 71, 72
Northern Native Broadcasting, 340
nuclear weapons debate, 59–60

O
Obama, Barack, 290
O'Brien, Greg, 328
OMNI Television, 215, 218, 257
Ontario Hydro, 105
Oosterman, Wade, 308
Orloff, Monford, 138
Osborne, Ron, 179, 181, 182, 183, 184–85, 186, 187, 189
Ostiguy, Michel, 172
Owen, Dr. Taylor, 341

P

Pacific Cablesystems, 135–36
Pacific Salmon Foundation, 105
Packwood, Bob, 142
Pai, Ajit, 124
Paproski, Steve, 63
Parkin, Jeannie, 288–89
Pattison, Jimmy, 294
Pauli, Steve, 202–3
pay TV, 110
Pearson, Lester, 59–60, 61
Pegula, Kim, 272
Pegula, Terry, 272
Péladeau, Pierre Karl, 237, 238
Pelley, Keith, 259
Peters, Ray, 72
Phelan, P.J., 196
Philip B. Lind Emerging Artist
    Prize, 293
Phil Lind Initiative, 54–55, 341–42
Phil Lind Multicultural Artist
    in Residence, 301
Phil Lind Scholarship Fund, 293
Phillips, Bill, 317, 318
Phillips, Janet, 317
Phillips, Willy, 317, 318
Philp, Bruce, 224, 233
Pierson, Ted, 78
Powell, David, 193
Poyntz, Ross, 46, 66
Premier Cablevision, 85, 86, 87,
    97–100, 103–5, 106, 111, 274

Q

Quebecor Inc., 237
Quello, James, 185–86

R

Rae, Bob, 172
RAI (Radiotelevisione Italiana),
    298–300
Ralph C. Wilson, Jr. Foundation,
    272
Rankin, Anne, 197–98. *See also*
    Lind, Anne
Reagan, Ronald, 119, 121, 144
Reeves, Bob, 339
Regenstreif, Peter, 53, 61–62

Reich, Robert, 341
Relentless (Rogers), 89, 182
Rennie, Bob, 295
Ricci, Nino, 299
Richardson, Doug, 171
Ridley College, 9, 44, 45–50, 52, 58
Riker, William, 53
Road Warriors, 109, 110, 155, 156,
    185, 190–91
Robarts, John, 45
Robinson, Mowat, 47
Roblin, Duff, 66
Rogers, Alfred, 38, 219–20
Rogers, Edward (TR son), 271, 338
Rogers, Edward S. Jr. (Ted)
    birth, 32
    business skills and knowledge,
        87, 125, 131, 152, 160, 165, 179,
        180, 217, 238–39, 266–67, 281,
        334–35, 342–43
    and calendars, 323, 324
    and CCL, 90–96
    character and personality, 96,
        112, 134, 244–46, 249
    and Cisneros, 132
    and commercial deletion policy,
        77
    company's move into sports,
        235–36
    concern over brand damage,
        276–77
    and CRCT MH acquisition,
        189–90
    death, 74, 270
    decision to leave U.S. market, 151
    disagreements with PBL, 160–61
    disagreement with Osborne, 182
    early radio career, 73
    elected chair of CCTA, 76
    and Godfrey, 241
    health, 223
    honours awarded, 328
    lack of technology skill, 330–31
    meeting with Drossos, 130–32
    Minneapolis venture, 119, 121
    opinion of Bell, 165
    opinion of sports broadcasting,
        255

opinion of Unitel venture, 163
PBL contacts about job, 72, 73
PBL meets, 60
PBL on, 330–31
PBL's appreciation of, 56
and PBL stroke, 7–8, 225
political activity, 62
pranks pulled on, 331–33
and Premier, 97–99
purchase of Blue Jays, 237–39
relationship with PBL, 73–74,
    133, 242–49, 334–36
and Shaw family, 284–85
temper, 170
travels with PBL, 329
and Unitel-Rogers conflict, 176
urges PBL to operate cable
    system, 102–3
Rogers, Edward S. Sr., 220
Rogers, Loretta, 180, 243, 281, 306,
    338
Rogers Cable. *See also* Canadian
    Radio-television and
    Telecommunications
    Commission
attempts to move into U.S.,
    108–10
B.C. swap with Shaw, 277–78
buys Western Cablevision, 107
and CCL, 91–96
and CFTO, 73, 74
commercial deletion by, 77
critics of, 104
division of Minneapolis market,
    123–24
early challenges facing, 74–75
enters U.S. market, 110–25
expands in U.S. market, 127–30,
    136–37
financial health of, 74, 84, 125,
    128, 136
increase in channel offerings,
    79–80
innovations in programming,
    82–83
leaves U.S. market, 118
need for increased programming,
    79–80

new programming, 82–83
number of subscribers, 109
ownership of, 73
and Premier, 97–100
and RAI, 298–300
and Shaw relationship, 281–82,
    284
takeovers by, 85, 86, 87
Rogers Cablesystems
California acquisitions, 143–48
financial health, 145, 154, 160
and Oregon acquisitions, 136–37
and Portland acquisition, 135,
    138–39, 140
rate hikes, 145
during recession, 139–40
selling of U.S. acquisitions, 151,
    153, 155–59, 160–61, 165
Rogers Cantel, 181
Rogers Communications Inc. (RCI)
acquisition of MH, 183–90
clash with CP, 175
costs of California expansion, 145
and CPAC, 208–12
CP-Unitel deal, 166–70
damage to brand, 275–76
financial health, 154, 176, 219
leaves Unitel deal, 177
and long-distance competition,
    168, 170–75
multilingual programming by,
    215–16
negative option controversy,
    273–75
ownership of networks and
    specialty channels, 257
purchase of Blue Jays, 235, 236,
    237
rate increase requests, 166
and sale of U.S. assets, 154
and sports broadcasting, 254–56,
    260–64
and sports content, 253
as stock investment, 160
stock price, 219
and Vidéotron, 236–37
and wireless competition issue,
    305–9

and wireless infrastructure, 154, 306

Rogers Group of Funds, 75, 164, 214–15

Rogers Media, 207, 239, 240, 242, 259, 265–72

Rogers Network Services (RNS), 177–78

Rogers Telefund, 214

Roland, Ellen, 201, 291, 292, 328

Rosencrans, Robert, 127

S

San Antonio Spurs, 130

Sanderson, Sandy, 103, 228

Savage, Graham, 95, 110, 135, 136, 176, 324, 333

Schwab, Herbert, 115

Schwab, Mildred, 115, 136, 140–41

Scott, Ian, 309

Scott, Kitty, 290

Scott, Mitzi, 110, 146

Seagram, Philip Frowde, 48–49

Seaway Trust, 216, 217

Selig, Bud, 238

Selkirk Holdings Ltd., 72

Service, Robert, 21

Shaw, Brad, 283, 303

Shaw, Jim, 278, 282–85

Shaw, JR, 208, 282, 283, 284, 328

Shaw Communications Inc., 159, 274, 277, 281–82, 303, 309

Shaw Direct, 284

Shea, Kevin, 109, 328, 330

Sheehy, Lee, 109, 119, 125, 146, 185, 319. *See also* Road Warriors

Shier, Reid, 291

Shoemaker, Michael, 90–91

Shopping Channel, 207

Short, Bob, 77, 81

Sierra Club Ontario, 221, 315

Siren, Janne, 291

Sobek (whitewater rafting company), 313–14

Sole, Leslie, 76, 218

Songs of a Sourdough (Service), 21

Spencer, Stuart, 144

Spicer, Keith, 181, 188, 190, 211, 212–14, 310

sports broadcasting, 2–3, 254–56, 260

Sportsnet, 2–3, 227–28, 239, 253, 254, 255, 256–57, 258, 259

Sportsnet One, 257–58

Sprint, 280–81, 335

Stanfield, Robert, 62, 63, 66

Starz, 147

Steelhead Society of B.C., 105

Stein, Ken, 208

Stentor Alliance, 280

Stern, Lenny, 233

Stevens, Ted, 317–18

Stiglitz, Joseph, 341

Stinson, Bill, 166, 171, 176, 281

St. Marys Cement, 11–12, 37, 219–20

St. Marys Museum, 39

St. Marys Portland Cement Company Limited, 38

Storen, Mike, 131

Storer, 108

Storer Broadcasting, 121–22, 123, 124

Stursberg, Richard, 168, 169, 171, 172, 233, 292, 322

Sunnybrook Health Sciences Centre, 4

Super Sports Pack, 263–64

Surtees, Lawrence, 163, 280–81

Sward, Jim, 217

Swift, Jack, 45

T

Tagliabue, Paul, 262, 267

Tanenbaum, Larry, 265, 266, 267, 271

Taylor, E.P., 197–98

Taylor, Ken, 122

Teeter, Robert, 63

Tele-Communications Inc. (TCI), 111, 253

Telelatino (TLN), 298, 299, 300

Telus, 278, 279, 306, 307, 308, 337

Temple, Paul, 102, 322

*The Washington Diaries: 1981–
    1989* (Gotlieb), 113
Thompson, Fred, 116–17, 144
Thompson, John, 68
Time Warner, 188
Toronto Blue Jays, 235, 236, 237,
    238–40, 242, 255, 257–58
Toronto General Hospital, 5
Tory, John A., 166, 243, 337, 338
Tory, John H., 7, 8, 57, 166, 224,
    227, 231, 240, 243, 244, 262,
    319, 331–32
Trudeau, Pierre, 62, 63, 71, 113,
    143
Trump, Donald, 271–72, 289, 341
TSN (The Sports Network), 3, 253,
    254, 256, 259
Turner, Ted, 110, 153, 183
Turner Broadcasting, 153
Tyrrell, Edith, 14–15
Tyrrell, Joseph Burr, 14

U
UA-Columbia Cablevision Inc., 127,
    128, 129, 130, 156–57, 316
UA Communications, 128
United States
    alien ownership provisions, 113,
        116, 117, 144
    anti-Canadian stance, 143
    broadcasting changes in, 110
    cable TV industry compared
        to Canada, 115–16
    cable TV industry in, 107–8, 116,
        117
    PBL interest in, 341–42
    Rogers enters, 110–18
    Rogers expands in, 127–30
    Rogers leaves, 118
*United States v. American Tel. &
    Tel. Co.*, 123
Unitel Communications Inc., 163–
    65, 166, 168, 169, 175, 176–77,
    279–81. *See also* CNCP
University of British Columbia, 52,
    53, 61, 293, 295
University of Rochester, 53–54,
    60–61, 149

Upper Canada College, 43, 44,
    292–93
USA Network, 154
U.S. Cable Center, 161

V
Valenti, Jack, 213
Vance, Sharon, 171
Van Hasselt, Caroline, 89
Vaughan-Graham, Julie, 231–32
V-chip, 212–14
Veilleux, Gérard, 209–10
Verizon Wireless, 305, 306, 307,
    309
Verveer, Philip, 123–24
Viacom, 137
Vidéotron, 236–37, 238, 303
Viner, Tony, 5, 103, 228, 239, 240,
    241, 242, 257
von Finckenstein, Konrad, 302–3,
    310

W
Walker, Dick, 66
Wall, Jeff, 288
Wallace, Ian, 288
Walton, Amanda, 171
Wansbrough, Chris, 220, 221, 222
Warner Communications, 139–40
Warren, Sally, 328
Waterland, Thomas, 138
Watson, Blanche, 32
Watson, Colette, 5, 164, 212, 319,
    320–21
Watson, Colin, 98
    airplane mishap, 316
    and *Ask Us,* 90
    and calendars, 323–24
    and Cantel dispute, 281
    and CCL, 95
    contemplates setting up business
        with PBL, 151–52
    handling of TR, 245
    leaves Rogers, 333–335
    and negative option billing, 274
    and PBL hijinks, 146
    on PBL's stroke, 224
    relationship with TR, 176

travels with PBL, 328–29
and U.S. cable operations,
    153,154
and U.S. market, 107–8, 109, 110,
    112, 117, 129, 130
Watt, David, 164, 168
WBEN-TV, 77
Welch, Bob, 67
Welsh, Syd, 87, 98, 99
Western Cablevision Ltd., 107, 274
Wheeler, Susan, 164
Wheeler, Tom, 116, 117
Wickson, Malcolm, 53, 61, 63, 64
Wickwire, Lyn, 110
Wilkinson, Bill, 14–15
Wilson, David, 93
Wilson, Martha, 171, 174
Wilson, Mary, 272
Wilson, Ralph, 265, 266, 268, 271,
    272
Wire Wars (Surtees), 163, 280–81
WTBS, 110
Wylie, Andrée, 254

Z
Zeta Psi, 50, 53, 198
Ziniak, Madeline, 218
Znaimer, Moses, 83, 216

About the Author

For 40 years, PHIL LIND was the right-hand man to Ted Rogers, the late CEO of the massive Canadian communications company. Lind provided the strategic compass to channel Rogers' entrepreneurial brilliance and shape a powerful organization with vast holdings — wireless, cable, telephone, Internet, and media assets — along with the Toronto Blue Jays and a significant stake in Toronto's other professional sports teams. Lind has been inducted into the Order of Canada, and the U.S. Cable Hall of Fame for his role in expanding Rogers into the United States. Phil is also a collector of contemporary art, including such Vancouver superstars as Jeff Wall and Rodney Graham, and is a keen fisherman.

ROBERT BREHL, an award-winning journalist formerly at the *Toronto Star* and *Globe and Mail*, now operates his own consulting firm, abc2 communications inc. He is the co-author of best-selling books *Relentless: The True Story of the Man Behind Rogers Communications* and *Hurricane Hazel: A Life with Purpose*, and author of other books, including the bestseller *The Best of Milt Dunnell*.

384
.509
2
LIND

Lind, P.
Right hand man.
Aurora P.L. JAN19
33164300355927